# HOMETOWN HEROES

# HOMETOWN HEROES

## A CROSS-COUNTRY ROAD TRIP
## INTO THE HEART OF HIGH SCHOOL FOOTBALL

## THERON HOPKINS

SKYHORSE PUBLISHING

Skyhorse Publishing books may be purchased in bulk at special discounts for sales promotion, corporate gifts, fund-raising, or educational purposes. Special editions can also be created to specifications. For details, contact the Special Sales Department, Skyhorse Publishing, 307 West 36th Street, 11th Floor, New York, NY 10018 or info@skyhorse-publishing.com.

Skyhorse® and Skyhorse Publishing® are registered trademarks of Skyhorse Publishing, Inc.®, a Delaware corporation.

Visit our website at www.skyhorsepublishing.com.

10 9 8 7 6 5 4 3 2 1

Library of Congress Cataloging-in-Publication Data
Hopkins, Theron.
The eighty-yard run : a twenty-week, coast-to-coast quest for the
heart of high school football/Theron Hopkins.
p. cm.
Includes bibliographical references and index.
ISBN 978-1-60239-284-7 (alk. paper)
1. Football—United States. 2. School sports—United States. I. Title.
GV959.5.H66 2008
796.332'62—dc22
2008020503

Cover design by Brian Boucher
Cover photo of the Katy High School Tigers by Ramiro Reyna

Print ISBN: 978-1-63220-298-7
Ebook ISBN: 978-1-63450-023-4

Printed in the United States of America

"Not the victory but the action; Not the goal but the game; In the deed the glory."

Memorial Stadium
Lincoln, Nebraska

"There's something these boys get out here on the football field that they don't get anywhere else ... I don't know what it is."

Johnny Mims
Vicksburg, Mississippi
August 2003

# Contents

# Week One—Coach the Ones You Got

## Blanco High School Panthers: Blanco, Texas

T'S SUNDAY, AUGUST 3, 2003, and Danny Rogers, the head varsity coach of the Blanco Football Panthers, sits in his Ford truck and watches the evening settle over his team's new practice field. In less than twelve hours, his coaching staff and players will arrive for the first day of practice. From the driver's seat of his air-conditioned pickup, Coach Rogers surveys the summer grass that he mowed himself only a few hours before, the new goalpost that his 310-pound offensive tackle welded and planted behind the north end zone, and the neat row of plastic blue fertilizer barrels that a local rancher donated to simulate a "skeleton" defense during "two-a-day" offensive practice drills. The stage is set and waiting for his players.

This quiet scene is a pleasant one for Coach Rogers, and the picture in his mind of what will take place here tomorrow is enticing for a man who has devoted much of his life to playing and teaching football and for whom the calendar is marked by the University Interscholastic League's designation of the first Monday in August as the first official day of football practice in the state of Texas. For Coach, for eighteen thousand or so of his colleagues, and for a hundred thousand Texas schoolboy football players, tomorrow is New Year's Day.

But it's not all celebration and reverie for Coach. Even though the Panthers boast a healthy stable of offensive backs, and even though those backs will have a seasoned quarterback to get them the ball and a massive offensive line to clear wide swaths of ground for them to advance it, and even though their defensive front seven can be deemed "formidable," Coach is nervous about the defensive backfield. As he sits here, just hours before the first practice, he is unsure about who he'll put back there, or even who might show up tomorrow to help him stabilize this potentially tender area in the Panthers' hope for a return to the 2A state title game that they won only two seasons ago.

Not that there's no hope. Yesterday he was on the phone with a kid who hurt his knee last season, and who plans to sit out football this year in order to stay healthy for basketball season. If there's some way that he might change his mind, he'll be an instantaneous fit at strong safety, the position he competently held down last year until he was hobbled by the knee injury. There is also the rumor of a "move-in," a sophomore who claims he started at varsity defensive back for a big Austin school last year as a freshman. But Coach shakes his head at the prospect of some flashy "blue-chip"-type player magically appearing in the locker room tomorrow morning ready to save the day. "He might be a tenth-grader, and he might be from Austin, and he might be a 150-pound defensive back, and he might even show up in the morning wanting to play football. But if this kid really does exist, there's usually a reason that his folks are moving out this way, and it's not because he's a big-time starter at a big-time school, and he wants to come give little old Blanco a hand."

Then there is the kid who is milling around in the fieldhouse weight room right now, a young man who has waited for the last couple of hours with the intent, Coach is certain, of talking about his future with the team. He has played for the Panthers the past three years, he's a defensive back, and he's really good. "The kid could help us," Coach says. "But he spent the last two months of school last spring sittin' in the gymnasium bleachers during athletic period, mockin' his friends who were down there workin' hard to get ready for football this year, because he decided he didn't want to play. And now he wants me to let him back on the team." Coach reaches to flick the air-conditioning knob to "Maximum," shifts his truck into "Drive," and says, "He was supposed to meet with me a couple days ago, but he didn't show up. He can wait a while longer."

As he makes a meandering loop around Blanco, Coach thinks hard about this young man, this ex-player who says he wants to be a player once again. And he reflects on what he is prepared to say upon his own return to the fieldhouse, and it is this: "This meeting will be for me to tell him, 'Don't show up tomorrow.' How can I let him back on after last spring? What would that show the rest of the kids? That you can just sit around and do what you want and still play? Of course, his family will hate me for the year, and I'll have to talk with them, probably tomorrow. But this is the right thing to do for the kid and the program. Consistency for the program, and show the boy that he's accountable for his actions."

By the time Coach swings his truck up the long school driveway, the orange halogen parking lot lights have blinked on and a big-wheeled black Dodge pickup sits idling in front of the fieldhouse like an army tank. In the driver's seat is Davey Behrends, the massive offensive tackle who built the practice goalpost, and beside him on the bench seat is A. J. Mann, the team's fullback and middle linebacker. They have come by the schoolhouse at this late Sunday evening hour just to "check in" and "see what's goin' on."

Coach says to them, "How you boys feelin'? You feelin' ready?"

And they reply, "Yessir."

"Well that's good," Coach says. "We'll see you boys in the mornin'."

"Yessir," they reply, and as Coach steps up onto the sidewalk, they give him a nod, and the big Dodge rumbles off into the dusk.

Waiting for Coach inside the fieldhouse is the would-be returnee, and he is flanked by two of his non-football-playing friends. Coach nods to them all and shakes hands all around, and then motions for his ex-player to join him in his office. When he closes the door and turns to start his speech, this kid, who looks every bit a football player and every bit a guy you'd want standing poised seven or so yards off the ball staring down a wide receiver, says, "Coach, I come by to check out my helmet." So Coach motions for him to have a seat and then sits down across from him and says, "Son, you're not going to be needing a helmet," and then, over the course of the next ten minutes, he explains to this seventeen-year-old boy why. Then the coach and the kid stand up from their chairs to shake hands, and the kid leaves to find his friends for the walk back into town, and Coach stands there for a few moments in the stillness of his office, just stands there, and then he makes his final rounds of the night, to shut off the lights and lock the doors before he climbs into the cab of his truck to head off through the darkness to his house on the hill to try and get some rest for tomorrow morning.

And tomorrow morning comes early. Coach is back at the fieldhouse at 5:30 a.m., and he's not the first one in. That honor belongs to Tesch, the team's offensive coordinator, who showed up at five to get his weight room workout in before his responsibilities for the day begin. Tesch is from Nebraska, but he's been down here in Texas for several years now, on the move from coaching job to coaching job, always in search of the right fit, and he seems to have found it here. Two years ago, when Coach took over the program, his first order of business was to call his buddy Tesch and say, "Man,

I need your help." And Tesch responded by immediately moving his family to Blanco and buying his first house ever. "It was scary," he says. "But it was time, and this is the place for us."

By six o'clock, all of the coaches have arrived, and the morning sun has just started to peek above the Central Texas hills, offering up the promise of yet another boiler-room–hot day. But the coaches don't know it because all their early morning duties keep them inside the fieldhouse. Dowell and Johnston are at the training room ice machine, filling up the water coolers and packing the ice chest with ice and towels. Dowell not only coaches the offensive and defensive lines—"The Fat Boys"—but is also the school's varsity basketball coach, and he's experiencing some guilt and worry about the kid who plans to lay out of football in hopes of an improved basketball season. "The other guys give me a hard time about it," he says, "and they're just kidding me around. But still, you feel bad. This kid could probably help us, and it almost feels like my fault. But what am I supposed to do? I can't make him play."

Johnston is in charge of the defensive backfield, where that basketball player would be if he was on the field, and the thought of going through the season with a skeleton crew back there is nerve-racking. At twenty-eight, Johnston is the junior member of the staff. He lives with his young family down in San Antonio where he coached for a time at 5A powerhouse Converse-Judson. But the hours were too long there and the attendant pressures way more than he wanted out of his coaching career, so he hired on at Blanco to coach football and track and teach P.E., a welcome relief from the Judson grind.

Across the training room from the two fellows on ice duty are Mouser and Jackson, who have their attentions focused on the industrial-grade washer and dryer. As he begins the arduous task of sorting and folding the mountain of laundry, Mouser thinks about his son, Blake, who will be walking through the fieldhouse door soon to start the first day of his last season of football. Mouser has an older boy who has been through the program and graduated and gone off to Texas A&M to continue his studies, and Blake will likely join his brother in College Station, where he will prepare for a career in education. With his father's build—a sort of "low center of gravity"—and, according to Mouser, his mother's high intelligence, he has no designs on continuing his football life after Blanco. And his father is proud of his son and the future that awaits him. "He's real smart," he says, "and he's a good kid. He'll make a fine math teacher."

Working with Mouser on laundry detail is Jackson, who coaches the wide receivers and defensive ends. He also teaches history at the middle school, but yearns to teach at the high school, where he would have more of a chance to share his enthusiasm for Civil War history. He is from Massachusetts, but has only been back home a time or two since he came down to Texas in the early 1980s to attend Abilene Christian University. He devotes his summers to studying the Civil War and visiting the sites of its more memorable battles. He is already red-faced and sweating from his early morning labors as he says, "They don't tell you about these duties in school when you're thinking about becoming a coach. The kids come in and say, 'Wow! How did the weight room get painted?' or, 'How did my practice clothes get so clean?' or, 'How did the water jugs get filled up and out here on the tables?' All of these questions can be answered by the point of a finger at the coaches."

As his assistants work at their chores, Coach devotes himself to the annual opening-day task of dragging out a cardboard box full of used cleats from the equipment room to the hallway where he dumps the tangled wad of shoes and laces onto the concrete floor and begins patiently to unknot laces, sort out shoes, and line up matched pairs against the hallway's cinderblock wall. This motley cleat assortment represents a stroll through the recent history of Blanco Football. The shoes have been donated to the program by outgoing seniors, and they all bear the scrapes and scars and tape and dried mud of practices and Friday night games that have already faded into the blur of yesterday's memory. But even though they may symbolize the school's football-playing past, these used shoes aren't representative or symbolic of anything at all for some of the players who are just now starting to drift into the fieldhouse. Instead, they are a very tangible opportunity to wear a pair of football cleats out onto the practice field today.

Coach's first customer at the cleat clearinghouse is sophomore "Wild" Bill Cunningham, who lives with a foster family in town and who has shown up early this morning with the goal of finding himself a sturdy pair of shoes that fits. As the boy digs through the black-and-white pile, Coach says, "What size you wear, Bill?"

And Bill replies, "Eleven, Coach."

"Well, you better get in there and find you a good pair of elevens." Bill nods his head and continues his search, while Coach finishes up his sorting job and drifts back to the coaches' office. After a few more minutes of this hunt, Bill looks up to see Johnston, his position coach, hustling out of the training room with a Gott cooler full of ice water.

"Dollar Bill!" Johnston says. "You fixin' to show me somethin' today?"

"Yes sir, Coach," Bill says, but his brow is furrowed because he's not thinking about who he's got in "Cover Two" pass coverage; he's got his mind on finding the shoes that are going to get him out to the practice field.

Bill is not the only player who is here early. A few kids join him at the shoe pile, while others head into the training room so that Dowell can fit them for a helmet. These headgear applicants are all underclassmen, and for many of them this is their first day of high school football. "There's gonna be some hubcap-size eyes out there," says Coach. "Especially when we put on the pads and start hittin' some. You get one of these tenth-graders lined up across from big old A. J. or Davey, and it's scary, man. He might not want to do it. But he's gonna have to do it. That's how you start knowin' you're a football player."

Before one of these upstarts can face A. J. or Davey across the line of scrimmage, he has to face Dowell to secure a helmet and pads, and Dowell is not overjoyed to be distributing equipment at this late date. The coaches have been down at school for the last week and a half, and almost all of the upperclassmen have made time to get down to the fieldhouse. But many of these younger guys haven't—not because they don't care, but because they don't know. This is not new to Dowell, so instead of chiding them, he turns to the first skinny freshman in the door and says, "Let's get you outfitted."

Because they are already outfitted, and because they are, after all, upperclassmen, most of the older kids take their time about making it down to the fieldhouse. Whereas the JV locker room is lined with tousle-haired boys seated in front of their lockers in their practice jerseys and cleats, contemplating the physics of an on-the-field encounter with A. J. Mann, the varsity room is strangely desolate. One junior who has made it in early is Pepe Mancha, and he is the kind of kid who doesn't look like much when you see him sitting in front of his locker humming a Christian rock song and adjusting his ankle supports. But when you see him chase down a pass or return a punt, it becomes clear just why he needs those braces, and it's because he has a way of "breaking down" and changing direction that can leave an opposing player infuriated, a spectator breathless, and Coach shaking his head and saying in his understated rural Texas way, "He's good, man."

By eight o'clock, all the younger kids have their gear, all the older kids have found their way down to school, and everyone—sixty-one players and six coaches—is gathered in the weight room underneath the gymnasium bleachers. The basketball player is nowhere in sight, and the phantom "savior" defensive back from Austin remains no more than a rumor, but Coach says, "We work with the ones that are here," and Dowell echoes him with, "If they ain't here, we can't coach 'em."

All is quiet and all eyes are on Coach as he steps through the weight room door to stand in front of his team and coaching staff and says, "Welcome to the 2003 edition of Blanco Panther Football." Then he goes over the team rules—" 'Yes sir,' and, 'No sir,' is how we answer here, and that's it … Be here and be on time, and if you're not gonna to be here or be on time, call and let us know … No swearing around here or out on the field … No hazing. The seniors will tell you it happened to them when they were freshmen, but they're lyin' … "—and then he says, "Some of you are wondering and worrying about what it's gonna be like out there. You work hard and listen and learn, and you're gonna do fine. Watch what these older guys do, and learn from them. We won't let you quit. If you feel like quittin', come see me, and I'll talk you out of it. Most of all, this game is about having fun. We want you to have fun out there, and we want to do this together."

And then there is a pause, and a sort of peace falls over the room, and Coach looks out over his team—the nonchalantly talented kid and the kid who "couldn't hit water if he fell out of a boat"; the one who equates football with life and the one who is here because his friends are here; the confident one and the one who is scared beyond all reason about what might happen out there; they're all here—and he says, "What do you say, boys? Let's go play some football."

In Blanco, before you can play some football you have to do some stretching, and this means two long lines of underclassmen facing two lines of juniors and seniors. It means a variety of responses from the players—some do it; some go through the motions; some don't even pretend like they're doing it. And it means mild cajoling from Coach to "get good and loose now … all stretching, no baloney. You guys with muscles, stretch 'em."

It's still early enough in the day that the mostly green grass on this new practice field is wet with dew and the slightest hint of a breeze from the southeast can help a person with the right imagination almost call this morning "cool." This is the first day that the Blanco team has practiced here, and the new situation is mostly a good one. The team no longer has to trudge the quarter mile across the county road to the stadium, wearing out their cleats on the asphalt, and carrying blocking bags, tackling dummies, water jugs, and anything else they might require for practice. It's also good for the stadium grass that now the team and the band won't be grinding it into the dirt as often as four times a day. But what's not so good is that the same rocks that are dug out of the ground to construct homes across the county, and have had a number of years to work themselves out at the stadium, are also right here, underneath the team's new practice facility and, with every step of a cleated foot, more and more of them will fight their way to the surface.

· · ·

It's DAY ONE of summer practice and legs are fresh and spirits are high. This shows in the first "Team Pursuit" drill where five players line up on one sideline and a lone runner stands cradling a football on the other. At a "Hut" from Coach, the ball carrier hurtles himself at these defenders, with spins and deer-like bounds, with all-out sprints, and all with the intent of getting around or over or through this hoard of anxious pursuers. This is designated a "non-contact" drill—part of the first four days of no-contact before they can don their pads on Day Five—but this doesn't prevent anyone from getting in that first thump, which is so much a part of preparing to play a varsity football game, and is almost impossibly unavoidable with a gang of energy-charged teenagers who are out here on a soon-to-be hundred degree summer day in large part for the physical aspect of the game. In short, they can't wait five more days to hit and be hit.

After Pepe and his gang of runners accept this daredevil mission, it is on to the rest of the first day of practice: through the individual offensive and defensive drills, where Dowell has his linemen working on "get-offs" against the blue fertilizer barrels, firing out on "Hut," punching into the plastic barrels, performing a quick "ground roll," and then moving upfield. As Ray Noah, the offside offensive tackle, shows particular fervor and talent for this drill, Dowell remarks, "Ray is mean, low, vicious, and nasty."

Up next is the "Pass Skeleton," where Nathan White lines up with his talented group of backs and ends to run play after play against a scout team defensive backfield. After that comes "Team Conditioning," where Coach spreads everyone along the goal line to start them sprinting and says, "You fat guys don't go down to the end and hide," and Dowell replies, "They're fat, Coach. They can't hide."

The two practice sessions are split by a forty-five minute break that many of the players use to get something to eat. Jackson mentions that he overheard some of the younger kids talking about Dairy Queen. "Well," says Dowell, "we're making offensive linemen here. You don't get offensive linemen feedin' 'em salads." Dowell has what one might call an "offensive lineman build" himself and the coaches all work at giving him a hard time about it.

Johnston shares a narrow corner desk space with Dowell, and he elbows his partner through his "Panther Pride" T-shirt and says, "Dammit! Quit hoggin' up all the room."

Coach chuckles from his spot on the floor where he uses a bookshelf of old game videos as a backrest. "I'll tell you right now. Dowell, he don't care. When he come here he was skinny, and look at him now, and he don't even care."

At this, Dowell unlocks his hands from behind his head and drums on his very ample torso. "That's right," he says. "You don't think this takes work? You think these kids can't learn somethin' from this kind of dedication?" Then he gives his best I'm-a-lineman-for-life grin, swivels around to his desk, and picks up a screwdriver and helmet to replace a wobbly facemask.

By a quarter to eleven, the players are back at school and in meetings with their individual offensive coaches. The first thing Dowell does when he reaches the room where he teaches world history is to make a beeline for the thermostat—"Fat boys like cold," he says—and then, once his junior varsity linemen are seated, he starts going over the terminology that they'll be using for the rest of their Blanco football careers. As Ky McNett watches Dowell plot out blocking schemes on the whiteboard and listens to him say things like, "A counter is a trap for the tackle," and, "A trap is for the guard to pull and hit someone in the ear hole," he gets a look on his face that says, "I am almost completely lost."

Dowell stops his lecture and says, "What's wrong, Ky?"

"Coach, I know what to do, but the words and names don't mean anything to me."

Dowell replies, "On Friday night I need to be able to talk to you and know that you understand me and what I'm talkin' about. I need to be able to say, 'Choke,' and know that you know what I'm sayin'. You gotta know these things if you're gonna help the team."

When the team heads out for its second practice session of the day, they are greeted by Linscomb, whose official vocation is to keep the Panthers and a number of other Central Texas teams supplied with equipment, and whose unofficial vocation is to supply an overly generous quantity and debatable quality of his idea of wit and wisdom on a bi-weekly basis as he makes his rounds across the Hill Country.

Linscomb is a sixtyish fellow, stylishly attired in pleated shorts and a polo shirt with tasseled loafers and no socks. Of all the many teams on his sales roster, he seems to have a very special place in his heart for the Blanco Panthers. "They got a way a' doin' things around here," he says. "You see how that quarterback hands the ball to his wing? That's what you call 'close tolerance,' and that don't come easy. That takes work and that takes coachin'." He changes gears suddenly, raising his voice to talk about his business. "And I'll tell you another thing, Son, I got me an American job. I work for a livin'. I don't got no one handin' me nothin'— I don't sell. I don't eat. You know what I'm sayin' here?" And then he calls out to Coach, "Hey, what you say? You got time for Subway after all this?"

"You buyin'?" asks Coach.

"What, it's not enough to have me here, supplying you all with all this worldly knowledge and athletic equipage?"

Coach turns to the salesman with hands on hips in a show of mock perturbation. "You meet with these other coaches, and you're treatin' 'em to steaks and shrimp, and you ain't even offerin' us a sub sandwich?"

"Okay, okay, I'm buyin," says Linscomb.

By one o'clock, the humidity and the slowly settling reality that today is the first of a long string of hot, hardworking, two-a-days has sapped much of the team's early morning antelope energy.

But as Coach calls for them to pull off their helmets and take a knee in a team huddle to close down practice, he is feeling fine. "Good first day today," he says. "It was good how you picked people up if they messed up. That's the way to be. Remember, if you don't know, ask. Don't go fifty percent due to not knowin'. But good work out there. I know it's hot, but we got lots of cold water, and don't be shy about drinkin' it. And get plenty to drink at home, and eat something good. And, I'll tell you what: You looked like a team out there. That's the way it should be now through December. Now let's get a break and get out of here. And who heard Linscomb say he's buyin'?"

There's a laugh at this, and the tired team rises up to Coach, who is in the center of it all, and their arms and hands come up and in, and there is a loud, all-voices bark of "State Champs!" to finish off the first day of this 2003 season for these Blanco Panther kids. They trail off their new field in small clusters, pitching footballs toward the ball bag, kicking at chunks of upheaved stone, scraping mud out of their cleats on the fieldhouse sidewalk, and calling out to each other, "Catch me a ride," and, "Meet me at C. J.'s," and, "You ain't workin' today are you?" And their worry for the day—at least their football worry—is done.

For the coaches, their football day is far from done. After they've followed Linscomb in their big, brush-guarded trucks to the Subway up on Highway 281, and after they've listened to him discourse on the new "Oh-A-Sis" water cooler that they've got to try, and reminded him about who's picking up the bill, it is back to the fieldhouse to wash clothes, sweep floors, empty trash, re-rack weights, discuss personnel, and plan for tomorrow's practice.

By mid-afternoon, almost everyone is done with their duties for the day, and the assistants head home to stretch out under the air conditioner on the living room carpet, or, in Mouser's case, to "open me up one'a them ice-cold Michelob Ultras from out the 'fridge—they hard to beat, man—and then get in the pool with my arms hung over the side, and sip that beer and look up at the shade of the big oak out back. If you want to get cool, that's one hell of a way to accomplish it."

It also looks as if Coach might have a chance to get away from school for a short while before he has to come back this evening for the weekly Booster Club meeting that his job requires him to attend. This is not one of the athletic director duties that he relishes, and, starting at lunch and continuing on throughout the afternoon, he has made his dread known to anyone within earshot. As he and Tesch draw up tomorrow's schedule on the office whiteboard, he says ruefully, "Booster Club tonight. Man, am I pumped." As he accompanies Johnston out to the practice field to start the motor on the rolling water cannon sprinkler system, he says, "I am pumped. We're gonna argue about lettuce and tomatoes and should we use plain or seeded burger buns at the snack bar."

But just as he gets up from his desk, there's a tentative-sounding knock on his office door, and in walks Justin Stone, the phantom athlete everyone has been wondering about. Just as Coach had promised, he's not a crackerjack defensive back and he's not from Austin. He's a tenth-grade kid for whom his parents have moved out to Blanco to give him a better chance in a smaller place, and "he thinks he wants to play some football." He's also a kid who Coach will take down to the equipment room to get him his helmet and pads, and then point to the shoe depository on the hallway floor and say, "If you need a pair, we got lots," and who, tomorrow morning will be introduced to the assembled team by Coach as, "Justin Stone, a new Panther from Smithson Valley. Take care of him." Soon after, he will feel a part of things as he trots off with the offensive linemen for individual drills and feels a slap on the back and a shake of the hand from his fellow sophomores and hears a "hey, man," and a "you stand here."

Coach eventually does make it home in time to see his wife, Lisa, and his daughters, Reagan and Landry, off to San Antonio for Reagan's gymnastics class, and in time to spend a few minutes with his son, Tanner, in the family's swimming pool. "This pool is the best thing we've done here at the house," Coach says. "It seems like this is the only place where me and Tanner get to spend much time together." They have a basketball hoop rigged up above the pool, and the two engage in a water-soaked game of one-on-one. This is a good diversion for Tanner because he has a tank-full of nervous energy to burn. Tonight is his first night of Pop Warner practice, and he can't wait to start. "I just hope they don't put him at quarterback," his father says.

After a dinner of sausage and beans, it's back down to school, where the town's Pop Warner teams meet on the high school's practice field. Tanner clatters in his cleats across the parking lot asphalt to join his squad, and Coach has a few moments to sit in his truck and watch the goings-on. For him, the first official day of the new season is drawing to a close. He just has to make it through tonight's Booster Club meeting and its twenty-minute discussion on whether to switch from soft drink cans to plastic bottles and charge an extra quarter, or to just leave things as they are. And maybe after he puts his kids to bed he can spend a couple of minutes in his chair in front of the TV to see what's going on with his Dallas Cowboys and their pre-season camp and try not to think about his defensive backs, or about picking up the phone to call that basketball player and say, "Hey man, when you comin' in?" or about what he'll say to the banished player's parents when they call, or about the laundry or the shoe pile, or "Wild Bill," or the new kid. If he makes his way through these things and anything else the last few hours of this August Monday might bring his way, then, hey, he might be ready to face tomorrow and whatever it has in store for him and his team.

. . .

BUT HE HASN'T seen tomorrow yet. He hasn't heard Pepe's ankle "pop" from across the practice field or seen him crumple to the ground at defensive cornerback. He hasn't heard Garrett Granberg— a Blanco graduate who has come by to help out at practice—say, "It's playing football here that got me ready for college." And he hasn't seen Big Davey walk into his office to tell him, "Coach, I might have TB."

He hasn't seen Wednesday either, when he arrives at the field-house sleepless because of a night spent at the emergency room in Austin with Landry, with Lisa almost inconsolably frightened, and with Tanner afraid, trying to be tough for Reagan on the long truck ride to the hospital in the wake of the ambulance that carried their mother and their sick baby sister. The record-breaking summer heat had triggered a midnight febrile seizure in the little girl. "She was shaking. Her eyes were rolled back in her head. It felt like she wasn't breathing for about a minute and a half. And there ain't nothin' you can do but hold her there and call the medics. And there ain't really nothin' they can do except try and get her cooled off." He tells all this to his team in the pre-practice huddle, and then he goes on to say, "It makes you think something about your life. It goes fast, man. You got to enjoy your life. You got to appreciate it."

Nor has he seen Thursday, when his freshman quarterback, Tanner Wilbanks, throws a ball so end-over-end, weak, and off-target that Coach says, "I think that's the worst pass I seen all week ... and that includes two Pop Warner practices." Or late that afternoon, when Davey again comes to Coach in his office to explain that the TB scare was a false alarm. He doesn't have it, and the co-worker he thought he contracted it from on a summer construction job doesn't have it either.

Or Friday, which is the first day in full pads and the first day of full contact. As the team trudges out to the field for the early morning practice, Dowell predicts that the anticipation of contact will far exceed the reality. "They're tired, their pads don't fit right, they're not used to them, and they're not used to hittin'. And my problem is, I'm excited, too. But I'll only end up mad when my big old linemen start wallowin' around on each other instead of hittin' someone."

Coach tries to get things started on a positive note by saying, "It's hot everywhere in Texas, boys. Let's keep our heads up and play through it." But Dowell's forecast holds true. As players drag around the field in the humidity, Tesch shouts, "You guys don't want it! You just want to wear that jersey with your name on it on the sideline!" Then Coach, who coaches the linebackers, yells at Seth Garza, "Why are you backpedaling? Our linebackers don't backpedal. I don't know who your linebacker coach is, but he ought to be shot." And then, in a move that contradicts every-thing you have ever heard about football and everything you've ever heard about how to treat football players, Coach calls the team together to say, "We're cutting it short this morning. No special teams and no conditioning. Everyone's tired. Let's come out ready to improve this afternoon." And then Coach does the same thing at the afternoon practice, saying, "Thank you for your effort today. This first day in pads is always tough. You boys get home and rest your legs. We gotta pick up the intensity tomorrow. Be ready."

And Coach hasn't seen Saturday, when Pepe comes back as dexterous and dangerous as ever, making everyone miss, and making Coach observe in frustration, "We can't tackle him," and then in resignation, "Well, no one else can tackle him either." Or a freshman running back—Jacob Noah, Ray's little brother—who "gets in there and gets after" the first-team varsity defense, and his eyes aren't like hubcaps, but more like ice picks, as he seeks out senior defenders to crash into. Or the new kid, Justin Stone, who jumps in on the "Scout Team" defensive line and almost immediately makes a big hit on a first-team wingback, steer wrestling him to the ground and then jumping up to the shouts and shoulder pad slaps of his new teammates. Neither has Coach gathered the team up in the post-practice huddle to say, "That's a good way to end the week. You all finished strong and finished playing like a team."

• • •

THE POP WARNER practice has yet to begin, and there are a dozen or so youngsters in too-big shirts and shorts and long socks charging around the field with a football in tow, feinting and high-stepping and all-out sprinting in a miniaturized version of the performance the high school boys put on earlier in the day. There is an unfettered joy in their cries of, "Go!" and, "Run!" and, "Throw the ball here!" And in the fearless careenings of these future Panthers, in their whirring legs and arms, with this *world* all around them, there is a picture of why we came up with this game to begin with. And Coach says, as he looks out at his son and the other boys, all of them running, "That's a tough picture to beat." And it is.

# Week Two—Where They Start and Where They Finish

## Warren Central High School Vikings: Vicksburg, Mississippi

**T**HE FIRST WEDNESDAY of the first week at Warren Central Junior High School is designated "Helmet Day," so when the fifty seventh graders who participate in athletic period football gather at the fieldhouse door to slip off their shoes and stack them along the brick wall, they hustle to their lockers, sit down on the red bench, and wait for Coach "Bumper" Brogden to set down his big-bottomed plastic coffee cup and start issuing the directives that they will strain to follow for the hour-long class period.

But, after the tardy bell rings to officially begin the period and before he sets down the cup, Bumper makes one final eye-sweep of the room in search of any shiny objects that might be glinting from one of these twelve-year-old's ears. He rattles the cup with his take from the last two days and says, "Anyone wearin' a earring, it goes right here. And Momma can come down and get it."

As Bumper shakes the cup and stalks around the room, kids who remembered to unclasp their tiny stud earpieces and deposit them in their pockets on the way to the fieldhouse, kids who have never had an ear-piercing, and a few kids who have forgotten the rule or, more likely, have forgotten their earrings and are now plopping them into Bumper's cup like gold doubloons into Captain Jack's treasure chest all frantically paw at their earlobes and glance nervously at their neighbors.

These seventh graders' assignment for today is to sit at their lockers and wait for Bumper to shout out their names from the equipment room. But not long after Bumper deposits the coffee cup in his office desk drawer and heads to the adjacent room where the long rows of gleaming red football helmets lie waiting, it becomes clear that there are a couple of obstacles on the road to getting these helmets distributed.

One roadblock is the soon-discovered realization that a lot of these kids have never donned a regulation tackle football helmet before. Not six players into the long line of helmet applicants, assistant coaches Wilson and Smithhart and their gang of restless charges hear a mini-explosion from the other side of the equipment partition. This results from Bumper's headgear-fitting work with a young man who tries to twist a too-small helmet onto his head like someone might screw a bottle cap onto a Coca-Cola bottle.

"Whoa, Big Dog!" Bumper exclaims. "Don't be breakin' my helmet!" At this, he marches out the equipment room door, swinging behind him a large-sized helmet, and demanding the attention of his fifty antsy players and two assistant coaches. He thrusts the helmet above his head, like a war trophy for all to see, and says, "This helmet ain't designed fo' yo' comfort. It ain't a cotton T-shirt. It's designed to keep you from gittin' kilt, so don't expect it to fit like a pilla'."

The "kilt" pronouncement works as a "before and after" dividing moment. The "before" is a squirreling mass of arms and feet and fingers and hammer-bobbing knees. The "after" is a fifty-kids-as-one, dead-quiet focus on a twenty-eight-year-old man with a helmet in his hands. And Bumper uses these few minutes of silence to demonstrate the proper way to put on a football helmet. First he shows them all the wrong techniques that kids have been employing back in the equipment room. "This ain't no ball cap to be rested comfortably atop yo' head," he says, as he flips the helmet up onto his own tow-headed mop. Then he takes a stab at Big Dog's corkscrew maneuver. "If you at all like havin' yo' ears, you won't be doin' this." And then he shows them the right way to fit their headgear onto their heads. "You take yo' index fingers and yo' thumbs, and you have 'em meet in a loop in both ear holes, and you pull 'em out on both sides."

As the hoard of youngsters makes practice loops with their own fingers and thumbs, and as he secures the helmet in place, Bumper is, for an instant, transformed into the ballplayer he once was. This illusion is short-lived though, as Bumper unsnaps his helmet, pulls it off his head, and says, "Awright, who can't git they helmet on now?" and then plunges back into the equipment room with Big Dog shuffling behind him.

Also short-lived is the peacefulness in the room. Once they have mastered the index finger and thumb loop, these kids are back to slaps and giggles and a general uproar that exceeds the now halcyon-seeming pre-kilt and post-earring rumblings. As Big Dog emerges from the equipment room with a triumphant smile on his face and a right-fitting helmet in his hands, Bumper calls out ominously, "Hey, I'm fittin' ta' come out there. And we fittin' ta' go to the Jungle."

This threat brings a strained calm to the masses as only three days into the program, they are already veterans of "The Jungle" and know that it means "Gorillas," and know that "Gorillas" means squatting down on their haunches, and then, at the coach's whistle, performing a ballerina-like leap skyward combined with a fist-beating of their chests, and a cry of, "Gorilla One!" and then, "Gorilla Two!" and so on, up into the dozens, or hundreds, or whenever Bumper gets tired of blowing the whistle. This uncomfortable picture succeeds in reining in the troops, and they devote the next couple of minutes to red-faced pantomimes and headshakes as they work to perform the high-wire task of staying quiet and watching their teammates slink into the equipment room one at a time, and then return to their seats with the coveted red helmet. But before long, the junior high locker room is back to the edge of mayhem, and there is a ringing call from behind the wall. "Next time I hafta' walk out that door, we goin' Gorilla for the rest of the week!"

The next couple of minutes proceed in the only way they can: with the false calm, followed by the storm of voices and creaks and falls and genuine childhood laughter, all produced by these kids who want to follow directions, but whose bodies and age will not let them do so. This is not ADD; it is the helicopter hovering over the canyon of puberty, and the coaches know it. But this doesn't stop Bumper from appearing in the equipment room doorway to say, "Awright men, iss' 'Gorilla Time,' and then, "You s'pos'ta be at the top'a the food chain. You s'pos'ta be able to reason and think and sit and not talk. You s'pos'ta be able to take directions"; nor does it stop Wilson from ascending a ladder to a lofty perch where he can sit on an overturned milk crate to oversee all fifty kids as they leap and crouch, leap and crouch, leap and crouch; or Smithhart from pursing his lips around his new chrome-plated whistle on this, his third official day as a coach in the program, poised to set off the echoing calls of, "Gorilla One! Gorilla Two! Gorilla Three!" All so that Bumper can return to the equipment room to continue handing out helmets, and so that these boys can continue to learn what it means to be a Warren Central Viking football player.

• • •

ABOUT THREE MILES away from Bumper's Nordic indoctrinations, past the Battlefield Inn and the Beechwood Lounge and just off

Highway 27, Mr. Joe stands inside the wide-open fieldhouse back doors to greet the Warren Central Football Varsity as they filter into the locker room from their morning of academic classes across campus. Each boy pauses at the door to say, "Hey, Mr. Joe," and to slip off his new-school tennis shoes or desert boots before padding across the paint-sealed and spotlessly clean cement floor to his red-painted wood locker space, where he has a few moments to sit and look. And what he sees is a stream of blue and red banners that commemorate the team's recent district and state-playoff successes, strung from the low-slung rafters. He sees the weight room circuit that Coach Oakes sets up four days a week in a labyrinthine scheme that allows half of the eighty-plus players to do their in-season "maintenance" workout in this finite space, while the other half watches film in the "Red Room" down the hall. And, in the middle of it all, in the middle of this place as clean and orderly and well-provisioned as a church-run hospital, he can see the diminutive Mr. Joe, the fieldhouse manager, in his plaid collared shirt and pressed pants and running sneakers, as he nods to player after player, as he shakes hands and pats shoulders, as he adjusts the laundry he washed and started drying last night and then folded early this morning, as he scans the floor for any accidental paper cup or piece of tape or lunch wrapper, as he *works*, which is something he has done for almost every day of his life since he started chopping cotton in Eagle Lake, Mississippi in 1938 for fifty cents a day. "I never been late for work," says Mr. Joe. "I never missed work. I took half a day off once for my momma's funeral."

Into this tranquil scene strolls head coach Robert Morgan, who has been with the program for thirty-five years and is beginning his eighteenth year as the man in charge. He surveys the locker room for a few moments and says, "How's ever'thing percolatin' today, Mr. Joe?"

"Good, Coach. Good. Just gettin' these boys lined out. And that is full-time work right there."

"Well, Mr. Joe, you the man for the job then." At this, Coach walks down the hallway, past row upon row of team pictures and awards, to have a seat behind his office desk where he takes a moment to thumb through the glossy Sears catalogue–sized "press guides" that the Vikings receive annually from places like Ole Miss and Tulane and the University of Florida. Of special interest to him is the Mississippi State booklet that features, in the players' section, a picture and short biography of his son, Brett, who is entering his sophomore season as a Bulldog defensive back. On the wall behind Coach is a portrait of Brett in his college uniform, along with pictures of his older brothers, Rob and Josh, also outfitted in their maroon and white MSU gear. The elder two have earned their degrees and now work in the construction business. "I'll tell you what," Coach says, "they momma raised them boys right. My boys … they a good lot." Coach picks a railroad spike up off his desk that is etched with the words "Viking Toothpick." The spike makes an echoing "clang" as he taps it on the hard wood of the desk and chuckles, "We gotta couple 'Git Tough, Stay Tough' drills for these boys today. We gonna find out which a these hosses can plow and which cain't."

One "hoss" who can plow is senior lineman Adam Huell, whose rampage in today's mid-practice "Oklahoma" drill doesn't so much put one in mind of a plow horse as it does a bullfight where the bull is winning. But this Viking Toothpick–type performance doesn't come until after the team's daily twelve-minute run in their shorts and shirts that Coach says, "Gives 'em a chance to talk and wind down from school—'Did you see so-and-so? She looked good, din' she?'"

Coach Brewer has his linebackers gathered around him for some individual work and he is unhappy with their effort so far. First, there is the backer who moves half-speed and "thumps" half-hearted in a "sideline pursuit" drill, and this sour showing is enough to make Brewer say, "That's all you gonna show us? If that's all you got, you ain't got no heart, you got a thumpin' gizzard." Then, as he explains to the group this kid's error and how to correct it, Brewer discovers that one of his charges seems to have his eyes on the pom practice that's taking place across the way on the stadium track, instead of on his "Contain" lecture. "I'll tell you what, Son," Brewer growls, as the young man snaps back to attention, "I remember growin' up in my fam'ly with five kids in the house. We learned to sit down, stop, and listen. Your mama didn't teach you that? 'Cause I'm fixin' to."

The wide receivers and quarterbacks work on "fade" routes with Coach Graham, but today the correct execution of the drill is just not occurring. While Graham forms his receivers into two lines facing downfield and settles on a couple of quarterbacks to throw to each line, Coach sets up an orange pylon on each sideline to signify the point where player and ball should meet, and then stands back to watch. He witnesses a grab bag of poor throws and muffed catches. Coach Tyrone, who works as the offensive coordinator and who has been with the program for twenty-five years, has already predicted, "It's gonna be sluggish out here these first few days of pads." And "sluggish" is a good word to describe these early-season fade route efforts.

As one pass drops fluttering to the manicured grass, nowhere near the receiver or the orange "target," Coach says, "I'ma git me a quarterback that can git it down there. If he don't catch it, I want it goin' out of bounds."

As another, this time decently thrown pass, is bobbled and dropped by a young receiver, Graham calls to the boy as he chugs after the still-rolling pigskin, "Wha's a matter … ball too heavy?" As sophomore Chico Hunter, a starting defensive back and sometime quarterback as well as Warren Central's version of "The Natural"

("You'll be hearin' about him playin' college," says Coach. "Just you watch. That boy's what you call a 'slobberknocker'"), winds up and floats a pretty spiral toward the pylon that is promptly dropped, Coach says, "Cheek, don't worry about it none. You thowin' it good. They just ain't catchin' it." And finally, as a ball skids along the ground at a receiver's feet, Coach says in exasperation, "We thowin' at the pylon. Hell, I'll go down and git a gul outta study hall. Maybe she can git it down there."

Things aren't going much better over with Coach Tyrone and his running backs. He has a row of blocking bags set up like sideways dominoes with the idea that his players will zig-zag between them, but the boys appear lethargic in the sticky afternoon heat. They are having some real trouble maneuvering through this bag course in the ungainly pads that they are not used to wearing. Instead of making clean "cuts" between the bags, many of these usually fleet-footed runners find themselves jumping and stumbling over them while trying to switch a ball that suddenly seems greased from hand to hand. "This ain't a 'hop drill.' It's a 'cut drill,'" says Coach Tyrone, who has a way of smiling when he chastises his players, and who delivers the bad news in such a soft, unassuming voice that it almost seems as if he is congratulating them.

But he's not congratulating anyone when he sees yet another football squirt through a kid's arms and onto the turf and says, "'Five points' means both hands on the ball," or when a succession of backs make it at least somewhat successfully past the last bag and break into a sprint, only to slow down to a jog long before they reach the light standard, and he says, with a headshake and a grin, "Sprint past the pole. It ain't a sprint and a ease up," or after he's seen plenty of what he believes are half-hearted and bumbling efforts from his group that he abandons the "Cut Drill" in favor of "Up-Downs," the big brother to "Gorillas," where the participant jogs in place, drops flat and springs back up, and then drops down again … and again, and again, and again. … until Coach Tyrone directs his heavy-breathing crew back toward the bags and says with a smile, "Now les' try this one mo' time." The boys make their next, much crisper rounds through the bags and past the pole, and it's clear that his quiet message has made its way through.

There is not much to cheer about over with Coach Oakes and the linemen either as they work on a "Get-off" drill, where big Joe Wallace, a sophomore tackle, settles down awkwardly into his "three-point" stance, Coach Oakes says, "Gimme a punch. Strike it like a cobra. I'm coiled up. I'm coiled up. I'm coiled up … and, 'Bam'!" And with this, Oakes gives Joe a strong "hand shiver" in the shoulder pads. "Now tha's you. Tha's what you got to do. Just like a cobra." But Joe is no cobra. He is a roundish fifteen-year-old kid whose new practice pants are too small, and whose pads don't seem to want to stay in place. He works to get back down into his stance, all the while fiddling with those pads and pants and Oakes says, "You got to leave them butt pads alone. You got to focus on your business." Coach Brewer chimes in from his drill across the way with, "If he can bruise his butt, tha's one hell of a fall."

One area of the practice field where things are moving smoothly is the far end of the field, where Will Clark, "the best kicker in Mississippi," and a pretty fair soccer player as well, boots football after football in high, dead-on arcs through the practice goal post. Coach stands back to admire yet another ball as it sails up and over the uprights and into the stand of willow and ash and wild cherry trees beyond, and he says, "I like the soccer team. They keep me in kickers." As footballs continue to soar end-over-end through the cloudy afternoon sky, and then land with a leaf-shattering "thud" in the woods beyond, a few of Will's teammates trickle over from their water break to watch him apply shoe to ball.

Vaughn Mims, a senior captain and starting middle linebacker, calls out, "Man, tha's the position to have. Make a million dollars and you don't do nothin'."

"Tha's right," says fellow senior captain and starting free safety Jason Williams. "Jus' stan' on the sidelines. Iss' cold ... take your jacket off, make the kick, come back, put your jacket back on, stan' next the heater."

This razzing garners a smile from Will. Then he booms the last of his practice bag of balls through the goal post, and he and his gang of three apprentice kickers disappear into the trees with bag in tow so they can fill it back up and kick some more. "I'll be proud when he leaves," says Coach. "He's about to break me. He's done busted out all my balls and wore out my shoes."

But then, just as Will and his kicking lackeys report to Coach that it's time for them to get on to their study hall, and Coach responds with, "I cain't believe that. You kickers got more places to go than a Jesuit priest," before sending them on their way, and just as the humidity and oppressive new practice pads seem to have gotten the best of the Viking Varsity, it is time for them to "Git Tough, Stay Tough." At Coach's call of, "Oklahoma!" a charge of energy ricochets through the team, almost seeming to bounce from helmet to helmet like the thick splats of rain that have started to drop from the gray clouds above.

"Oklahoma" features a row of eight blocking bags, lined up side-ways to create seven two-yard–wide "chutes." On one side of each chute is an offensive "blocker" and, three yards behind him, a "run-ner" with a football tucked solidly under both arms, whose com-bined job is to get the ball through the chute and to the green grass of the open field beyond. On the other side of each chute is a defen-sive "tackler" whose job it is to stop them. Surrounding the twenty-one players, who are at the ready in the seven chutes, is everyone else, and, if you have seen the movie *Gladiator*, you have a pretty good idea of what this whole cheering, jeering mob looks like about now: They want to see some collisions ... and then they want to get in there and get a lick in themselves.

Even here in this most primal of football drills—you run; you block; you tackle; and let's see who's toughest—things start out rusty enough for Coach to say, "You about as flat as a half-baked biscuit." But then something about the rain and the mud and the churning cleats transforms this part of Coach's dream field into a barrow pit; the high-pitched exhortations of this seething crowd, the settling of plastic pads and nylon jerseys and teenaged flesh and bones into a more comfortable communion; it shovels this holy muck of slips and slides and fumbles and frustrations into a forgotten furrow and tramples over it with the hits and hollers of "Oklahoma."

And now is when Adam Huell crouches down into his tackler stance, taut and angry and ready to show James Henderson just who exactly is in charge here. Earlier in the fieldhouse, as Adam pulled up his socks and strapped on his pads, James had stood over his best buddy, taunting, "We hittin' today, Boy. You fittin' ta' find out what pain all about," and Adam had looked up at his friend and calmly replied, "Back it up," and then gone about his business. Now James cradles the ball behind a big senior blocker who, when Coach blows his whistle, looks like he's stepped on a skateboard, as Adam throws him over a blocking bag on his rabid-dog express to the ball carrier. But James is not quite ready to follow his blue-jerseyed escort into the mud, and is, at least in his mind, ready to "back it up," and the collision that follows is ram-horned and resounding and brings a roar from the multitudes, but Adam is just mad enough, and James enough stunned, that Adam "wraps him up" and deposits him onto the turf like

you might flop a sack of meal onto a truck bed. Then Adam strad-
dles his fallen friend and says, "Who hittin' now? Who backin'
it up?" And James punches the ball on the ground and leaps to
his feet saying, "Les' go! Les' go!" And then there they are in the
chute again with a new blocker, but at the blow of the whistle,
the same result, as Adam this time shoves the blocker straight
back into James and then bear-hugs them both to the ground to
whoops of glee from the congregated.

All this is too much for little Larry Warner, who Coach says is
"no bigger that a popcorn toot. But he tough as a nickel steak."
Larry is a junior and a back-up offensive back, and his number
hasn't been called yet to step into the Oklahoma foray, and he can't
wait another instant for it to be called as he hollers, "I'm a git me
some!" and jumps in, not to run the ball, but to block. The kid he's
up against is an ample-sized lineman, and Larry proceeds to attack
him like a bulldog pup might a rib roast, and knock him back and
flat, and the field full of boys and men is jumping now, and Coach
says, "Can you do it again, Larry?" and Larry lets loose a joyous
shriek and lines up and does it again, and then yells, "Bow up,
boys!" as he springs back to his feet in a spray of mud and grass,
and he's saying, "Who gonna tote it? Who gonna tote it?"

And the next thing you know, it's big Joe lined up in his best
cobra stance and his sagging pants are forgotten as his teammates
say, "C'mon, Joe," and "Stop up that hole, Joe," and "You the one,
Joe-Joe," and he drives his three-hundred-plus-pound bulk of a body
into the chute, only to be pushed down and stepped on and run
over, and, as he drags himself out of the mud, he says in his gentle
giant voice, "Nice play, Derrick. I'll get you next time," and the two
boys shake hands, and then next time comes, and the whistle blows
and this time Joe throws Derrick to the ground and wrestles down
the runner in a lightning-flash burst that is as much a surprise to

him as it is to his teammates and coaches who howl in celebration at his feat, and he and Derrick are crouched on hands and knees in the muck, and they're smiling, and it's clear that this right here is where they want to be. They can't imagine another place.

But there is one more place the team needs to be before they can start to think about leaving the practice field for the day. Coach has saved his other "Git Tough ..." drill for the end of the day. He calls it "Make Five, Take Five," and the object of it is nearly as simple and battle-bitten as today's Oklahoma drill: the football is set down on the forty-yard line, and it's the job of the offense to advance it over the goal line against a defense that is charged with stopping them. For every play that the offense gains at least five yards, they get to "Make Five," and the ball is moved five yards closer to the goal-line. For every play that fails to gain at least five yards, Coach "Takes Five," and moves the ball five yards back and away from the goal line.

Today's practice-closing drill pits the "Blue" offense against the "White" defense that features Chico Harris, so it is not such an outlandish thing to witness when the Whites, after allowing four straight "Make Five" plays, "bow up" to stop the Blues cold and begin to shove them further and further back toward their own goal line. And, even though its the end of practice and the beginning of a cool shower and a "long ride home" await everyone—players and coaches alike—once the Blues make their way into the end zone, the Whites seem to be in no hurry to go anywhere.

As the Blues bend down with hands on knees and heavy breathing in the huddle, and then make their slow way toward the ball to set up for yet another play, the White nose-guard, who has had a big part in stuffing several previous running plays, settles into his "four-point" crab stance and calls out, "Send him, baby. Send him right here." And the "weak-side" cornerback explains his own contribution to this defensive dominance to his backups on the sideline with, "I knew I mighta' got ranned over, but I'm just tryin' to make a tackle," and these future Blues and Whites nod their agreement, and all up and down the defensive front, white-shirted kids offer up challenges to the worn-out Blues saying, "Bring 'em to me," and, "Send him here," and, "You don't want none 'a this." But Coach Brewer says, "Les' quiet it right down and play ball. They don' need you flustratin' 'em. They got to work this out. You all ain't sportscasters yet. They don' need you agitatin' 'em."

The Blues eventually do stand up and fight, but not until the Whites knock them around for a little while longer and Coach says, "Tha's a perfect example of how to get run over," and not until Jesse Pedyfoot, his ill-fitting and mud-soaked practice pants drooping around his hips, gets his fill of the abuse and says to his bedraggled offensive mates, "You follow me, you'll get there," or until Oakes says to senior tackle Scott McKinnie, who is dizzy and swooning in the traces, and who wants to come out bad, "You worked six years to get up here. Now, you gonna wallow, or you gonna bow up?" or until Jesse does get them there with a final gasp of a fullback plunge that caves in the defense enough to "Make" that final five yards as he collapses over the goal line.

· · ·

THE VIKINGS CONCLUDE this all-pads day with a round of conditioning sprints that is accompanied by a break in the rain, and by exuberant team claps and shouts of "Vike!" after each length of the field. And by Coach saying, "They'll sleep good tonight." Then, after the last boy straggles in from the last sprint, he calls out to his team, "Hug your buddy!" and he watches like a happy dad as these kids who have devoted much of the last three hours to beating on each other, do just that. They shout and laugh and slap pads and shake hands and, yes, hug one another in a way that makes it easy for Coach to call them in tight around him, and then say to them and to his coaches, "We'll learn how to win together," and then to stand alone in the soft halogen glow of the new practice field lamps, and in the midst of all these trees, to watch his boys drift back in toward the now-darkened shadow of the fieldhouse where they pause to strip off their muddy cleats before stepping into the lighted frame of the locker room doors to say, "Hey, Mr. Joe."

# Week Three—The Big "If"

## Valdosta High School Wildcats: Valdosta, Georgia

O N TUESDAY EVENING, an hour or so after the muggy afternoon football practice has ended, Rick Darlington takes a break from his job as head coach of the Valdosta Wildcats to eat some dinner. It's raining hard, one of those deep Southern rains that helps keep afloat the Okefenokee Swamp, which can't be more than twenty miles south of where Coach hydroplanes his black Dodge Ram pickup along Highway 84 toward Waycross. Perched next to him on the wide-bodied armrest is an open Styrofoam to-go box full of fried food and ketchup packets and plastic cups of ranch dressing. On the other side of these victuals sits Welton Coffey, Coach's offensive coordinator, who takes a moment between condiment-soaked bites and an animated "Flex-Bone" offense discussion to nestle back in his bucket seat and gaze out at the scrub pine forest and sea-gray sky, and at the rain that drums down on the blacktop and truck hood and runs in canal-wide rivers at the lip of the road. "Yeah," he says. "This is the life of a high school coach—eatin' Church's chicken and drivin' the back roads of Georgia."

The two men are on their hurried way to a Georgia High School Association football clinic in Ware County, where their attendance is mandatory and where they expect to hear the usual lecture about sportsmanship and about how the game officials are doing the best job they can, as well as get a confirmation of the rules changes that will affect the upcoming season. In many ways, though, there is nothing "usual" about the instructions they'll be listening to when they arrive at the meeting because almost everything here is new to them. Coach was hired in March to assume the head coaching and athletic director duties at Valdosta, and he convinced Coach Coffey to come north with him from Florida. This was not an easy decision for either of these men, who both left head coaching positions and pretty much all things familiar to them to come up here for this new challenge. Coach came from Orlando, where he and his wife and their four children lived in a one thousand square foot duplex, and where, two seasons ago, his Apopka High School team won the Florida large-school state title.

The following Tuesday, at the celebration in the school's gymnasium, Apopka alumni, Warren Sapp, approached Coach and said, "What you all need?"

"What?" Coach replied.

"What you all need?"

"Well," Coach ventured, "the boys have been talking about championship rings." Later that week, a twenty-five thousand dollar check arrived to pay for the eighty rings.

Coach Coffey left his job at Jacksonville's Raines High School, which is not only a place he led to a state championship—a first for a Jacksonville city school—but also where he grew up and played his own high school football in the mid-1980s.

When Coach asks him why he left home for this journey into the unknown, Coffey replies, "The opportunity to work with kids."

"But there's kids back in Florida, too," Coach counters.

"True … true …" says Coffey. And with this vague response a couple of hard facts hang in the moist air between them—one fact as tangible and obvious as the windshield-wiper blades squeaking furiously in front of their faces, and one intangible, but maybe even more magnetic and more real for a couple of fellows who have devoted so much of their lives to football and who burn for competition. The plain truth is that, in this profession—the education profession—where money and salaries are a mostly taboo subject, both coaches have seized this Georgia job offer as a chance to increase their income and their families' lifestyles dramatically, and not in a swimming pools and movie stars kind of way, but in a way that, for the first time in their young teaching careers, they both live in houses where their families can spread out a bit, and they can both see down the road to where their own children might be interested in attending college and how they might start to pay for it. Apart from the salary scale inequities between the two states, however, there is also this: The Valdosta Wildcats are the winningest high school football team in America and these coaches simply cannot resist the opportunity to be a part of this almost mythical tradition, even with the understanding that, if they don't win soon enough and often enough, they'll be fired.

If Coach needs historical proof of the gleaming guillotine hanging poised and oiled over his shaved head, he has to look only as far back as the gentleman he's replacing, Mike O'Brien, who began as an assistant here in 1981 and who took over the head job in 1996. Over the next seven years he won seventy games and a state title in 1998, and then, after an eight-win 2002 season, was unceremoniously fired. He can also look at the Valdosta coaching career of Nick Hyder, which began in 1974 after his predecessor compiled a 17–3 record and was let go after two years, and included 249 victories, seven state titles, and three national championships, before ending in 1995 when he died of a heart attack while eating fried chicken in the school lunchroom. In 1988, Hyder said, "I've been here for fifteen years and the other day at the store I heard a woman say, 'There goes that new coach.' And I'm sure it'll be that way if I'm here another fifteen years."

Coach Hyder as the new coach for the entirety of his nearly 250-win tenure, Coach O'Brien's not-good-enough ten-wins-a-season pace, and Coach Darlington's own slippery foothold in a job where he hasn't yet stalked the sideline in an official game, can all be traced back to Wright Bazemore, the rock upon which this Winnersville myth—and reality—was built. Between 1941 and 1971, with three early-career years away from the school for his overseas service in World War II, Bazemore piled up 268 wins and fourteen state titles. But, more important than those victories or the impressive additions to the school's trophy case is what retired Coach Jack Rudolph calls, "A tradition that helps the new kids maintain tradition." There is a certain "way things are done" at Valdosta, and "Baze" started it all, as well as kindling the fire of the heightened expectations of winning and the obsessive impatience with losing. "Coach Bazemore was just like my daddy," says Ronnie Pitcock, who grew up in the shadow of Cleveland Stadium, where the Wildcats play their home games. "He instilled in us a belief in discipline and the priorities of God, family, and country. The only way to play football at Valdosta was Baze's way. The way he taught us and the way he treated us … you just didn't want to let him down."

Or, as Jerry Don Baker, a former teammate of Pitcock's who now serves as a fellow assistant coach, says about a mini-controversy that is brewing among the staff concerning who should be in at quarterback—Cedric Hatten, a compact senior who can really run, or Scott Shuman, a rangy sophomore who can really throw—"I told Coach to put in the thrower, play the other kid at wing-back. Tha's what Baze woulda' done. Tha's my coach right there. Baze is my coach." And so, Coach will be battling Coffee County and Wayne and Lowndes Counties, and all the other on-field opponents that he and his coaches and players will face this fall, and he'll also be battling the ghost of a man who built the tradition that drew him like a brilliant and inescapable light into his long shadow, where you either win and hold on to your tenuous place in the shade or lose and get swallowed up by the darkness.

But it isn't symbolic darkness facing Coach right now. It is a very real darkness that is settling over the roadway and making the rain look like lit matches thrown into his truck's headlamps. It is fast approaching seven o'clock, the meeting's start time, and the coaches still have a way to go to get to Waycross, which gives them a chance to continue their free-flowing discussion about the direction of the offense that they work together to direct, and that is new to everyone at Valdosta except for the two guys sitting in the truck right now. Coach can't get over Cedric Hatten's speed or the unteachable "moves" that brought to mind some of the kids he worked with down in Florida, where, according to Coffey, they have a "natural swagger" that you don't see anywhere else. "When we had the two other guys in there today, they made some pretty solid eight- and ten-yard runs," Coach says. "With Cedric in there, those little gains could become touchdowns." But Coach is also nervous about Cedric's inconsistency. When he has the football, anything—good or bad—can happen. "Right now," he says, "Cedric is the worst option quarterback I've ever had … but he could be the best."

For his part, and as much as he enjoys watching Cedric run with the ball and wondering what might happen when he has it, Coffey is convinced that they need to "spread things out more … more 'Gun' and more 'Trips' and less 'Triple Option.' " In other words, Coach Coffey doesn't want to watch his Wildcats run with the football as much as he wants to watch them throw and catch it. He envisions a reliance in their offense on a quarterback positioned five yards behind the center, and varying formations of receivers that force defenses into choosing who they're going to fully cover and who they're going to leave in "single" or "man-to-man" coverage. "If they don't cover people in the 'Gun,' then we gotta immediately go 'Bubble,' " he says in his adamant, almost preacherly, fashion. And when he says "Bubble," he means that he wants his quarterback to look out at his receivers, who'll usually be spread out two a side, discern which side has the "weak" coverage, say two defenders versus two receivers, as opposed to three defenders versus two receivers and, at the snap of the ball, get it out to the "inside" or "slot" receiver so that he can make the catch and then loop or "Bubble" around his outside receiver, who is heading down and toward the middle of the field to take out one of the two defensive backs. "That's five yards right there, for sure … unless somebody misses a tackle, and then who knows? Three times five is fifteen; first down, move the chains. That's somethin' you can't defend. We make the right reads and get the ball there, there's no stoppin' it. We do enough of that, they start walkin' guys up to try and defend it, tha's when we go to our verticals, and jus' throw it over the top of 'em. Or we go vertical and send a guy underneath. Once you get started with all that, and once you get the defense thinkin', they not gonna know what to do. They won't know what's comin' next." The more Coach Coffey talks about his offensive vision, the more excited he gets. "We got four receivers who can do it!" he says. And Coach nods his head in semi-agreement as he thinks about the "4.2" speed and the shock-therapy quickness that Cedric provides when he's got his hands on the ball. "You are right on, Welton," he says as he tosses their supper box onto the jumble of notebooks and videotapes that are splayed across the back-benched seat of the Dodge truck. "But the run opens all that up."

• • •

SOMEWHERE UP AHEAD of the Ram pickup, through the dark and the rain along Highway 84, is a Valdosta school van that carries the rest of the Wildcat varsity staff to the same rules meeting. Tim Horton, who has been here since 1987, is sitting high in the driver's seat. For the last two years he has worked as the team's offensive coordinator, calling the plays from the sidelines, and, in many ways, helping to set the tone and the tempo of practices and ballgames with his directives. When Coach took over last spring, Horton was given the option of accepting the role of slot-backs coach and equipment manager or finding something else to do with his weekday afternoons and Friday evenings. By staying on with the team, he has sent the message, in effect, that Valdosta Tradition, the importance of this team, and the chance to be a part of it and be a contributor to it, far outweigh the personal glory and satisfaction of being the guy wearing the headphones on the sidelines who says on a third down and short yardage situation in a big game, "We're gonna throw it here, and we're gonna see what happens." In fact, the thrill of being a part of the Valdosta mystique may be greater for him even than any of the other coaches or players involved. Unlike his coaching peers, who are either near-lifelong Wildcats like Pitcock and Baker and Bob Bolton, or, like Coffey and Richie Marsh, came here from other winning programs, Horton played his high school football at nearby and supremely mediocre Telfair County, close enough to Valdosta to see the Wildcat glow, but too far away to feel it. It was like a dream fulfilled when he was hired on here as a freshman coach, and that dream only got better as he moved up in the ranks. "I'll tell you what," he says, "standin' on the sidelines, callin' those plays ... sometimes I had to remind myself that it was me doin' it ... it was really somethin' ... when it first happened, it was almost like it wasn't me, like I was above it all watchin' someone else." And that's why he remains here today, driving the van and checking out chin straps and making sure his slot backs will know exactly what they're doing out there on a Friday night. "You get a chance to be a part of something special," he says. "You got to hold onto it."

A big part of "holding onto it" for these coaches who have been here for so long is working their way through the departure of Coach O'Brien while at the same time settling in to work with Coach Darlington and his brigade of transplanted Floridians. When Horton thinks about O'Brien, who is busy trying to rebuild his own career along with the struggling program at Woodstock High School up near Atlanta, he says of the semi-surprising Valdosta dismissal, "He deserved better." Or when Baker's wife, Miss Polly, talks about the many years "that we were all together here and all the things we did," she compares it with family and she says, "It's hard to say goodbye to family." And Pitcock says, "The firing was a shock. A lot of people were put off by the way he was let go."

But, serving as a balance to the general dismay over O'Brien's dismissal and the puncturing of this cloistered world where Horton, a fifteen-year Valdosta veteran, was far and away the newest member on the varsity staff, is the fact that, as Bolton puts it, "The last few years got stale in some of the things we were doin.'" Included in that was a locker room that Coach calls, "The worst I ever saw—food on the floor, trash and filth everywhere, pee-yellow lockers, stained walls, nasty rubber floor-mats. It was uncomfortable to be in there." So, as a first order of business upon his arrival, he met his staff with brooms, mops, brushes, paint, and brand new rolls of carpet, and, in two long Spring Break days, they transformed the Bastille-like atmosphere into a place where a kid can change into his practice gear, take a shower, watch film with his teammates, or even eat his lunch, in comfort. A daily "Pride Patrol" vacuums, sweeps, mops, and picks up any wayward gum wrapper or notepaper that players and coaches somehow missed during the day.

The weight room has also received an extreme makeover since Coach's arrival, with the Touchdown Club chipping in one hundred thousand dollars to purchase all-new weight racks and carpeting, which gives ninety-six Wildcats a chance to train together during their afternoon athletic period and gives Marsh and Bolton, the two coaches who lead these grueling workouts, the chance to say things like, "If you ain't got a funny look on your face, then you ain't doin' what you s'posed to be doin'," and, "Thowin' up's a good thing," and, "I'm proud of the way you workin'. But I don' wanna reminisce, just carry this through game night."

There are some other changes that, although not as physically obvious as the "new" locker and weight rooms, are nonetheless creating ripples in the tapestry of Valdosta tradition ... like the Wednesday afternoon practice before Thursday evening's scrimmage against Thomas County Central when the team steps out onto the practice field outfitted in "shells and shorts"—or helmets, shoulder pads under practice jerseys, and, instead of the usual practice pants, only their athletic shorts—and Baker blinks his eyes at the bare legs that he has never seen out here before, and shakes his head like Dorothy when she woke up in the Land of Oz. "You seein' a first right here," he says. "This ain't never happened at a Valdosta practice ... never. This is full, livin' color history, what this is."

Or like Coach and Coffey's new offense that replaces the "Pro-Set" that, according to Horton, "We've used for sixty years." The old guard has concerns about what many of them see as a radical change. "We went from a very simple system to a complex one," says Bolton, "and a lot of these kids are confused. Being confused makes them less aggressive, and a confused kid is not a kid you want to have out on a football field." This is a concern for the Valdosta veterans and for Coach and his "new guard," who have flavored their risk in coming here with the introduction of this new plan of attack, and not only on offense, but on the defensive side of the football as well, where Jeff Rolson comes in as the fourth member of the Florida contingent. He was Coach's defensive coordinator and assistant head coach at Apopka. He bypassed the possibility of taking over the program there in favor of packing up and coming to Valdosta for similar responsibilities here. "I figured this is where the Lord wanted me to be," he says. "You're always looking for the biggest challenge you can get and this is a challenge, so here I am." And the big challenge for him right now is helping his ballplayers to get comfortable with his attacking defense. But he has confidence in this scheme that proved so successful back home in Florida and confidence in his Valdosta defenders' ability to master it. "They're used to the old defense and the new defense is making them think too much instead of react," he says. "They'll get it. It just takes time."

Yes, time, that chief healer among all elements, which, combined with effort and the supreme focus that a program like Valdosta demands from its participants, should help these kids to "get it." And it should also help these new coaches to feel more comfortable here at Valdosta, and for the veterans to shake off the untimely departure of their old friend, O'Brien, and fall in with the new system and new order of things. But these football men aren't waiting on time to make that happen. Instead, they are working—together and every day—to make it happen. Coach took the first step in this process by meeting with each veteran assistant and offering him continued responsibility with the team, perhaps not in the same capacity, as in Horton's case, but as a part of this hallowed organization where every position is important.

Coach Bolton, like Pitcock, is pleased to have the opportunity to continue forward with the team. "There's been a renewment here at

Valdosta," he says. "And I think things are going well between the new and old coaches." He does see some differences in approach, such as the new emphasis on repetition, with everyone in almost constant forward motion, as opposed to a past focus on "alignment and assignment" where "time was never a factor." "We'd be out there till seven, eight o'clock—till way past dark—and it didn't matter. We were gittin' it right before anyone went home … and that's somethin' that Baze started, and we've just held to it." Things are a little different now though. "We use practice cards, and we got a schedule, and we stick to it pretty tight." But there is a cornerstone that the veterans and the newcomers share that transcends any type of offense or defense or ideas about the right or wrong or just plain different way to practice and play the game. "The new and the old has bought into the same philosophy," says Bolton. "They love football and they love to win … just like us."

Even now, as "the new and the old" bounce along together toward Waycross in the school van, there is a familiarity and respect generated among them that feels genuine. Marsh is in the midst of explaining how "the Lord and Coach Darlington brought me up here from Florida, and I'm thankful for it," when he grabs a handful of Bolton's meaty shoulder and turns the talk to the team's poor showing in their first scrimmage last week against Camden County, an off-kilter performance that has the entire staff jumpy and on edge. "We were lookin' good in camp all week," he says. "And then Thursday we didn't look so good." He shakes his head at the not-so-distant memory of a game so filled with Wildcat penalties, gaffes, and mental blunders, that veteran players had been approaching coaches all week to express their embarrassment, and Rolson was prompted to say to the gathered team, "This is disappointing compared to my idea of Valdosta Football before I got here. Is this team living on the past? Are you tired … outta' gas? Or are things over?"

Even though none of the coaches are even close to quitting over this one dip in the road, Marsh especially wanted to put the game behind him and behind the team as quickly as he could. "I was worried and ready to hit it hard over the weekend," he says, "but Bolton says to me, 'There's always next Thursday,' and I figured they won that many state championships, tha's good enough for me ... I'da' been in trouble 'thout Coach Bolton sayin' that."

Bolton nods at Marsh and settles back in his mid-van seat, saying, "You gotta work smart. A tired coach, you work him all weekend, he'll come in tired on Monday and he won't be ready to give you his all come Friday."

Or Thursday, when the Wildcats will have a chance for a little redemption in their second scrimmage, this time against Thomas County, a smaller school, but a no-less-menacing opponent. "They got some 'Boy Dogs,'" says Baker. And they do, since they are returning seventeen of twenty-two starters from last year's 4A state runner-up team and promising to be a stiff test for the Wildcats, who after the Camden County debacle are in search of some confidence as much as anything else before heading into their regular season schedule.

But Rolson, for one, is more excited than nervous about playing this first preseason home game, even though it is his defense that will be charged with the daunting task of containing Erik Walden, the Thomas County quarterback who throws great and runs even better. "I can't wait to get over to that stadium and hear the guys bang on that tin," he says. The "tin" he refers to is the alleyway corrugation between the Wildcats' concrete dressing room underneath the home stands at Cleveland Stadium and the field that is named after Coaches Bazemore and Hyder; and what the players do before they charge out onto the turf, in another tradition that dates back to Baze's days, is stand in that tunnel, with helmets raised high overhead, punching deafening dents in the tin roof and whipping themselves and their packed-house fans into a fury that, on the nights when they used to pound opponents into submission, could be petrifying for a visiting team. This frenzied atmosphere has waned in the last few years, and the challenge of reviving it is a big part of why Rolson and Marsh and Coffey and Coach are here, and why Pitcock and his fellow veterans aren't quite ready to say goodbye.

As far as Coach Baker is concerned, much more than just plain old football, it is what Valdosta Football is all about. Over the course of his decades at this school, he's had numerous offers to head up programs elsewhere in the state, but he's turned them all down. The closest he's come to departing Valdosta was in 1994 when he actually accepted the head job at Coffee County.

But when he and Polly sat down with their kids to discuss the move, their oldest son, Don, who was starting his sophomore season as a Wildcat, said, "You can go, but I'm stayin'."

"Right then I got them chill bumps up and down my arms," says Baker. It was also right then that he excused himself from the family discussion to call Coffee County from the kitchen telephone and say, "I can't take the job." The same thing happened four years later when he was again offered the Coffee County position and his son Cliff was entering his senior year.

"Well, I guess you can guess what he said," says Baker. "And you can guess them old chill bumps come right back up and down these arms."

The "chill bumps" that Baker describes are something that all these coaches seem to get when they think about the idea of a Friday night football game. But then, when it comes to the reality of that same game, and especially the reality of preparing for it, those chill bumps are all but forgotten. Back in the Dodge Ram, Coach Coffey, who has calmed down somewhat from his earlier offensive-minded furor, thinks that his players may have gone into the Camden County scrimmage too excited, too "high," and too eager to please. They have been hit with so much that is "new"—the locker and weight rooms, the offense and defense, the coaching staff shake-up, the "shells and shorts" on pre-game day—and also some revived traditions from "glory" years past, like the return to a staunch and consistent discipline; the week-long preseason training at Twin Lakes 4-H Camp, which was, as Coach says, "… as Spartan as we could get it … except they had air-conditioning," and which the Wildcats hadn't done since 1987; even "Make Five, Lose Five," which was purportedly invented right here at Valdosta and which had been abandoned in 1998 … until it was brought back this week to light a fire under these weary teenaged legs. In addition to this, there is also the almost ludicrous expectation of success in Georgia's 5A "Large-School" Division in which Valdosta is dwarfed, in terms of school population, by almost all of the teams they compete against. (For example, crosstown rival Lowndes County has 2,800 students compared with Valdosta's 1,800.) It all might simply be too much and may have caused this Wildcat team to go into last week's scrimmage wanting it too badly, if that is possible in a sport where "wanting it" is supposed to be such an integral part of success. "Emotion is good," says Coffey, "but it's just a feeling. It wears off after about two or three plays. What I want to know with our guys is: After they get in that first lick, then where they gonna be?"

· · ·

By the time Coach and Coffey have found where they need to be and found a spot for the big truck in the far back corner of the Ware County parking lot and hustled through the rain and puddles and the slick hallway of the almost-new main brick building to the school cafeteria, Brocky Brock, the head of the Albany Officials Association, has already begun to speak and the rest of the Valdosta staff is seated at a couple of tables right up front, the only seats available in the packed room when they arrived a few minutes ago. Even though Brock has already vowed that he'll keep this meeting as short and to-the-point as possible, he can't help but notice Coach as he makes his way around the side of the room toward his seat, and he can't help but interrupt his early "rule changes" monologue with an aside about his officiating crews and their primary aim to "get things right." And, as many of the other hundreds of coaches in the room turn their heads to acknowledge Coach's arrival, not with a nod or a wave or a whispered, "Hey," but rather with a blank, icy stare, Brock says, "Many of you coaches get upset about questionable calls 'cause your jobs are on the line … an' we unerstan' that. If you don't do better, you're gone. If you don't win $X$ number of games, you're gone. There are people sittin' in this audience tonight whose jobs are on the line."

As he pulls out a chair and offers up a quick grin to Baker and Bolton and company, who have already settled into this speech, Coach is pretty sure that the editorializing isn't directed entirely at him. But later—between the warning that, "When you get to Heaven, God ain't gonna be no football coach; he's gonna be a athletic director," and the story about the grizzled old coach who was happy that the state was switching from a four-man to a five-man officiating crew because, "That gives me one more to yell at"—Brock shoots a glance in Coach's direction and says, "We all have strong traditions, or we're rebuilding or starting one," Coach is pretty sure that it is directed mostly at him. And it's not just because, as Al Akins, another long-time Wildcat assistant, says, "Ever'body hates Valdosta, and ever'body wants to beat us," that he seems to be on the receiving end of these pointed words and these less-than-chummy looks. It also stems from the fact that these born and bred Georgians, who take their football and their Deep South heritage seriously, are none too happy with what they perceive as an out-of-state usurper horning in on their game.

Coach can feel it and Coffey can feel it, and, as the meeting adjourns and the van crew makes plans to head over to Ryan's Steakhouse for the beefsteak buffet, both men are eager to get back to the truck and get out of there. "I'm trying to decide," Coach says once they are safely ensconced in the pickup cab and headed west toward home, "and maybe you can help me. Would you call that a palpable dislike? Or maybe palpable loathing, what do you think?"

Despite the frosty reception at the meeting, Coach is happy to be in Valdosta, a place that he sees as having those small-town values, and a good place to raise kids. He's happy about his new house, which is quickly evolving into a home, where his family has a backyard, and he has a loft office over the garage with his computer and desk and TV and VCR, and a comfortable couch where his kids can crawl all over him while he watches game tape and figures out ways to get his offense into the end zone and how to hold onto his job for another week. And his coaching staff, "the old and the new," as Bolton calls them, with the way they seem to be coming together and maybe even starting to enjoy being together (As is evidenced at this very moment back at the buffet in Waycross, where Marsh grabs a dinner plate and promises to "put on a clinic," and Baker replies, "Let's see you do it"). Coach's team, too, who, even though they haven't quite "gotten it" yet, show him every day, in the way they work and the way they listen and learn, that they want to and will "get it" if he'll just stick with them, and there's no question about whether or not he will. And then there's Rolson and Marsh, and Coffey sitting right here beside him, quiet now and, like him, occupied with his own thoughts. These guys have found some kind of faith in coming here. And how much can that be worth? There is all of this … all of it.

He also understands, though, just as Nick Hyder did when he came down here from West Rome, that, no matter how long he stays, he will never be totally accepted. "I'll probably always be an outsider," he says, "no matter what happens with us on the field." But that's okay with him because it's sort of a dream come true to be the head coach of the winningest team in America. Besides, he's got a scrimmage to get ready for against Thomas County Central.

And how about that Thursday evening scrimmage? Well, Scott Shuman will throw a touchdown pass that causes Baker to exclaim, "He's slingin' it around like a Houston gambler"; and Cedric will run for a touchdown after Coach counsels him on the sideline, "Don't guess to get there … just run"; and the Wildcat defense will succeed in bottling up the experienced Thomas County offense, which makes Rolson breathe a little easier. Before the scrimmage, Coach will say to the team, "Play like it's Saturday afternoon. Don't put pressure on yourself. Have fun. Play loose." Afterward, he'll say, "We looked like we had more fun. We looked better and we were a little more fiery out there … and we executed better. But let's not be satisfied with this. Enjoy it for the next hour, but we got Wayne County next week," and then he'll send the whole crew over to the hamburger feed that the Touchdown Club has set up for them behind the east end zone.

. . .

BUT BEFORE THE scrimmage—sometime before Rolson hears the team pound their helmets on the rickety tin, and after the rain subsides and the sun peeks out in time to float above the live oaks and red oaks and the hickory trees—there is a moment of calm when a few of the coaches find themselves standing outside the locker room while their team dresses inside. And in the middle of this moment, Jack Rudolph appears through the chain-link gate to lean against the boarded-up snack bar and survey the field, which is as much his as anyone else's. He is, after all, the bridge, a bear of a man who came down here to Valdosta in 1966, after his NFL playing days with the Dolphins and the early New England Patriots, and started coaching defense until 1998, when the Wildcats won their last state title, and when he was good and ready to stop. He's the one who worked with Baze, worked with Hyder, worked with O'Brien, and these are his boys, Baker and Bolton and Pitcock, who gather around him now, who played for him and coached with him, and who connect him to this Wildcat team that will take the field any minute. And what else do they talk about but old times, the back-to-back seasons when they gave up two total touchdowns; the time against Tifton when Baker "got his ass knocked off"; but they're not old times at all because, as these middle-aged men lean against the snack bar counter listening in rapt attention to Coach Rudolph speak, all of their eyes, theirs and his both, are glistening, and they convey the same message, "We were there. No, we are there … right now." And, as he continues to talk and point out toward the emerald green field to a spot where this happened or where that guy made a tackle, coaches keep drifting over, Horton and Rolson and Marsh; Middleton, Akins, and Coffey, and they are all listening, almost witnessing, as this history scrolls out before them.

This is when Coach strides around the side of snack bar and sees his coaches, and he sees, in the middle of them all, Coach Rudolph, a man he has never met and yet knows who he is just by looking at him, just by the look of him, and he says, "Hello, Coach. I'm Rick Darlington."

The two men clasp hands as Rudolph says, "I know who you are."

"Well," says Coach, "I've been hoping we could meet, and hoping we could get together here soon and talk some football."

And Coach Rudolph replies, "I'd like that."

# Week Four—What It's All About

## Orange High School Panthers: Hillsborough, North Carolina

**I**T **IS THE** middle of the afternoon and the end of August in North Carolina, and Bill Hynus, the head football coach at Orange High School, scrubs out and sprays down $CO_2$ cans on a patch of concrete next to the school's pump house and baseball field and, oh boy, is it hot. The metallic canisters are hot. The asphalt driveway and brick pump house and cement sheet where Coach performs his task are all boiling hot. The vinyl driver's seat of the utility golf cart is like sitting on a waffle iron. And up above all this hopping-footed discomfort is a yellow ball of a sun that shines down like a smirking bully. The only thing cool is the hose water, and it's not that cool. Oh, and Coach, he seems pretty cool himself right now, feeling good on this Hades-hot Wednesday afternoon, wearing his paint-splattered "Panther Staff" T-shirt, his paint-flecked athletic shorts, and his black rubber coaching shoes.

And he's got good reason to be feeling all right about now. He's made it through his five classroom periods of algebra instruction; he's made it through his lunchtime parking lot duty in short sleeves and no hat and temperatures hovering around ninety-eight degrees; he's getting his prep work accomplished to go out this evening after practice and do one of his favorite things: paint the

Glen Auman Stadium field. His team, the Varsity Panthers, has a real chance to break an eight-game losing streak—dating far back into last season—with a victory in this Friday night's game against their new cross-town rivals, the Cedar Ridge Red Wolves, and his varsity starting quarterback will celebrate his fourteenth birthday tomorrow, a full day before the big game. So Coach is doing pretty okay as sweat rolls down his face, and he considers this first-ever meeting with Cedar Ridge, squints up into the gamma-ray sun, and says, "I never worried too much about my job security here. But if we lose this game, I might have to worry."

Luckily for Coach though, he doesn't have a whole lot of time to think about what might happen to his job if things don't work out exactly right against the young upstarts from across town. He's got too much to do right here, right now. First, there's this paint deal. Coach has got to wash these cylinders out, then pour white paint into them through a plastic strainer until they're half full, and then fill them up to the top with water. Then he loads the eight cans on the golf cart to move his operation over to a storage shed next to the football field, where he unloads them and hauls them inside to shoot them full of $CO_2$ gas before he drags them back out to the grassy area behind the end zone and lays them on their sides so they don't "gunk up" and are ready for tonight.

By the time the end-of-school bell rings, the canisters are lined up like shotgun shells on the stadium field, and Coach is back in his office inside the spanking new fieldhouse. He is thankful for the new bathroom in the new coaches' office that gives him a place to change out of his soaked painter's shirt and splash some of that semi-cool water on his face and try to look half-way present-able for the "No Child Left Behind" meeting that he is expected to attend in a matter of minutes in the school's newly renovated library. Before he can get out the door and to the meeting, though, he's got to spend a moment with his two "off-campus" coaches, Steve Neighbours and Paul Cecil, to discuss the film work they'll be accomplishing with the team while he is down at the library. "Now remember," Coach says, "we're focused on ourselves this week. We ain't even worried about Cedar Ridge and what they gonna do or might do. Hell, we know what they gonna do. They gonna give it to Devon Moore and watch him run with it."

Cecil considers all of this and repeats what has become the staff's mantra for the week, "We got to worry about us," but Neighbours is more concerned about the Red Wolves. "What I want to know is: how'd they come up with that name, Cedar Ridge? It ain't on no ridge, and it's surrounded by pines. How'd they get Cedar Ridge? It is a nice name. But what about Pine Grove or Pine Hills or Pine Forest or Pine Something? And when's the last time anybody saw a wolf around here?"

"Well," says Cecil, "there ain't no panthers neither, and you don't hear no one gripin' 'bout that ... but remember, we ain't worried about them."

Coach nods his head just as Josh Coburn, the lone senior on the offensive line, walks through the office door. Josh and his mom have the idea that Josh will be playing Division I college football at this time next year and they are doing everything they can to make that happen, including setting up a "re-take" of Josh's individual football picture so he looks bigger and sturdier than he does in the one he posed for on the team picture day. He's here for his game jersey and game pants because the photographer is standing outside, sweating through his shirt and ready to take the new picture. Josh has already gotten his hair cut and visited the dentist this week in preparation for this moment, and he says, "I'm a have 'em take it in the shade so I ain't squintin' into the sun."

"That's a heckuva idea," says Neighbours. "You know what you need though? Them 'Queer Guys Gone Straight'."

"No," says Cecil. "It's them 'Five Queer Guys'."

"Well whatever. You know what I mean," says Neighbours. "Where the gay guys work with the straight guy to get him straightened out."

Josh tries to imagine this possibility, but Coach shakes his head and says, "Josh, there ain't a makeup artist in the world could help you." With this, he gives him his jersey and black pants. "You get this done quick and then you get back with your teammates," he says.

Josh leaves the office, prepared to stand tall and look tough, and he's replaced in the doorframe by LeQuentin Breeze, the soon-to-be fourteen-year-old starting quarterback. LeQuentin has stopped by on his way to the locker room for no other reason than to say "hello," and, as he shakes hands all around, Coach says, "Quentin, we gotta get you a nickname."

The idea brings an ear-wide smile to the young man's face. "Tha's a good idea, Coach."

"That is a good idea," says Neighbours, "but not 'Cool Breeze' 'cause it's taken."

"Yeah," says Cecil, "and not 'Fresh Breeze' 'cause it sounds like a damn feminine hygiene commercial."

"Well, we'll think of somethin'," says Coach. "You keep gittin' better, and we'll work on that one."

"That sounds good, Coach," says LeQuentin.

"Awright then." And with this, he is off to change clothes and Coach is off to his meeting.

As he wends his way through the halls and toward the library, Coach isn't thinking about the test-taking strategies he'll be expected to discuss in the next few minutes, but rather about his freshman quarterback. "It ain't like he's a phenom or anything. He ain't. But he'll end up bein' pretty good … and he's what we've got. And," Coach says, "he's a good kid … a good kid." There are older kids wandering the hallways of school that Coach wouldn't mind having on the team to help out his young quarterback, but, for one reason or another, they have chosen not to go out for football this year. "There's one boy," Coach says, "a baseball player. Good athlete. He's a senior. Can throw with either hand. He should be our starter. Give Quentin a chance to ease into things. But he don't wanna git hurt playin' football. Jeopardize the baseball deal. So he sits out, and we throw our freshman into the fire."

The "No Child Left Behind" meeting goes as expected for Coach. He sits down at a back table with his offensive coordinator, Allan Gorry, and the two work hard to remain interested in the discussion as their fellow teachers sip on bottles of soda and nibble trail mix and bemoan the fact that the high number of students at the school who qualify as "Exceptional Children" is wreaking havoc with the state-mandated test scores. "If they'da had all this when I's in school, I'd a been classified ADD. Sittin' still was hard for me … hell, I'm havin' a hard time sittin' still right now. But in my day," Coach says softly to Gorry, "they had ways of makin' kids pay attention."

Coach's "day" was back at East High School in Huntington, West Virginia, and he was able to sit still and pay close enough attention to move on from there to play wide receiver at Marshall University, where he earned a math degree and then taught and coached for a few years in his home state before he started looking for a coaching job down here in North Carolina where, he says, "the pay is better and they provide you with some decent insurance." It is primarily football that got him through high school and into and through college, and football, and all the different things it means to him, is what keeps Coach here now. "I'm here for the combination of football and watchin' kids succeed," he says. "It's gratifying to see a kid who's gone off to college, on a scholarship's great, but just *go* to college and got a degree, and now's come back to say hello and let us know he still remembers us here, remembers the school. Tha's prob'ly the best part."

For Coach and Gorry, the best part of this meeting is when Ms. Purcell, who is running things, says, "Well, this gives us some things to think about for next time." But, until that moment, Coach takes big gulps of his coke and tries to convince himself that what he is doing here in the library is important to his school and his students. He understands that "wins and losses are a part of the job, but not necessarily the biggest part." The upcoming and seemingly "must-win" game against Cedar Ridge not withstanding, Coach believes that "they look at the whole picture here"—respect for the kids, academics, and so forth—and one reason why he has been able to carry on through some not-so-successful seasons is because he has made the importance of academics and the worth of the individual student integral components of the program. Coach hands a business card out to his players at the beginning of each school year that has on it his name and phone number, and he wants them to keep it in their pockets and feel like they can call him anytime and for any reason.

While Coach and Gorry fidget in their meeting, Neighbours and Cecil and Mike McDaniel are down at the fieldhouse with the team, watching film of last Friday night's loss to Chapel Hill. Coach McDaniel was a defensive lineman here in the 1990s and is in charge of the JV team, as well as the varsity defense, and he is sick of watching his guys lose.

As he sits in the dark with his varsity defenders and presses "Play" and "Rewind" and "Play" and "Rewind" on the VCR's remote control, he has a difficult time masking his anger at what he perceives to be the squad's lackadaisical performance. "You hittin' him like I hug my momma," he complains as he watches a linebacker slide off an enemy ball carrier. "I'm not tryin' to be mean to ya', but hit the son of a gun. You huggin' on him." On the tape's next play, Markise Poteat, an undersized junior defensive end, makes a solid hit to bring down the opposing runner and McDaniel says, "Good punishment here, Markise. Tha's what we need from ya'." As Markise nods his head and reaches to slap five with one of his congratulatory buddies, McDaniel interrupts the mini-celebration. "But not one out of ten times. You need to be hittin' hard every play."

As the first half of yet another eventual Panther loss winds down McDaniel has seen enough for today. He shuts off the film and calls for the lights. "You boys see what we need to do. I don't want to see no finger-pointin' except at ourselves. If you haven't been knocked down playin' football, then you ain't played long enough or rough enough." McDaniel pauses to look around at the defensive team that is seated on the concrete locker room benches or stretched out on the concrete floor. And all of them, for once, are intently listening. "Look," McDaniel continues, "we up against it right now. Ever'body knows we got a young quarterback, a young offensive line. I heard you finger-pointin' on the sidelines Friday night. I don' wanna hear it no more. Cheer the offense on. Cheer your teammates on. Git out there and hit somebody—hit him ... hit him ... hit him! Have it in your mind that you're gonna make a play when you're out there. And when you're not out there, you support your teammates."

One player who doesn't seem to be supporting his teammates today is punter Will Dickerson. As Coach hurries from the library meeting back to the fieldhouse, he glances out toward the school parking lot and sees the lanky, redheaded junior leaning against his father's black Hummer, laughing with some friends. "There's a kid who's on the team and could help us more … but all he wants to do is kick," he says.

Coach makes it back to his office, late for the film, but in time to ask, "Well, what'd we learn in there?"

McDaniel, for all his criticism in the film session, feels pretty good about the defense, but right now, he has some real concerns about the team's lack of offensive production to date, which has totaled twelve points in the season's first two games.

Gorry, who is a little sensitive about being in charge of this young offense, says, "It doesn't help when your punter kicks it straight up in the air."

"That's right," says Neighbours. "We did have that zero punt."

"We got these young kids up front," continues Gorry, "and they'll hit a guy, and then turn around to see if there's a hole created. We gotta get 'em to sustain them blocks."

"I agree with you," says Coach, "and the big reason our backs aren't runnin' hard as they should is 'cause I don't think they trust what's up front."

"If I could line up my offense and stand behind 'em to see what they're up against, I could just pick and choose, and we'd be movin' the ball," says Gorry. "But instead, I'm over on that sideline goin' crazy. We just gotta get over the hump, and we can be all right … get these kids believin' in themselves, believin' they got to keep fightin'. The problem is that not a whole lot of high school kids have that mentality to fight to the very end."

"Now, is it us that can't get 'em to push, or is it just society?" muses Coach. "But I got to believe that there are still programs out there where the coach says somethin' and it gets done."

In response to Coach's querying editorial, Gorry walks up to the whiteboard where he uncorks a marker and writes the number "30" with a slew of exclamation points after it and a fat circle around it, and, for emphasis, pokes the marker at the board as he pronounces, "We … scorin' … thirty—at least thirty—on 'em Friday night."

"Awright," says Neighbours, "the offensive guru has spoken."

As the offensive guru returns to slump back down in his seat, Coach sees Will the punter glide by the office door. "Hey, Will!" he calls out over the heads of his gathered assistants.

Will peeks in to say, "What's up, Coach?"

"Why weren't you here for film today?" Coach asks.

Will responds, "I was in tutoring with Mr. Cox."

Coach leans back in his desk chair, his clenched fingers drumming his ex-athlete's paunch. "Is 'at right?" he says.

"Yeah, I was behind and wantin' to catch up."

"So you was in with Mr. Cox," says Coach in his high, nasally, and mildly entertained West Virginia voice. "You weren't out in the parkin' lot showin' off no high-price vehicle?"

"Yeah Coach, tha's right."

As Will starts to back away from the doorframe and toward the locker room, Coach gets the picture in his mind of Friday night's punt that went straight up and landed almost at Will's feet. "Son," he says, "your hair flames above the crowd and your face turns the color of your hair when you lie. I know what you were up to and it wasn't puttin' in time with Mr. Cox, and it wasn't over here helpin' this team get better." Coach is smiling as he says this, and so is Will, and both smiles communicate pretty much the same thing, which is, "If this exchange goes any further, like to the promise of post-practice punishment, then the Hummer will be getting a lot more after-school use and Coach will be searching for a new punter."

So, Will offers up his best impression of a sheepish grin and Coach turns his attention to Gorry who has strolled back up to the board to demonstrate exactly how they'll get those thirty points. As Gorry draws Os and Xs and makes determined swooshes toward an imagined end zone, Neighbours says, "Ever'thing looks good on that whiteboard, don't it?"

If there's one person here at Orange High School who should know what things look like on the whiteboard, or the greenboard, or the blackboard before it, Neighbours is the man. He played football here in the 1960s and, after driving about ten miles up the road to attend the University at Chapel Hill, he set up an accounting business back here in Hillsborough and started helping out with the football team. He has been here long enough to coach Cecil, McDaniel, and Kevin Wright, who has just arrived for practice, and he was already a veteran on the staff when Coach arrived as a fellow assistant in 1990.

It has been a long time since Coach's days as an assistant. He now has one daughter in college, one daughter in cosmetology school, and a wife who moved with him from West Virginia. Mrs. Hynus has been mostly confined to the house for the last couple of years due to a chronic fatigue syndrome called fibrositis. Today is one of the few days when Coach is so busy down at school that he can't find the time to get home to deliver a McDonald's hamburger or at least check in to see how she's doing. "It's been tough on all of us," says Coach. "But mainly tough on her. She's used to bein' out and gettin' things done." She was able to fight through her illness to complete the orange and black plaster Panther statue that is stationed outside the fieldhouse door and that players and coaches don't walk by without a "good luck" tap on their way out to the stadium for a Friday night game. "I'm real fortunate," Coach says. "My wife, she understands what this football deal means to me ... and I think it means something to her, too."

This "football deal" also means something to the town of Hillsborough and its two high schools and that's why Principal Jeff Dishmon is standing on the team's practice field in his loosened tie and rolled-up-sleeves shirt while the players and coaches straggle out in the muggy heat. Before they line up for their pre-practice stretch, he gathers the team around him for a few words about this week's first-ever rivalry game. "This school is extremely proud of you boys," he begins, "and we'll be proud of you when you walk in the door Monday morning, regardless of what the scoreboard says on Friday. I want you to represent the school well." As he concludes his remarks, Mr. Dishmon notices senior running back Akil Stewart gazing off toward the scrub pines that line one side of the bowl-shaped practice field. "You got me, Akil?" he asks.

This snaps Akil back into the here and now and with a grin on his face, he says, "I gotcha, playah."

They begin the practice day with a Gorry-designed concoction called the "half-line" drill, where one side of the offensive line lines up on the ball with their backfield behind them and a "half-defense" lined up across from them. The object of this drill is for the offensive group to "go hard" for three plays, and for their three offensive coaches to watch them do it and to make sure they do it right. "That's been our problem," says Gorry. "We make that initial hit, but then we stop and look around as if to say, 'What do I do next?' We got to learn to play through the whistle." The drill starts out in positive fashion, with Gorry lining up the left side of his first team and explaining to his gathered offensive players, "I'm gonna put you in situations that might be adversarial. I'm gonna scream and yell and praise all day today. But we'll reap the reward on Friday night. When we beat Cedar Ridge fifty to nothin', you'll be beggin' me to do it again next week. What I want you to do is give me maximum effort. You linemen are gonna explode. Squat down and explode."

For the first couple of plays, that is just what happens—the center snap is crisp; the hand-off is flawless; and the offensive line runs over its overmatched defensive counterparts like a John Deere tractor scythes a row of wheat. This gets Gorry excited and exclaiming, "Pick each other up ... keep it up ... keep it up!"

But this period of good feeling and hard hitting is brief as the linemen start to let up on key blocks, and the backs start to look skittish and scared instead of bullish and bold. At first, Gorry tries to attribute it to the heat, and he says, "Stand up between plays, and get some air if you're tired." Gorry works to remain positive, saying to the chest-heaving Josh as he settles in for yet another play, "Get in a good stance. Now's the time, when things seem tough ... get in that good stance."

But McDaniel, who has brought his defensive specialists over to the drill to stiffen the competition for these first-teamers, can't resist saying, "He's too tired to get in a good stance. He wants to play in college, but he can't get in a good stance." This observation is followed by more half-speed effort and soft contact.

Gorry tries another tactic, exploding with, "We runnin' the sweep again next play and if one 'a you ain't blockin' we'll just start doin' up-downs! If we can't learn any other way, we'll learn by punishment! If you all can't learn, they can fire me, 'cause I ain't gonna let you play like 'iss! Hell, they won't have to fire me, 'cause I'll quit! I can't stand to watch it! You all are actin' like a buncha' damn superstars, and I ain't seen nothin' outta ya yet ... nothin'!"

But even Gorry's tirade proves ineffective to the point that Cecil pushes a second-teamer into the fray and drawls, "Do somethin' different today. Get out there and hit someone." And kids try to coax Will—who has concluded his solo punt practice for the day and wandered over to watch the rest of the team—into playing some offensive tackle, but Will says, "C'mon guys, I can't just jump in there." Coaches and players all snap their heads around in starved unison when they hear a loud "Crack!" that sounds like a big hit from down at the junior varsity end of the field, only to discover that it is nothing more than a cooler that fell with a thud off the managers' table.

This is practice for the remainder of this afternoon—through the individual drills where Gorry tries to jump in and shows LeQuentin exactly how he wants the "fade" route thrown, and succeeds only in demonstrating why he was a lineman during his own playing days; through the group drills where Wright grabs a "tackling bag" to jump in on the scout defense, and McDaniel calls out, "Good look, Coach, way to give 'em a look," when Wright delivers a big-league "shiver" to a surprised Big Josh.

During Team Offense, Gorry arrives at such a point of disgust that, when he screams "Run!" at his tailback to try and get him to run, Hugo Clard, a reserve receiver who is standing innocently behind the play, is so startled that he breaks into a sprint upfield and right through the middle of the half-speed play.

By this point, Coach shakes his head and calls in his team, and says, "Why come out here in this damn heat for two hours if you're not gonna have fun and beat on somebody? We got guys comin' out here and goin' through the motions and wantin' to go home. Well les' go home then. We'll come back out tomorrow and see if we got anyone who wants to play. Get a break, and get in, and tha's it for today. I seen enough."

As the players tramp up the newly mown hill and across the parking lot toward their cool shower and their ride home, the coaches hang back on the practice field. Wright leans on a tackling dummy. McDaniel adjusts the drawstring on his straw hat. Cecil and Gorry toss a ball back and forth. Coach bends down to retrieve an orange cone that his players have left behind and says, "This is s'posed to be fun, and right now it ain't." Neighbours chuckles and lets his gaze settle on Coach Wright. "You know," he says, "watchin' you out there with that defense today, prowlin' around like 'at … shore does bring back them memories," then starts his slow walk back to the fieldhouse, where he finds Akil and Josh bobbing their heads to some hardcore rap song that, to his wizened ears, sounds like gravel on a tin roof. He can't help but say to the two seniors, "If that don't get you up for a game, nothin' will." They stop in mid-bob, and watch him in open-mouthed silence as he strolls into the office.

Gorry, who has seen this generational mini-clash, says, "Wha's a matter?"

"Damn," Akil says, "He be tokin', o' what?" And Josh nods his head in shared bemusement.

"See boys, it's like 'iss," Gorry explains in his best concerned uncle way. "Coach Neighbours has a dry sense of humor, like Saturday night at the Improv. And most of it goes right over yo' heads. Tha's good though, 'cause, if you actually got it, you wouldn't be able to practice 'cause you'd be laughin' so hard."

Coach arrives at the fieldhouse in time to say, "See ya later," to Gorry and Cecil, who are headed out to the stadium to get a start on the painting, and to Neighbours who is going home to a hoped-for chicken dinner before he'll return to join the paint crew. McDaniel is waiting for him in the office and says, "We better get over to the gym." The two coaches are expected at an athletics meeting for participants' parents, and, thanks to Jim King, the school's athletic director, and to the absence of air-conditioning, the meeting moves right along.

So, before he can get too uncomfortable sitting on the hard-wood gymnasium bleachers, Coach finds himself where he has wanted to be all day—out on the field under the stadium lights with a paint-sprayer in his hand, swatting mosquitoes and swapping stories with his coaches. There are a couple of pizza boxes and a cooler full of punch on the sideline trainer's table, all headed toward the same temperature in the damp evening heat. Cecil's brother, Bentley, who played here with McDaniel and Wright, has joined the crew; he is a fan of this football team and the people who coach it. He helps them paint the field on Wednesdays; he keeps game statistics on Fridays; he remembers his own playing career here fondly, saying the hardest he ever got hit was a "friendly-fire collision" with McDaniel. "We was playin' defense and ran into each other. It was like a explosion. My ears was ringing for days after that"; and he has a hard time thinking of something he wouldn't do for Coach, who, he says, "Holds this whole deal together."

By ten o'clock, the field is next to ready for Friday night's game, except for the jungle-orange "O" that Coach will paint at the fifty-yard-line during his planning period tomorrow, for no other reason than "it looks good for the field and the kids and the folks up in the stands." Then, after he paints the "O" and after school, he'll meet with his team on the stadium field to go through their Thursday practice "walk-through" for Friday's game. The team will be in their shorts and game jerseys, all except for Ryan Edwards, a senior linebacker who is so hyped-up for the Cedar Ridge match-up that he comes out in his full pads and can't help but prance around, shoving his fellow players and getting "pumped," until Coach says, "I don't care what you got to do to get ready for the game … but not while I'm talkin'." This calms Ryan down enough for Coach to tell the team, "You know what you gotta do. You know what this game means. You know who's gonna be there and how many," and then to dismiss the team with a "Panthers!" break. This will leave him just enough time to drive the junior varsity over to Cedar Ridge, where he'll look on as McDaniel's JV team so thoroughly dominates the Cedar Ridge JV that, after the game, Wright asks one of the young Panthers, "Did you do what I told you to do?" and the player replies, "No, I did what I wanted to do. I told him what I was gonna do, and I did it."

And then it will be Friday and Coach will make his way through the sand-slow class periods, before facing the long afternoon, the march over to the cafeteria for Booster Club sandwiches, and the office wait, and the locker room wait, and the ankle tape and wrist tape, and the prayers and admonitions that, "This is ours, dammit! This is ours, boys!" And then the stadium and the game. Lightning rings the blue-black sky, and Coach can't stop sweating. With every snap of the ball, he pumps his fist or covers his eyes. And then it's late and fourth and six for Cedar Ridge, and Coach calls time and says to his defense, "Play to win," and they trot back out.

Gorry can't stop smiling, and he says, "This is what it's all about ... 'cause you never know what's gonna happen." And the Panthers find a way to stop Devon Moore who they couldn't stop all night, and LeQuentin ushers his offense onto the field to fall on the football and end the game, not with fifty points, or thirty, but with fourteen. And tonight, that's enough.

# Week Five—All the Little Things

## Bethlehem Catholic High School Golden Hawks: Bethlehem, Pennsylvania

**A**FTER A SHORT and fitful night of sleep and an early wake-up to attend morning Mass, Coach Chuck Sonon parks his silver Malibu near the back door of the Bethlehem Catholic High School cafeteria and readies himself to head inside and talk some football. As he gets out of the driver's seat and opens the trunk to retrieve the cardboard box that serves as his football office, he bids "good morning" to his offensive coordinator, Dan Kendra, who is leaning back against the side-door of his black Crown Victoria. The sun is already a bright disk in a promising blue sky; the faintest hint of an autumn breeze floats over the Becahi school grounds and over the town cemetery and neighborhood beyond; and, except for the whisper of air in the maple trees, there is an almost stock-still quiet and a calm in this scene that gives Coach the chance to "let go" for a moment and think about absolutely nothing.

But as the cars of his assistant coaches continue to turn off Madison Avenue and into the Becahi parking lot, Coach's mind is yanked back from its bucolic reverie and into the rough reality that looms over him and his team. Last night, the varsity Golden Hawks went into their season-opening game against Philadelphia Parochial League powerhouse St. Joseph's Prep as the nineteenth-ranked high school team in the country in *USA Today*'s pre-season poll, and with heady expectations to live up to that national notoriety. But now, on this Sunday morning, after a 40–6 walloping at the hands of what Coach calls "the best team we'll play all season … and that includes postseason" there is a palpable shift in priorities for the Hawks and their coaching staff. The national ranking will be gone when the new poll comes out on Tuesday, and this Saturday night loss by such a lopsided score will have, according to Coach, "all those people who don't like us saying, 'This is the end of Becahi Football.'" Unlike these "nonbelievers," he is not quite ready to accept this bad beginning as the death knell for his team's season, saying, "Let them have their fun. That game was much closer than the score indicated," and Coach is ready to work on a plan to resuscitate the Hawks' fortunes.

But there are some obstacles that stand between Coach and his goal of getting Becahi Football back on track, the first of which is that neither he nor any of his gathered staff possess a key to unlock the cafeteria door. So, Coach Kendra pulls out his cell phone to call Jimmie, the equipment manager, to ask him if he might be able to come down to school and let them into the building. While they await Jimmie's arrival, the coaches offer up their individual perspectives on what went wrong last night. They all agree that the tone for the St. Joe's game was set on Becahi's very first offensive play from scrimmage, when Coach Kendra called a "double-reverse pass," where senior quarterback Drew Wilson, in his own first play as the Hawks' starter, took the snap from center and pitched the ball to his tailback, who handed it to the split end, who pitched it back to Wilson, who heaved it downfield to another wide receiver, who was streaking toward the goal line. Up to this point, the team's execution of this play had been flawless. But then Wilson's long pass came up a bit short, and the ball bounced off his receiver's heel and into the welcoming arms of the

St. Joe's defender. This unfortunate ricochet cast an immediate pall over the Becahi sideline that it couldn't shake for the entirety of the contest.

But the coaches also know that it wasn't just bad luck that made the difference in last night's contest, and this concerns them even more. "Their speed shocked me," says Tony Cocca, the team's defensive coordinator, of the way the St. Joe's backs seemed to beat his linebackers to the field's perimeter on play after play.

Coach Kendra can't get over how mentally prepared St. Joe's was for this late August match-up. "They knew a lot more about us than we knew about them," he says. "None of our play-action stuff stood a chance. It was like they knew what we were gonna run better than we knew what we were gonna run."

Cocca agrees with Kendra about St. Joe's impressive preparation for the game, but he also adds, "You know why they scored so much?' Cause they're stronger than us. They're just a better physical football team."

"And," says Rich Mazza, the one-time Becahi head coach who now assists with the team's offense, "there were a lot of mistakes from some of our veteran guys."

Cocca shakes his head and says, "This game shows how ridiculous the *USA Today*'s rankings are."

The Golden Hawks found themselves members of the national newspaper's elite preseason "Top 25" on the strength of last year's performance—which featured only one loss, to a Parkland High team that went on to handily win the "large-school" state title—and because they returned almost all of their starters from that team. But one of the players they lost was Adam Bednarik, their quarterback who accepted a scholarship to the University of West Virginia, and who, says Kendra, "is one of those guys who could do pretty much anything you needed him to do." It is Wilson's job to step into these oversized shoes, and, judging by this opening night performance against St. Joe's, he has got a great deal of improving to do, and he's got to do it fast. "He had the proverbial 'deer in the headlights' look," says Kendra. "He was moving at one speed, and the game was moving at another speed, and it was like a blur going by him." But Bednarik is not the only player they miss, and the success of this season doesn't rest solely with Wilson's ability to catch up to the game. The Hawks also lost two top-notch receivers, who prowled the defensive secondary as well, to graduation, and there are a couple of gaps in the offensive and defensive lines that last night's shellacking made all the more glaring.

In some respects, Coach is relieved to have the added consequence of this mythical nationwide ranking off his team's back. This will allow them to forget about "expectations" and start focusing more on establishing their own identity. And, as Jimmie arrives to unlock the cafeteria door so the coaches can start to "break down" the film from last night's game, Coach—who has already watched the film a couple of times, and who devoted much of this morning's early hours to thinking about it—says to his staff, "We don't want to get too down on the players. We gotta band together. We gotta coach 'em up so we're not having those mental mistakes. What I'm seeing is a lot of little things … and they're all things that are fixable."

Coach is not the only one here in the dim light of the cafeteria who eschewed sleep last night in favor of watching the game tape. As soon as everyone has grabbed a Krispy Kreme doughnut and settled into a chair, and almost as soon as Coach presses "Play" on the VCR, Coach Kendra begins lobbing comments of disgust and dismay toward the flickering images on the screen. Even though he attributes the kicked and intercepted pass to rotten luck, Kendra is beside himself over his quarterback's play-time choices when he has another chance on the field. On the next offensive play, and with the team already down 7–0, Kendra has called a "Crack Screen," a play designed for the quarterback to sprint back from the line of scrimmage in a "deep drop." The offensive linemen hold their blocks for a count of "one-one thousand … two-one thousand," and then "release" their defensive counterparts, who will charge toward the quarterback while the offensive linemen race toward the sideline where an offensive back awaits them.

The actuality of the play is that Wilson takes the snap and fires the ball to his running back, Boomer Rice, before the offensive line has "released" their blocks, and before Boomer has made it anywhere close to the sideline. But it wouldn't have mattered even if Wilson had allowed the play to unfold in its natural progression because the St. Joe's defense "sniffed this one out," and the defensive linemen, instead of sprinting toward the quarterback, hold their ground. There is also a linebacker who "mirrors" Boomer, and who smashes into him, driving him into the turf the instant he hauls in the premature throw. "What is he thinking?" Kendra asks the room full of similarly appalled coaches. "Where is he looking? He takes two steps and dumps it off to Boomer."

But Boomer is not safe from Kendra's disappointed wrath either. On the next play, he is supposed to step up to the line of scrimmage to help provide pass protection for his beleaguered quarterback. But just as Kendra is ready to see this senior team captain deliver a blow to an advancing defensive end, Boomer offers up nothing more than a half-hearted shiver that the St. Joe's defender shrugs off as he continues on toward the unsuspecting quarterback. Kendra ruefully shakes his head and says, "Boomer, if he's not carrying the ball, he doesn't give max effort."

If there is anyone here who would know about effort, it's Kendra, who, at forty-eight years old, maintains the Paul Bunyan build that served him so well when he played quarterback at West Virginia, where Bobby Bowden was his coach, and fellow assistant Artie Owens—who is fifty and still looks highly capable of "putting on the pads"—his teammate. And when the two long-time friends talk about football, it is their college days in Morgantown that they remember most fondly. Both men were already married and the fathers of young sons, and the thing they remember most is on some days after practice when they would be on the field with their wives and sons. They may have been tossing the football around, or just sitting on the grass, relaxed and contented and free from their unwieldy shoulder pads and helmets, with their pretty wives chatting quietly by their side, and their baby boys rolling around and happy, and it would be peaceful, with everyone else having drifted off the field, and it was just them, and they were young and they felt good, and there was this world surrounding them, and it was, as far as they could tell, all theirs. "These were the best times of our lives," says Kendra, "and we were too young to realize it."

Right now, neither Kendra nor Owens is thinking about those days. Instead, all the coaches are thinking about the practice days ahead and how they are going to move the Hawks away from this St. Joe's debacle and toward playing like they are capable of playing. "Coming off the field last night, the kids are in shock," says Kendra. Coach shifts uncomfortably in his plastic chair, as yet another failed offensive series concludes on the film and the Hawks' exhausted defense digs in once again to try and stop St. Joe's. "I'm gonna talk to the captains tomorrow," he says. "Give them a refresher course about how they need to lead by example."

Then, St. Joe's rips off another big offensive run and Cocca is seething. "Boomer can't get to the play because he's lined up wrong," he says. "He's thinking he's Dick Butkus gonna get to the play and blow it up. I got news for you: right here, he's no Dick Butkus."

And then it's another St. Joe's score and another anemic "three and out" offensive display by the Hawks, and, as the film continues in this fashion, and the coaches become more frustrated, it becomes more and more clear why Boomer can't "get to the play," and why senior tackle Jeff Kocsis can't "fire off the ball," and why senior end John Bedics is "taking a lousy angle," and it's because they, and most of their fellow senior starters, play both an offensive and defensive position that keeps them from ever coming off the field for a rest or to get some kind of perspective on their team's situation—which is dire. "We're a good team, not a great team," says Cocca.

And, on this film of last night's game, it is painfully evident that they are lined up against a great team. "I knew going into this game that we wouldn't beat St. Joe's just by looking at their tapes," says Cocca. "They were a better team that would have to play their 'B Game' as opposed to our 'A Game' in order for us to have a chance. Instead, it was the opposite." The game tape continues to roll, and it is the same story repeated over and over again: A confused Becahi offense swarmed over by an exuberant St. Joe's defense that gives way to a fresh St. Joe's offense running roughshod over an exhausted Becahi defense.

"My biggest fear right now is our guys are intimidated," says Kendra. "They're playin' scared, like they think everybody in the country is lookin' at us. They're not. They don't care. They're not watching us."

A lot of folks will have the chance to watch Becahi in their Friday night road game at Lansdale's North Penn High School because the Pennsylvania Cable Network is broadcasting the match-up across the state as its "Game of the Week." And, instead of a game where the Hawks can "get well" with a confidence-building victory, the going will be anything but smooth against this next opponent. In addition to a numbers disparity (North Penn has a graduating class of more than one thousand, compared with Becahi's 740 total students), the word is that, even though St. Joe's may be the grid-iron pride of the Philadelphia Parochial League, a lot of people believe that North Penn is the best squad in the state. The thought of facing the two toughest teams on the block in rapid succession to begin this season and the chilling reminder that Becahi's athletic director, Bob Bukvics, has already penciled in these same two opponents to kick off next year's schedule prompts Cocca to crack, "Me and Kendra are taking a sabbatical next year ... only for the St. Joe's and North Penn weeks."

"Yeah," adds Kendra, "we'll go on a Caribbean cruise and let Bucky coach those two games."

But before they can turn their attention to the difficulties that North Penn might pose for their reeling Golden Hawks, the staff takes time, as Sunday morning bleeds into Sunday afternoon, to talk about what Becahi needs to do to make themselves a better team. And, in the midst of all this gloom, they are able to muster up a few rays of optimism. "Defensively, we played with 'em in the first half," says Cocca. "We had some little things that killed us. But it's all coachable, all correctable. The down linemen? We need to work on alignment, and they've got to get a piece of their guys ... keep 'em off our linebackers. And the linebackers? They were reading backs. They've got to read guards. The backs don't tell them anything. The guards tell 'em everything. Our defensive backs? They have to work on depth. We've got to have 'em at five yards and don't bail. They've got to come up for run support. And our pursuit angles were terrible. It's damn geometry. They have to work on pursuit, on their angles. That's gonna be conditioning for us this week ... pursuit ... get 'em to get to the ball."

The more Cocca talks about his defense and what they need to do to be more formidable, the more animated he becomes. This is in stark contrast to his disposition when the talk, or the film, or the team practice, or the game situation, turns to offense, which he views in the same way a plumber might view a clogged kitchen sink—something that is unpleasant but grudgingly necessary and must be dealt with in a professional manner. Whereas Owens and Kendra profess to "love football" totally and unconditionally, Coach Cocca is a little more fickle in his passion for the game that has been such an important part of his life for so long. He sums up his feelings when he declares, "I hate offense."

Meanwhile, Kendra, from his post behind the first-team offense, points at the scout team defense and says to Wilson, his gun-shy quarterback, "You got three reads to make. You gotta look off the safety. You gotta see the linebacker's drop. And you gotta know where the cornerback is headed. And then you got to get rid of the ball … right now! You got to have the guts to step up and deliver a strike."

Owens plays what he calls "that psychological game" with Boomer, replacing him at tailback with Brandon Carter in hopes of showing this headstrong senior that there are other guys who can run the ball if he doesn't want to go all out all the time. Boomer paces around manically behind the JVers and second-stringers until Sam Carrodo, one of the team's numerous volunteer coaches, takes him by the arm and says to him in a whisper, "You got to be a leader here. You got to keep your cool."

Coach has arrived from his job teaching math at Emmaus High School and he is counseling his starting offensive line and the scout team defenders across from them. "You can't form treaties," he says. "When you take it easy on each other, you lose. You gotta come off the line like Banshee warriors. You gotta go a hundred miles an hour. That's how we get better."

This is all important stuff for a struggling offense, but while it is going on, Cocca says, "I try to place my mind elsewhere." He is successful at this tactic until the Wednesday afternoon practice when he is shaken out of his solitary musings by what he perceives as a near-complete lack of effort by the offensive starters, who he also counts on to perform defensively. He marches into the middle of the offensive team drill and emits an increasingly shrill and breathless series of epithets that are partly an attempt to wake this crew up and partly a way of releasing his own frustrations. "You don't care!" he shrieks, and then he pounds on his chest and bellows, "You don't have it in here!" and, as he reaches a nadir of breath and hope, he gasps, "I'm gonna have a stroke!"

He continues to beat at his chest with a clenched fist as he retreats back toward his solitary outpost and Kendra takes up his rant, only with a tone more of state-the-facts observation than frustration. "You guys don't care," he says. "There's no senior leadership on this team. It doesn't matter if Coach cares, or me, or him. We can't play the game for you. You gotta care." And, with this out of their collective system, Kendra says to the first-team offense, "Reload," which is the Becahi parlance for: Let's run that play again. Everybody lines up, Drew Wilson barks out his crisp cadence, P. J. Donofrio centers the ball, and the Golden Hawks get back to getting better.

As Cocca continues to massage his chest, just to make certain that his "stroke" proclamation was nothing more than a threat, he says that as important as football is to him and these other coaches, and to the players, he thinks it is taken too seriously. "You get a packed school board meeting if someone tries to fire the coach," he says. "They try to change the English curriculum and one guy with a pocket protector shows up to complain." Whether thanks to his tirade or not, the offensive practice has settled into a productive groove with the staccato "pop" of shoulder pads and helmets and the reassuring calls of, "Good throw," and, "Atta' boy," and, "That's how to go for the ball," punctuating each play from scrimmage.

This renewed execution and hustle and all-around good feeling has softened Cocca a bit and made him think about why he's out here watching these boys run around in the drizzling rain. "It's just a game played by kids," he says, "and sometimes the fans and the parents forget that. Parents think their kid is special and going to school on a scholarship. But guys don't just walk into a living room with an open checkbook and say, 'How much do you want?' You got to be a special player."

The North Penn Knights have one of those "special players" in their offensive tailback, Kevin Atkins, who has committed to attend Boston College next year, and, as the Becahi coaches turn their Sunday attention to game tape of North Penn's weekend performance, it is clear why Boston College, and a lot of other schools, covet Atkins so badly. He is really good. Cocca is convinced, though, that beyond Atkins and his quarterback, who also has the breakaway speed and that natural swagger that only the best runners possess, the North Penn offense doesn't have much to offer. "Their passing game is miniscule," he says. "They really don't throw it, and judging by this tape, they can't throw it." The more he watches the Knights' offensive line "pack it in" with tight splits, and then watches the quarterback "quick-pitch" the ball to Atkins, who races around end with a couple of his hefty blockers as escorts, the more he is convinced that he needs to "put ten in the box" on defense to stop the run and make North Penn resort to their shaky and, so far, untested passing attack. He wants ten out of his eleven defenders right up on the line of scrimmage, daring North Penn to run the ball and one "safety man" dropped back fifteen yards in the middle of the field to protect against a surprise pass that Cocca doesn't think will come. "We're gonna have to keep 'contain,'" he says. "That'll be a big thing for the defensive engine, force 'em inside and don't let 'em get out to the perimeter and off to the races. I'm convinced that they'll line up tight and run the ball, and say, 'Becahi, you can't stop us,' and keep pounding it and pounding it until we prove that we can stop 'em."

On offense, Kendra wants to get junior wide receiver Kyle Newell out in "space," or on the line of scrimmage, but separated as far as possible from the scrum of bodies in the middle of the field in the high hope that he'll be isolated man-to-man with one of the Knights' defenders. This will give him the opportunity to catch a pass from Wilson and then use his 6'4" 220-pound frame and sprinter's speed to either run over his one defender for a seven- or eight-yard gain or "juke" around him where, says Kendra, "It's off to the races because the safety is way off on the other side of the field."

So this is one facet of the plan they have contrived to attack the North Penn defense and it will work if the Knight corner-backs are consistent in their eight-yard-plus cushions and Kendra's offensive formations can create the "space" to get Kyle and his pass-catching buddies in those desirable "one-on-one" situations. The Hawks offensive line will also have to hold back the wither-ing pressure of North Penn's hyper-aggressive defensive front for the two-plus seconds it requires their quarterback to take the snap, back away from the line of scrimmage, "set up," and throw the foot-ball; and Wilson must trade in his St. Joe's "deer-in-the-headlights" experience for the poise it takes to face the pressure and make the throw. But also, says Kendra, "We have to be able to run the ball."

On first impression, running the ball seems impossible against this rock wall of a North Penn defensive "front seven," especially after the St. Joe's game, where Coach says of the Hawks' ground attack, "We had a bunch of guys standing around and one guy fighting for his life."

Kendra doesn't want that to happen again this week. "Our backs shouldn't have to make three people miss just to get to the line of scrimmage," he says. And Kendra seems to have found a way for Becahi to at least try to run the football. His plan is to use the extreme athleticism and aggressiveness of the Knights' defensive front against them. They "come off the ball" so hard that Kendra thinks slow-developing and misdirection-type plays like "traps," "counter-traps," and "draws" just might work. These plays rely heavily on a defensive down lineman committing full-force to where he thinks the action appears to be headed, and then working the ball carrier in behind him, into and through the space that the defender has created with his own hasty departure.

Another running "series" that Kendra thinks he can count on to register some rushing yards against the Knights is variations of the quarterback "option" that North Penn uses in its own offense to great advantage and that the Hawks will try to use against them in their search for defensive shortcomings. Kendra, seeing the controlled recklessness with which these North Penn defensive ends "come across the line" and "crash down" toward the ball, wants to include, instead of the basic "option," a couple of variations of it: the "speed option" and the "lead option." "Speed option" dispenses with the fullback fake and with the quarterback read in the assumption that the end is automatically "coming hard" so that the quarterback takes the snap, takes a quick step or two down the line, and immediately flips the ball to his trailing back. The "lead option" sends the fullback along the line of scrimmage as a "lead" blocker instead of into it as a possible ball carrier or decoy, thus giving the offense one more man out on the perimeter to help clear the way for either the quarterback or his trailing back. "These guys just flat-out come off the ball," says Kendra of the North Penn defensive front. "We got to tell our guys, 'Don't look. Don't think. Just run.'"

And so this is what practice is about all week—running the ball, running to the ball, running to create space, running at correct angles, running with heads up and with the faith that "we can play with these guys." And Coach, he's running more than anyone and he's saying to his linemen, "You don't take the path of least resistance! You gotta take the broom and sweep the corners!" And he's chewing his gum, chomping it, his back teeth operating like a piston engine, and his face scarlet, and his voice wheezing as it rises and rises in the Friday night pre-game locker room and he says to his boys, "I don't like this place. They're rich and they think they're better than us. You play hard … and you punch 'em and you hit 'em and you swarm the ball … and you hit 'em and you hit 'em and you hit 'em and you hit 'em until they say, 'No más'!" And this is Coach's week, his life, right here in this halogen lamp–lit room ready to watch his team storm the field and play football, and he's ready to win, wanting to win bad, so bad. And his heart, what is it doing right now in the middle of his chest, after this week of worry, after so many weeks and years of worry and film and sweat-soaked practice, of alignments and angles, and those little things, too many to count, too many to try and imagine, for himself and for his team? What is it all doing in that heart of his?

But there's got to be more in his heart than football, than that desire, that will to win, to achieve. And on Wednesday, sometime between Cocca's stroke warning that precipitates the good strong end to practice and his own son's "Junior Hawks" practice that Coach tries to catch at least some of whenever he can, and the film session Coach hosts for the parents and the fans in the same dark lunchroom where he spends his Sundays, Coach gets in his car to drive over to Pott's, right next to the Moravian College campus, to order up a couple of cheese dogs and a chocolate milk, and then to sit on a sidewalk bench and feel this warm September evening settle in around him. And right now there's no football, no math class, no parent asking, "Why isn't my kid getting the ball?" No nothing, except a middle-aged man, relaxed and remembering. And the thing he's got in his mind is a trip he took many years before, a driving trip with his wife and his daughter, before his son was even born. This young family got in their car and headed west. They saw it all—San Francisco, Mount Rushmore, a truckload of potatoes in Idaho—but more than anything else, it was the Grand Canyon that Coach can't forget. "I couldn't believe it," he says. "I kept stopping the car to look at it from each slightly different vantage point; and it was different each time. I kept stopping the car and getting out to look and my wife was getting mad, but I couldn't help it. I just couldn't get over how big it was and how beautiful. It was really something."

As he says this, he's sitting on a scarred wooden bench on a tree-lined street in Bethlehem, Pennsylvania. But he's not really here. He's standing on the lip of the Grand Canyon gazing out at the most magnificent thing he's ever seen and might ever see again, and the old car is idling behind him, his wife and daughter waiting patiently in their seats, and the dry Arizona breeze ruffling his still-brown hair, the smell of piñon pine and the red rocks and blue sky. Coach is there in the middle of it all, tall and athletic, breathing deep and easy, not wanting to forget.

# Week Six—How Things Come Together

## Corcoran High School Cougars: Syracuse, New York

**H**ERE'S A NEW YORK story for you. Two kids—Ridwan and Wanzell—start hanging around together at school and after school, and gradually become best friends. They decide that it might be fun to play football for their senior year at Corcoran High School and so they show up for summer practice. Ridwan is small and fast and has played for the Cougars before, between school suspensions and grade probations and bouts of not showing up for practices and games. Wanzell is big and strong and has never played organized football. They both make it through the arduous summer training sessions. Ridwan is slated to start the season as the team's number one tailback and Wanzell has earned a job as a first-team defensive end. On the second day of school, though, Ridwan decides to cut class and head across town where he has a beef to settle with a student at rival Nottingham High School. He waits across the street from the school grounds, and, when this other young man approaches Ridwan, there is really nothing else for the two to do but start throwing punches. This leads to their arrest and the end of Ridwan's football-playing days because he never shows up at Corcoran again. Wanzell, who didn't accompany Ridwan over to Nottingham, hangs in there at school and with the football team, and he accepts an athletic scholarship to attend the University of Central Florida. He earns his diploma from Corcoran in June and he leaves Syracuse in late July for Central Florida. During his first couple of years there, he comes home to Syracuse a few times, and each time he thinks the same thing: *I got to get out of here*, because Ridwan and Ridwan's new collection of friends, who together have formed a group called "Boot Camp," keep trying to pull Wanzell back in. Six years after the summer morning that he showed up for his first official Corcoran football practice, Wanzell is married and working in Florida while his friend Ridwan sits in a jail cell on a racketeering conviction.

This isn't the only football tale of this hilly southwest section of the city. There's the defensive back who survived an ambush outside the front door of his house where he was shot six times only to wind up in the Auburn Correctional Facility a couple years later serving twenty-five years to life; or the big offensive lineman with limitless potential, who played his sophomore year and then drifted away; or the kid who was in too deep with the 110 gang over on Bellview Avenue and never made it.

There are also the kids who did make it, or at least seem to be making it, like Wanzell; or like LeRon Brown, who is playing community college football out in Coffeeville, Kansas; or Will Allen, who parlayed his Corcoran career into a scholarship at Syracuse University and who now plays cornerback for the Miami Dolphins. And what about Cordell Mitchell who started here nine years ago when Leo Cosgrove and Tim Schmidt were hired to take over a Corcoran football program that was in shambles? They began a revolution that has turned Corcoran into a city football powerhouse. After his one electrifying year as a Cougar, Cordell went on to play running back at Penn State and has now returned to Corcoran as an assistant coach while he finishes up his teaching credential.

And there is Omari Howard, the junior fullback who helped create the holes Cordell galloped through, and who stepped in the next season as Corcoran's "feature back" before moving on to a career at Central Florida. He too has come back to help coach while he decides whether or not education is the field for him.

In the midst of all this is Coach Schmidt, who arrived as Cosgrove's assistant and took over as head coach when his good friend accepted a job as the school's assistant principal. Schmidt seems an unlikely fellow to carry the fortunes of the Corcoran football program on his shoulders. He teaches English at the school and has the kind of willowy build and ingenuous smile that served him well as a student and basketball player at Le Moyne College on the other side of town. And he coaches football because "it's interesting," not because he can't live without it.

But underneath the breezy way he seems to approach the sport and the first impression of, "What is *he* doing *here*?" there is the understanding between him and his players, and the message is: "You stick with us, and you're going to have a better chance … we're going to have a better chance." "It can be pretty heartbreaking," says Coach. "Sometimes you get 'em, and sometimes you don't."

One thing that should help the program to "get" more kids and also to generate a more consistent base of support from the surrounding community is the rebuilt football stadium that is part of a six-million-dollar facilities renovation project at Corcoran. On Friday night the team played its first game of the season and its first game at home in more than two years, in front of a standing-room crowd eager to get a look at this first-class Cougars squad playing on the "field turf" of its new first-class stadium.

"It was a great night for Corcoran High School," says Coach. And, to make the night even better, the game pitted the Cougars and their No. 2 citywide ranking, against the No. 1–ranked Christian

Brothers Academy. CBA stormed out to a 35–14 halftime lead that Coach attributed in equal parts to his players' fascination with a sell-out home crowd and a CBA offensive blitzkrieg that the Cougars had devoted much of their preseason practice to stopping, but, says Coach, "Starting out, we didn't do it. We were too busy gawking."

Besides the new stadium and the big crowd, there were a number of positives in this opener against CBA, not the least of which was the Cougars' rousing second-half rally that brought them back enough to almost win the game. "A lot of CBA kids were limping around in the fourth quarter," says Coach. "We started playing physical, and they didn't know how to handle it."

Coach feels confident that his team will see CBA again in the playoffs, but first the Cougars need to get ready for this week's game against the Auburn Maroons. "We don't need to panic," he says of the team's 0–1 start. "We need to stress the importance of understanding what they're supposed to do. Everything we do in practice leads to the same goal."

Assistant coach Jack Altman agrees that each kid needs to take responsibility for his individual assignment. "You get ten people doin' their job, and one doesn't," he says, "you see what happens … and it's not good."

Dane McShane, who drives over from his P.E. job at Danforth Elementary School to work with the team, also thinks that each player on the field needs to know how what he does affects the team as a whole. "When we go 'Team O' and 'Team D' we need to isolate each position," he says. "So these guys can see how things come together."

Before things can come together, the team needs to come together, and the first place they do that is in Coach's classroom right after school. As they filter into the room, the talk today starts off with Friday night's sold-out game against CBA.

"Man," says Xandar Burke, the team's intimidating senior defensive end, "startin' out, that field was weird to play on."

"Yeah," agrees junior running back David Goddard, "but after you get used to it, tha's some comfortable stuff." But David is not completely satisfied with his team's performance on that new and comfortable field. "They shoulda' give me the rock more. When we were in the 'Red Zone,' they shoulda' give it to me. I know what to do when I got the rock."

"Yo', man," says Xandar. "Movin' the ball, that wasn't our trouble. You see our defensive backs back there? They was playin' scared. They got to get better."

Raymond Rice, a senior defensive back, has more pressing matters on his mind than a football game. "I need ta' eat sumfin'," he says.

"Why din' you eat lunch, nigga?" asks Xandar.

"I did," says Raymond. "Skinny people got to eat more'n one time a day."

But Xandar won't be dissuaded from his defensive game critique. "You see the way our safeties was droppin' back and they was just dumpin' the ball right in front of 'em? Now why's they doin' that?"

"I'll tell you why," says senior left tackle James Brown. "'Cause they idiots."

Tim Sheard, the gifted senior quarterback and team leader, looks up from the bag of pretzels he has been sharing with a few teammates. Coach has exited the room to get some errands done around school before his academic day concludes and the football day officially begins, and Sheard—or T. J., as his friends and coaches like to call him—is remembering his days as a freshman in Coach's English class, in a school where the kids aren't necessarily perceived as having a penchant for listening and learning and following directions. "Yeah," says T. J., "sometimes Schmidt would just get up and leave. He'd stand here for maybe two minutes after he give you an assignment, and then he'd just walk out the door ... and it'd still be mad quiet in here."

Coach knows he will always have to deal with some tough kids in the classroom, which leads him to contemplate his own tenure here, and that of his fellow faculty members. "Most of the people on staff have either been here a long time, or they just got here. Last year we had to replace three people before Halloween. They just got eaten up. It can be tough. But I would say that if you're here five years, you're not going anywhere ... you don't want to go anywhere."

And there are, if you look around, too many good reasons to stay ... like Tyrell Ford, for instance. He's the offensive lineman who usually has a smile on his face that is even more considerable than his 6'7" 330-pound body. Coach found him early on in his freshman year wandering the halls at the end of the school day, and said, "Are you playing football?" When Tyrell said he wasn't, Coach said, "You're coming with me," and took him down to the equipment room to check out pads, and then to the locker room, where he showed him how to change into them, and then out to the practice field, where Tyrell has been ever since. "He's not a great player," says Coach. "But he contributes and he's out there instead of somewhere else."

Before it's time to go back out there on the practice field, it's time for Coach to show back up and go over some of the finer points of the CBA game with the team. To his defensive line and linebackers Coach says, "You look at the film and there's a lot of guys saying, 'I was getting held, getting held, getting held.' You weren't. You were getting handled." To his kickoff team he says, "They started their drives on the forty. We started on the twenty. We got forty-one pretty good athletes here. There's got to be somebody who can kick it high and down to the ten-yard line and today we're gonna find him." To his hefty offensive line he says, "We got no surge out of you all night. You just hit and stopped. You're not driving anybody. You spent most of the game underachieving and that has to change this week." And he still has enough left over to say to his defensive backs, "You guys may as well have been at the concession stand for that first half, because you weren't covering anybody."

And here Coach pauses for a moment to gather his own thoughts and let these little observations sink in. "But ..." he continues, "then there was the second half. It would have been easy to tank it with that big 35–14 up there on the scoreboard. But you didn't. You kept playing. It's a credit to you guys that you hung in there and made a game of it. You're all here, and nobody's tanked it still ... and I believe we'll see these guys again down the road."

Coach feels comfortable criticizing his team and telling them as a group where their shortcomings lie and what they need to do improve them. But when it comes to individual criticism, or "calling a kid out" in front of his peers, Coach treads warily. "You can't do it unless you're absolutely right, and it's obvious you're right, and everyone out on the field knows you're right, including the kid, and you're confident of this ... and then you can do it. Anything short of that, you can't publicly question the kid. I've done it before," he says, and here his eyes get narrow and his brow wrinkles up and he shakes his head like a guy getting ready to walk a tightrope. "But you've got to be real careful."

One kid who Coach is trying to be real careful with right now is Anthony Dean, his high-strung senior linebacker. Anthony missed the team's compulsory Saturday morning weight room workout and Coach has listed him and a few of his teammates as unexcused and eligible for post-practice "Catch-Ups."

As soon as he hears his name though, Anthony explodes in protest. "That ain't right!" he says. "My gran'moms was in the hospital!"

Coach can only say, "You needed to call in and let us know, and you didn't do that, Anthony. That's unexcused, and that's time after practice."

Coach excuses the team from his classroom and everyone heads down to the locker room to get ready for practice with Anthony's voice echoing in the hallway and the stairwell. "You don't know! She there right now!" he shouts.

Coach would like for Anthony to have a chance to do his Catch-Ups and for the team to go through its practice drills up at the stadium field, so everyone gets changed, and the footballs and kicking tees and water coolers and orange cones get loaded onto the golf cart, and the whole crew—except for Altman, who has the fortunate duty of driving the cart—trudges up the winding, quarter-mile, hillside trail that leads to the stadium and the surrounding construction site that will, in a couple of years, be Corcoran's all-sports practice complex.

And for these kids, to stand at the cusp of this steep hill, in the shadow of their new aluminum bleachers, and gaze across the few miles of trees and houses and church steeples, toward the Carrier Dome, where the Syracuse Orange play their games, is something akin to all those movies where the Brooklyn boy leans against the wrought-iron fence to look across the East River at all those big Manhattan buildings and whispers to himself, "Someday that'll be mine." For most of this crew, outfitted in their burgundy and white practice jerseys and their second-hand orange pants that Coach got for a bargain from the Syracuse University program, the closest they can even hope to get to that dream is the possible high school title game. But for a couple of these players—notably T. J. Sheard—there is a real chance that someday that could be theirs. "I want to play at SU," T. J. says matter-of-factly, as he considers his options for next year.

But Altman isn't sure that's such a good idea. "Get out of this city," he tells T. J. "You don't have to go far away. They got Division I schools an hour from here—Penn, Penn State, Pitt. How about Bucknell? I'll get you into Bucknell."

T. J. just shrugs his shoulders and straps on his helmet. "Nah," he says. "SU, tha's the place for me."

And Coach thinks Syracuse U might be the place for him. "We worry about our guys," he says. "But T. J.? He's a little different. He could handle it. He could handle being that close."

. . .

THE TEAM HAS time to take in this panoptic cityscape view because, after their mountainside trek over the creek and up through the trees and past the gravel piles and bulldozers, they find themselves waiting on the soccer team that was supposed to be through with its stadium field practice by 4:30, but due to a scheduling mix-up, it becomes increasingly clear, as the American footballers continue to sit and wait, that the kickers and headers are nowhere near close to concluding their day. This miscommunication is something that Coach is becoming accustomed to and can't really complain about because his athletic director, April Wertheim, has been assigned to take on the athletic director responsibilities for Nottingham in addition to her Corcoran duties. Coach says, "April's new job is tough because it's already more than a full-time job with one school."

When it becomes apparent that there's no end in sight to the soccer practice, Coach calls out to his troops and they all head back down to practice on the old dirt and dead-grass field.

But once the team has wended its way back down the slope, through the trees, and over the creek to form up into their stretching lines on the hardpan dirt of the old practice field, Coach witnesses a mostly halfhearted attempt at the team stretch and a similarly weak effort as the squad sleepwalks through its "form run," and after he listens to some complaints about the heat, he does what any self-respecting coach who wants to light a fire under his team might do: He starts yelling, wrathfully and indiscriminately.

"You're fired!" he screams at his fullback, after a particularly slothful attempt at a block. "Dewayne!" he says to one of his seniors. "Get in there! I want to see someone hit someone!" After minimal offensive results and a continued lackadaisical approach, Coach wants to beef up his scout defense to make the offense work. "Xandar!" he hollers, "Get in there right now! Where you're play-ing, that's where we're gonna run. I want him crushed!" Coach yells. "I want him double-teamed and crushed! I'm tired of every-one wanting to win and no one wanting to pay the price!"

While Xandar's first play at scout defensive end results in another "no gain" for Coach's sputtering offense, the JV squad that is prac-ticing on the next-door field begins a slow jog around the two fields, where the perimeter is marked by a dense pocket of woods on the side opposite the school buildings. Suddenly, the gang of fully padded and helmeted underclassmen finds itself accosted by a couple of yelping Labrador retrievers that leap out at them from the forest, their human companions straining at the other end of their tethers. This canine surprise creates bedlam among the JVers, who scramble headlong away from the woods and the dogs, some of them scaling the mesh backstop, some of them running over one another as they retreat back toward the tennis courts, and some of them scurrying right into the middle of the varsity practice, just as Coach says to his guys through the sweat and labored breathing,

"I got a news flash for you. Our record is 0–1, and you're practicing like we're 8–0. We're the fastest team in the league and we can't run the sweep … and it's not because our tailbacks can't run. It's because our fullback and guards won't get out there and look inside to block!"

He runs a forearm across his cheek and then turns to see the swarm of JVers charging pell-mell through his practice. "Get off my field!" Coach bellows, and this is enough to get most of the pack doing just that at a spirited trotting clip.

But there are four stragglers who stop to look at Coach, and then continue to saunter across the varsity practice pitch. "Off my field!" Coach repeats. "And I want you running!"

This order is met with a slowing of the gang of four's oozing gait and mutters of, "Damn, man," that are within easy earshot of Coach, who says, "Either run, or keep walking right to the locker room." This changes nothing for the boys and their pace, and Coach follows them over to the JV practice field to huddle with them and their coach, Jesse Long, and the next thing you know, they are, the four of them, stripped out of their pads and headed in toward the school building.

Coach heads back over to his team and he is doing everything in his power to hold his anger in check as he calls them around him and says, "You know, the thing that Corcoran is known for is 'playing through' until that one big hit when somebody just rips someone's heart out, and then it's like a swarm of piranhas. I've been thinking for three days what's been missing, and that's what it is—nobody made that first big hit Friday night. And today it looks like the same thing. It seems like the only time I can get anything out of you is when I'm barking at ya and right now that's not even working. There is not a guy out there who wants to lay the wood to somebody and I'm sick of it. We're going to start playing some football right now, or guys are going to start losing their jobs. We're going to find some football players before we leave this field."

And with this, the team does start playing some football. McShane escorts his linemen over to the blocking sled and they work in shifts to grunt and groan and shove the padded iron frame around the field in a fit of pure intensity. The backs and ends work through their blocking and tackling drills with Coach as they drive through one another and body after body bounces off the withering grass, and then they're up and ready to do it again.

Practice finishes strong with Tyrell and his line-mates driving folks off the ball and a steady rotation of fullbacks sticking their heads in there to hit somebody. Coach says to his gathered troops, "It's about time you got a little cranky out there," and he can't help but think this latent orneriness will carry over to tomorrow's practice and on through Friday night's game, where his team really needs to be mean. After the "Cougar!" team break, he sends his backs and ends to the weight room, and then jumps in line with his "Big Boys" for their round of conditioning sprints. The shoulder pads and helmets come off, and Anthony Burgess and Tyrell—the really big boys—get ten-yard head starts, and there is Coach, running and smiling and chugging along right in the middle of it all, and saying, "Let's go, boys. We're looking good," and you can forget about Anthony Dean's Catch-Ups, at least for today, because everyone is feeling pretty fine right now, and why mess with that?

But eventually Coach is going to have to mess with it by saying, "Anthony, we've got to take care of that absence, or you won't be playing on Friday."

Anthony is going to reply, "It ain't right, I ain't doin' it."

And Coach will have to say, "That's your choice, Anthony. But it's something we can take care of and get behind us real quick."

As the week goes on, Coach's varsity crew seems to be waking up. Tuesday is more hard-hitting than Monday, and Wednesday has Tuesday beat by enough for Coach to say, "I'll sleep better tonight. I've always had an expression that Wednesday is the day you figure things out … Wednesday tells the story. Monday, you're kind of searching. Tuesday, you're feeling things out. Wednesday will tell you how you'll play Friday." And Wednesday is also the day when Anthony Dean decides he wants to play bad enough to do his Catch-Ups. He takes advantage of the bag drill that Coach sets up to end practice on the steep hill that slopes up from the practice field to the school building. As wave after wave of players and coaches high-step it over the bags and up the hill, laughing and joking and punching and pushing all the way, Anthony joins in with extra groups, doubling up on everyone else's repetitions, so he can erase his unexcused absence, without anyone but him and Coach really knowing that he backed off his earlier iron stance.

But even Anthony is giggling, as two normally agile backs stumble simultaneously over a bag and collapse in a heap on the green hillside turf. "All right!" Coach says. "A double … but I don't think the Russian judge is going to like that one." For the final few waves, Coach stands atop the hill and fires footballs to his players as they leap over the bags.

Big Anthony Burgess makes a dexterous catch that defies many of the physical laws that govern his ungainly body. "Hey, yo!" he cries out. "I could be a tight end."

But McShane, out of breath from his own hill exertion, isn't buying this. "There ain't nothin' tight on your body," he says. And Coach sees this as a good place to end things until Thursday's shorts and helmets "walk-through" on the stadium field with no soccer team in sight.

After "Team O" and "Team D" and every one of the specialty units, including that kickoff team that had better get better, Coach calls the squad together on the permanent burgundy Cougar head at the fifty-yard line and he has one thing to tell his team. "Play with real passion tomorrow night," he says. "And I don't mean coming out of that locker room whooping it up. We're all a little insecure—all of us—and we've got to overcome those insecurities. I'm going to ask you to lay it on the line. Go for the interception. Go lay out for the ball. You got a chance to lay someone out? Pop him. Don't play cautious. You're a good team. When you get that opportunity, grasp it … 'cause you may not get a chance on the next play."

It's an hour-long bus ride out to Auburn and so the team gathers outside the locker room at four-thirty on Friday afternoon in their burgundy game pants and with their helmets and shoulder pads and white jerseys bunched together and slung over their shoulders. But when only one bus arrives, Coach makes the phone call that helps him discover that the second bus was accidentally canceled. He takes a breath and calls the transportation yard and they promise to have another bus over to the school as quickly as they can. Then it's him and his skill guys—the backs and ends and runners and kickers—boarding the one sure bus and headed west, while the linemen wait for another forty-five minutes until a short bus swings into the school parking lot, and there are some chuckles and a "no way" or two, and then they pile aboard, cheek to jowl, sitting in the aisle and the stairwell, but everybody is on and safe, and it is off toward Auburn, in distant pursuit of that other yellow bus.

Perhaps the odd-looking Corcoran arrival has its comic value for some of the suburban Maroon faithful. But that will be their only chance at a laugh this evening because, as Coach had hoped and predicted, the Cougars have come to play some football. Even during pre-game warm-ups, as the teams stretch and pop pads and shag punts, Altman stands at the mid-field dividing line, takes a moment to study the smaller, slower Auburn team, and says, "This could get ugly."

But it doesn't start out ugly. It starts out almost like a dream with the Cougars marching purposefully down the steps of the horseshoe-shaped stadium and into the bowl-like arena, with Coach trailing in their wake hand-in-hand with his elementary school son, and with the western sky lit up like the Grand Canyon turned upside-down. Then Coach is on the sidelines, engulfed by his mob of players, and he says, "All the good Corcoran teams play with a swagger ... and tonight's the night we get the swagger back." This doesn't take long. Three minutes into the game T. J. throws a sixty-five yard touchdown strike to David Jordan, and the Cougars never look back from here. The Xandar-led defense that was coached this week to, "Go 'base' and kick ass," does just that. T. J. ends up with 464 passing yards to lead an offensive track meet that the Maroons can't even pretend to keep up with. The Cougars are bigger, stronger, faster, and better than Auburn. They should manhandle the Maroons, and they do.

This doesn't stop the team from basking a little in the glow of their performance. Amid the nonstop chatter and glee and chants on the sideline, you can hear Tyrone Burke ask a JV kid if he's going to see some playing time in tomorrow morning's junior varsity game. When the sophomore answers in the affirmative, Tyrone says, "Good. 'Cause I'm gonna be there ... with bells on."

And Coach can't help feeling pretty good about his team and this night. Post-game, he's got the boys gathered around him again, and he says, "Take a knee." Then he heaves a giddy sigh to show them how he feels and how he hopes they are feeling about now. "That's better," he says. "That's what we're talking about ... flying around. You could actually hear pads out there. Tonight you had that attitude, that step, and we're headed back in the right direction." And Coach is really smiling now and he says to these boys, "You know, I haven't heard a good 'Oooh' in a long time. Have you got one?" Of course they do. So forty-one Corcoran Cougars open their mouths and raise their voices, as a team, a family, in a long and low and glorious, "Oooooooh!!!" And all this for Coach, who can't think of anywhere he'd rather be than right here, right now, in the midst of these teenage boys who are thinking the same thing.

# Week Seven—On the Road

## Washington High School Tigers: Massillon, Ohio

**W**HEN THE MASSILLON Washington Tigers travel, they don't travel light. First, there are the buses: ten gleaming charters—two for the team, three for the band, and five for any parents, boosters, fans, or students who don't feel like making the sixty-mile drive west through possible hurricane conditions. And even though it might be okay for the "rooter" buses to cruise over unaccompanied by anyone in an official capacity, this isn't the case for the Massillon Swing Band or for the varsity Tigers, who are accompanied by Massillon town police cars. Then there is the team's equipment manager, Jerry Vance, and its head trainer, Mike Lewis, who both arrive at Arlin Field with their respective crews a couple hours before the team buses pull up at the stadium gates. Jerry drives a Massillon Boys' & Girls' Club van packed full with footballs and water coolers and chinstraps and mouthpieces and anything else that he and his student assistants might possibly need to help the Tigers succeed. Before the team bus has even crossed the Stark County line, all of this gear is in place in the locker room and training room and on the Arlin Field visitors' sideline, and Jerry is striding back and forth across the damp turf to check and double-check and triple-check that he and his staff are ready for the team's arrival. The same goes for Mike and his gang. The athletic tape is stacked in pyramids on the scarred wooden tables, the dry white towels are laid out, and Mike and his assistants stand in the middle of this small-scale triage unit in their white polo shirts and medical fanny packs, going over their mental checklist of what to do and when to do it.

Then there's the Swing Band's equipment truck that transports wooden risers and hats and capes and the real tiger-skin tiger suit for the band's student mascot. And somewhere in the midst of this parade of Tigers and Tiger fans rides Obie XXXIV, the Tigers' tiger cub mascot, in the comfort of his very own white-barred tiger cub cage, and accompanied by Don Shonk, Bob Hollender, and George Mizer, this season's "Obie Crew," who sit shoulder to shoulder on the front bench seat of Massillon's "Tiger Van" with all of their collective focus trained on keeping Obie happy and healthy and exercised and fed, not just tonight but also throughout the Tigers' fall football schedule.

Maybe the only ones, besides Obie, in this thousands-strong westward migration who aren't thinking about pride and tradition and the general joy of being some part of this fabled Massillon football dynasty are the players and coaches who carry the responsibility of maintaining it. Not that they don't relish being the focal point of this football-mad Ohio town. But right now they've got to block out all of the outside noise about the mantle of Tiger Tradition that they carry and concentrate on the game ahead of them. This trip to Arlin Field is not about some dream of Massillon magic; rather, it is about the reality of defeating the Mansfield Tygers as yet another step in their ultimate goal of winning the Division I state championship.

No one on the team bus is more aware of the importance of this visit to Mansfield or of its place in the "big picture" than Rick Shepas, the Tigers' head coach. He took this job, and the position of school athletic director, five years ago with the idea of bringing a state title to the school and the town.

Not that Massillon hasn't won its share of state, and even national, championships; they have. But, since 1972, when Ohio started playing to crown a champion in a statewide playoff system, the Tigers have yet to win the Division I title that was theirs twenty-two times before the inception of post-season play. They have come close, making it to the semi-finals a few times, and even to the title game twice, but the big win, the opportunity to say, "We are the best," has always eluded them. And so Coach left a rebuilding job at western Pennsylvania's Seneca Valley for the chance to guide Massillon to an historical first in one of the tougher football coaching challenges in the nation.

If ever there was a town that is defined by its football team and the devotion it has for that team, Massillon is the place. Although the Tigers started playing football in the late nineteenth century, the program didn't start to hit its stride until Paul Brown, a twenty-four-year-old Massillon native, turned down a Rhodes scholarship opportunity to return home to coach the Tigers in 1932, amassing, between then and 1940, an 80–8–2 record, winning six state and four national titles, "putting Massillon on the map," and casting a long shadow of excellence over the program that thrives to this day. The street that runs in front of the school is named after him. The 20,000-seat stadium across that street from school, where the Tigers play almost all of their games, is named after him. There is a bronze statue of him out in front of the stadium that is the centerpiece of the Tiger "Walk of Pride." He is the "Legend" by which all of his successors are measured.

But more than the victories and the recognition that Massillon has come to expect and even demand from this team, Brown brought the town together in a way that many people here believe only high school football can do. Says Al Hennon, the Massillon superintendent of schools: "Paul Brown brought unity to this community in the Depression. People of all economic and social levels got involved, and this has lasted to this day." Perhaps the biggest contribution that Brown made to the town and the team was his formation of the Massillon Tiger Booster Club, which today boasts more than 2,000 members and is responsible for, among many other things, the $1.2 million artificial turf field and the electronic scoreboard at Paul Brown Tiger Stadium. But when he started the club back in 1934, he didn't have such lofty goals in mind. Many of his players were showing up at practice hungry and he was looking for a way to help get them something to eat. He approached members of the community for assistance, and they chipped in to a cause that has grown stronger and more influential with each passing year.

Twenty-two years later, in 1956, and in a nod to the legacy that Paul Brown had begun, Dick Reichel, noticing that an increasing number of Massillon boys were becoming troubled products of single-parent homes, formed an off-shoot branch of the Booster Club called the "Sideliners" that exists to this day as sort of a Big Brother program, matching community members with juniors and seniors on the football team. Among other activities, every Thursday evening during the football season the Sideliners meet at the Elks Lodge for dinner with the team and coaching staff.

There are also the "Orangemen" and the "Touchdown Club." Both organizations are dedicated to promoting and supporting Massillon Football and both sprung up from the Booster Club that began in the depths of the Great Depression when Paul Brown approached a couple of civic leaders and said, "My kids are hungry. Can you help us out?" But he wasn't purely a philanthropist. Junie Studer, a senior member of the Booster Club Board, says, "Paul Brown recognized he was in the entertainment business." Brown didn't only get the community involved by coaching teams that won football games and by saying, "We need you," he also showed the town that they needed their high school team by transforming the Friday night games from a mere athletic contest into a complete Massillon football experience. He recruited George "Red" Byrd to take over the musical direction at the school, and thus the Swing Band was born. The two men were next-door neighbors and on Saturday mornings they would sit on their back porch rockers, and then Brown would say, "You know, George, that was quite a crowd the football team drew yesterday evening."

Byrd would always reply, "No, Paul, the crowd was there to watch the band."

When Coach Brown resigned his Massillon position to accept the coaching job at Ohio State, he took George Byrd with him, and the two duplicated their on-field success and off-field argument in Columbus, while the traditions they had begun at Massillon continued to flourish.

These are the traditions that had such a magnetic pull on Coach Shepas. When he accepted his previous Pennsylvania coaching position, it was with the promise that the only high school job that could get him to leave was at Massillon. "When I handed over the keys at Seneca Valley," he says, "there were no hard feelings. They knew this was the place I wanted to be." And now that he's here, he says that there is not another high school coaching job in the country that he could possibly want. "I'm here because I love the football atmosphere," he says. "There's no better place in the country to watch high school football."

But Coach isn't the only one who is drawn to Massillon football from afar. A number of the players on his team have come from somewhere else to be a part of this Massillon mystique. Sometimes this can be a good thing, as it is with Steve Hymes, Massillon's smiling senior quarterback, who moved to an apartment here at the beginning of his junior year because he absolutely could not resist the opportunity to be a Tiger. "A lot of people think it would be cool to be in high school and have your own place," he says. "But it's not. It was boring and lonely. I'd get home from school and practice and just sit there looking at the walls until it was time to come back to school." But this isolation was worth it to Steve. His father has since come over to live with him, and, after Quentin Paulik broke his wrist on an opponent's helmet a couple weeks back, Steve has gotten to live out his dream: to start at quarterback for the Massillon Tigers.

Or with Lashawn Edge, a senior backup tackle, who arrived here this summer not for any kind of football tradition, but because the state moved him to a group home in town. On Monday morning he walks into Coach's black and orange tiger-carpeted office and Coach sets aside his paperwork to look up at this imposing giant of a kid and say, "Big Gulp, what's goin' on?"

Lashawn pulls a couple crumpled dollar bills out of his pocket and starts fiddling with them, folding them back and forth with his meaty fingers. "They's botherin' me in class," he says.

"Wha'd'ya mean, 'botherin' ya?'" asks Coach.

"They's teasin' me, callin' me gay, and one of 'em tried to grab me from behind, and I grabbed his arm so he wouldn't do it, and they wrote me up and sent me to the office."

Coach shakes his head as Lashawn continues to look down at his fingers and his money. "You're gonna have people tryin' to antagonize you," Coach says. "You got to learn to walk away from all that. They're not gonna cut you any kind of slack down there … you know that, right?"

"Yeah," Lashawn mumbles.

"That's right," Coach says. "And you got to understand that. Now who's gonna stick up for you around here?"

"You," says Lashawn.

"'Me' is right," says Coach. "But if I'm gonna keep doin' it, you got to do your part. You got to walk away and remember you're part of somethin' here. You got me?" Lashawn has shoved his dollar bills back into the front pocket of his saggy jeans and he does his best to look at Coach when he says, "Yeah, I got you."

One kid Coach and his Massillon Tigers don't have is David Phillips, the standout tailback for this week's opponent, the Mansfield Tygers. And this is one case where the town's irresistible pull maybe isn't such a good thing. Aside from the long-standing traditions that might just set Massillon apart from any other place in the country that even pretends to like high school football (like the Booster Club president's custom of placing a miniature orange football in the hospital crib of every newborn Massillon boy), Coach has established some important traditions of his own, one of which is a propensity for helping kids extend their football-playing careers past high school. In his five years at Massillon, he has helped thirty-five of his players find a college that would give them a chance to combine academic and athletic pursuits. Some of his guys have gone on as "big-time" recruits to Division I universities, but with many of them, their desire to keep playing football outweighs their size and speed and ability to do so, which is where Coach really lends a hand. "These Division I schools, they're gonna find the guys they want," he says. "But there's a lot of kids, they're not gonna get a shot like that, and so I try and help 'em find a place where they can play … if they really want to play." Coach gets a particular satisfaction in placing kids in one of the many Division III colleges that dot the landscape in this part of the country and which play a brand of football that Coach refers to as its "purest form." "You get a kid going Division III, and you know he just loves to play."

And this is where the problem lies with David Phillips, who, along with his parents, saw a move to Massillon both as a chance to play for the Tigers and as a clearer path to a college scholarship, which is fine and within the boundaries of the rules, just as it was within the rules for them to make the hour and fifteen minute drive east on Highway 30 to do some house-hunting and to try to meet with school officials about a transfer. But it wasn't within the rules when a couple of overanxious Massillon fans felt compelled to get involved. This is when the Ohio Athletic Association stepped in to take a look and when Superintendent Hennon began his own internal investigation of the matter. "You've got to have the zealots around the program or you don't have a program," he says. "But, in this situation, we had some people go overboard … and we're dealing with that now." Mr. Hennon is also heading up the school's cooperation with the OAA and says, "I expect our district to be fully cleared of any wrongdoing very soon." As for David Phillips, it was back to Mansfield Senior. Instead of preparing with him, the Massillon Tigers spend this week preparing for him.

One of the guys charged with helping to get ready for David Phillips and his offensive mates is defensive coach and math teacher Jamey Palma, who utilizes his Wednesday morning "planning period" to studying videotape of his defensive backs' "run fits" from yesterday's practice on the big screen TV in the staff offices. Coach Palma devotes a couple of minutes to watching each defensive practice play. He presses "Play" and "Rewind" and "Play" again, studying the pre-snap reads and post-snap reactions of his strong and free safeties, and two cornerbacks.

He spends several moments watching one particular play where the scout team offense is lined up strong to the right, in a mimesis of Mansfield's signature "I" formation. The particular position that Palma studies is his free safety, who is lined up on the opposite side of the field from the tight end and seven yards off the line of scrimmage on the weak side and whose job it is, on any running play that "flows" away from his side, to step up or "fit" into the line of scrimmage gap between his defensive tackle and his defensive end.

The thing that bothers Palma about this play is that, as the offensive tailback takes a hand-off, the defensive free safety takes an outside route around the defensive end. As he continues on this incorrect course, the scout team tailback cuts back across the grain and into the gap. The safety recovers to make the tackle, but not before the runner has gained five yards. It is clear that Palma also noticed this mistake yesterday and took the time to "coach him up" because the next play on the video is a repeat of this play, only this time the free safety goes to his correct run fit and stuffs the runner at the line of scrimmage for no gain.

Although Palma and Coach and the rest of the staff devote so much of their time to finding what's wrong with their team's execution, technique, preparation, and performance, and looking for ways to improve each, there seems to be no shortage of additional people willing to point out what's wrong with their program. Even on a Tuesday evening when Coach meets a few members of his staff down at the Irish Exchange after practice for a round of iced tea, buffalo wings, and caramel sundaes, he sits on his bar stool with his back to the wood-paneled wall, vigilant of everything and everyone, not just at the table, but also in the entire place. He compares his coaching job here to that of a soldier in Vietnam. "You got to always have your head on a swivel," he says. "You got to always be looking for who's in the vicinity, and who they're with, and what they might be saying or thinking, or about to say or think." But he accepts this under-siege job reality almost cheerily, saying, "You're always gonna have the people who are supporters … and you're gonna have those people looking for ways to tear you down." He didn't arrive here with illusions of a harmonious paradise, he wasn't blind-sided by the mostly positive sense of ownership that this town claims for this team, and he remains pretty much ready for anything that might come his way. "When I came in, I changed some things, and I've tried to stay true to what I think a program should be," he says, "and that's what I'm gonna stick with. You got to be aware of what people are saying and thinking and doing, but if you spend all your time listening to criticism and trying to please everyone, you'll just end up chasing your own tail. It'll drive you crazy."

One day last spring, Coach had parked his Jeep Cherokee and was strolling up to the door of Rockne's Bar and Grill, where he does his weekly radio show every Saturday morning, when he noticed one of the Booster Club members at the center of the "David Phillips Saga" headed up the sidewalk with a couple of lunch companions.

As Coach held the door, he said to the Tiger supporter, "This doesn't look good, buddy," to which the fellow nodded in somber agreement. This two-second exchange, and all of the implications that the town newspaper could conjure up, appeared on the front sports page two days later.

"When I first got here, I tried to be as open as I could with the media," he says. "But you get tired of seeing things you say and do get twisted around over and over again just to fit into whatever story it is they're trying to print."

When he is asked at the Monday Boosters Club meeting about the looming storm that threatens to wreak havoc on the Tigers' offensive attack, he repeats the question into the microphone, and then responds, "My answer for foul weather is to show up with twenty footballs and keep switchin' 'em in and dryin' 'em off. We will maintain a dry ball." When he's asked about the Tygers (who earned the "Y" half a century ago when Mansfield and Massillon agreed that the loser of that year's game would change the spelling of their team's nickname) and what kinds of problems they might present this week, he repeats the question, and then says, "Well, defensively they over-pursue the football, so we're working on some misdirection plays to try and take advantage of that. Overall, they're big and fast and pretty physical. As far as looking like a football team, for my money, they look as good as anyone in the state." When he's asked about the chances of a state title on the near horizon, he doesn't mention the fact that Massillon's population is aging, and the school's population is shrinking, and the factory jobs have all but dried up, and that the Tigers are starting seven sopho-mores, and that Massillon's schedule is considered by many to be the toughest in school history. Coach just says, "In order to win a state championship, you gotta have that strong belief, like that Jim Jones had with his bunch … they were all drinkin' the punch." This gives the gathered boosters something to contemplate as he continues. "A coach should be evaluated based on when he doesn't have talent to coach. What does he do then? Any coach can look good when he's got a lot of talent and a lot of team chemistry." Coach has a pretty good grip on the lectern, and he leans forward to conduct a slow scan of the room before he goes on to say, "This coaching staff has been pulling off miracles for the last five years. But I love the football atmosphere here … that's why I'm still here. As far as that other outside stuff is concerned, I don't care. You folks should be asking yourselves how I'm still standing … how I do it." And with this, and a "see you all Friday night," and a knowing, but good-natured grin for all his true believers in attendance, he turns the microphone over to Coach Palma, who will spend the next forty-five minutes watching a Mansfield scout film with the club, while Coach heads back to his office to work in the nighttime quiet.

There is also plenty of work to do in the daytime, and Tuesday's and Wednesday's full pads practices are conducted, for the only time this season, on the uneven grass practice field that is usually occupied by the freshman squad. The water bucket the team managers keep handy to dunk old practice footballs in so the quarterbacks and their backfield mates can work on their rain-game ball-handling is also unusual, as is the miniature island of mush that kicking coach Bill Shaffer tries to create with a couple bucketfuls of water for Max Shafer, the team's kicker and punter, to practice his craft in fake foul weather.

Coach adjusts his ball cap atop his smooth-shaved head and turns to address his first-team offense, which, for the first time, includes big Lashawn at right tackle. The sophomore starter, Kyle Brown, has been trying to make a go of it with two painful stingers and an inflexible neck and shoulder brace to try and protect them, but today he comes out late from the training room, with a grimace on his face and an inability to move his shoulders or neck or head. "I hate this thing," he says.

Coach smiles like a guy who experienced a stinger or two in his own playing days and says, "Quit whining. You don't like it, take it off. Have a seat." And so young Kyle does just that, and the next thing you know, Lashawn has gone from fending off some punk kid trying to grab him in English class to starting on the offensive line for the Massillon Tigers. And the more Coach watches him operate in play after offensive practice play, the more he is encouraged by the fit. "Give 'im a drink a that Gatorade, Gulp!" he says after a pancake block where Lashawn's man ends up "on his back, counting clouds," as offensive line coach Paul Salvino likes to say. After another effort where Lashawn shoves his man completely out of the play, Coach hollers, "Hey, hey, don't quit on the play. Don't quit, just finish it. Who needs Kyle Brown when you got the Big Gulp right there? The Big Orange Drink from 7–11!"

A. J. Vennetti, the defensive ends coach, is not so pleased with the way his man is getting pushed around and says to this scout-teamer, "If you're gonna do that spin, practice it at home because you're goin' nowhere."

Coach is still feeling good about Lashawn's newfound prosperity and so he says to Vennetti about the downtrodden defensive end, "He got him a girlfriend, Coach. He's a tough kid turned soft. You got a girlfriend; it's like kryptonite."

Maybe it is the girlfriend that is wreaking havoc with this scout team defensive end's toughness, but also somewhere in his mind— and the minds of everyone else out here on the practice field—is the calamity that took place up in Cleveland last Thursday when a St. Ignatius player named Mark Tupa shattered a couple of ver-tebrae in his neck in a head-to-head collision in a freshman game. While these Massillon kids play football under the blue skies of an early autumn Ohio afternoon, Mark lies in an intensive care bed at Cleveland Metro Hospital in a medication-induced coma, fighting for his life. Coach makes the time between a Wednesday-morning meeting with a disgruntled volleyball parent and the team's after-noon practice to drive up to Cleveland and deliver a football signed by his Tiger players and staff. When he enters the pediatric wing's waiting room, Coach is greeted with hugs and handshakes from Mark's mom and dad and his grandfather, Tom, as well as some family friends who are here to lend support in this vigil. And when Coach hands over the football to Mrs. Tupa, she smiles and says, "This is gonna mean a lot to him when he wakes up."

So, the rest of us wonder, what happens to everyone else while they wait for Mark to wake up? What do the Tupas do, and the young man he collided with, and Mark's St. Ignatius teammates, and the Massillon kids? What do they do now? The only possible answer is: They carry on. The Tupas sit and wait and act brave and get ready to do everything they can to help their boy walk out of the hospital. The St. Ignatius team has a game this Saturday against McKinley, and they've got to be ready. And the Massillon Tigers? They board their two charter buses after school on Friday to start making their way toward Mansfield.

After Coach distributes sandwiches and sports drinks from the Booster Club to his players, he wants to know who is worried about dehydration. Max the kicker shakes his head and then grins when he realizes the absurdity of his response. But Mike White, a senior running back, is looking a little peaked, so Coach says, "You better get you one 'a them Propels. That'll fix ya right up." Then Coach reaches into the lunch boxes for packets of Little Debbie's cakes, which he flings randomly down the aisle. As these sweets zing past defensive tackle Vince Volpe's head toward the back of the bus, Salvino says, "Look. It's Volpe's ultimate dream—snack cakes flying through the air."

The bus ride over is quiet and relaxed, with the kids retreating into the sanctuary of their headphones and the coaches engaged in quiet conversation up front. The talk drifts easily from topic to topic, like Coach's anticipated groundhog hunt after Saturday morning's radio show. There is no talk about the game because there is no need to talk about it. Mansfield has been thoroughly scouted. The pre-game plan and game plan for offense, defense, and special teams is ingrained in their memories. The Massillon Tigers are ready to play some football.

Before the team launches into its many rounds of pre-game meetings and warm-ups, Coach says, "I like to give the guys pretty free reign to do what they need to do to get ready for the game." Most of the Massillon players spend the hour and a half that they have to themselves upon arrival clad in their black game pants and dri-fit undershirts, but they all seem to have their own individual pre-pre-game rituals. Some kids perform little moves and wind sprints on the game field. Others remain engrossed in their headphones, or pace the field, or sit in the stands, or stretch out in the locker room, or visit the trainers to get taped and bandaged. There is no extracurricular giggling or gossip, no pointing up into the stands as fans of both schools begin to find their seats, no gawking at a cheerleader or hearty "Hey yeah!" to a passerby, nothing but the football business at hand.

This unflinching focus proves unfortunate for the Mansfield Tygers, who, in person and pre-game, look every bit as menacing as Coach has forewarned his Monday night Boosters. But, after Salvino tells his linemen, "There's nothing that gets me more fired up than playing on the road. People are against you ... and our number one goal is to be nasty"; after the Swing Band marches onto the field and up into the grandstand to the beat of their own rousing rendition of "Hold that Tiger"; after "that tiger," little Obie XXXIV has been carted to his sideline spot and fed his first hamburger and chicken meal of the night; and after Max boots the opening kickoff into the fading remnants of the hurricane winds; it doesn't take long to see which is the better team.

Of course, that's only if three game minutes doesn't seem too long a time, because that's how long it takes for Massillon's swarming defense to drive a stunned Mansfield offense into early submission, and for the Massillon offense to take the field and do what it has grown surgically effective at accomplishing during Coach's tenure, which is score touchdowns. As the Tygers line up in their customary "I" formation, defensive coordinator Tyrone Partridge and Vennetti and linebackers coach Chris Albrecht call out simultaneously, "Toss right!" The Tygers go "toss right" to David Phillips, who gets buried for a loss under an avalanche of Massillon defenders. The Tygers again come out in their "I" and the defensive coaches call out, "Left tackle! Watch the left tackle!" The Tygers try a deep left-side hand-off to Phillips who is again swallowed up before he can make it to the line of scrimmage. The Tygers come out in split backs and try a deep-out throw toward their own sideline, and Billy Relford, one Tiger who is a legitimate Division I prospect, nearly "picks it, and takes it to the house," except that the excitement of streaking toward the opposite end zone gets in the way of him catching a ball that hits him squarely between the numbers. But this minor glitch doesn't really matter, because the only other time in the game that Mansfield attempts to throw his way comes in the second quarter, and he does intercept the ball, and this is when the real fun begins.

If you have ever settled in to watch a first-rate symphony orchestra led by a veteran conductor who wields his wand with a nonchalant confidence, and without a lot of histrionics, and can then imagine the Tiger offense as that orchestra, and Coach as the conductor, then you might have a reasonable idea of what the Massillon "Spread" looks like when it is running really well. And tonight it is running really well. But it isn't the lightning quickness with which they score that is the most impressive feature of this offense, nor is it the crisp execution of these scoring plays and so many others, or the way the Mansfield defense is set immediately on its heels in bemusement at its circumstances. No, the most stirring particularities of this offensive display are the way the conductor and his orchestra work together in such seamless accord, and the enthusiasm with which this symphony is performed.

The "Spread" offense goes huddle-less, and so, immediately upon a play's completion, there is a frenetic scramble by the Tigers to get to their new spots at the new line of scrimmage. The five linemen align themselves in traditional fashion along the ball, and their job is to stand with hands on hips and wait. The usually four wide receivers hustle to various positions along the line of scrimmage—usually two split out on each side of the ball, but sometimes three on one side and one on the other, or some other combination—and, once they've reached their destination, they simultaneously cock their heads toward the Tiger sideline to stare wide-eyed at Coach. The quarterback hustles up to his standard shotgun position five yards behind his center, and he is joined almost always by a single running back. Then these two join the receivers in their seconds-long vigil, so that there are five heavy-breathing offensive linemen staring longingly at the fast-approaching goal line, and six skill guys with unanimous attention on Coach, who is preparing, through hand signals and raised fingers and the occasional hollered message, to direct all of them to their next destination. The quarterback then barks out instructions to his linemen as they crouch down into position, and then, before the befuddled defense can scratch its head over what happened on the last play, the center snaps the ball and the race to the end zone is on.

And, if you are ever in the mood to watch a guy who knows what he is doing as he directs this offense that is based primarily on quick-hitting passes and runs, and on numbers—as in who is covering whom and how many and where—Coach is the fellow to watch. "It's amazing how he figures it all out," says Salvino. "He can get our guys into a formation that he somehow knows will make the other guys run a certain defense, so we can run the play he wants against that defense. You stand there and watch him do it, and you're like, 'How did he do that?'" He does it with no headphones and no notes, just a grid in his mind maybe, that he can translate to a bunch of excited teenage kids who like nothing more than to run up and down this grass field.

There is a blemish or two in this exhibition, like when Steve Hymes throws an interception near the end of the second quarter that gives senior offensive tackle Tim Dewald the chance to make a diving tackle near the Massillon goal line, and that prompts Coach to say to his quarterback in the halftime locker room, "Don't throw to the two safeties. Make the read, throw the ball like a dart, and play the game the way it's supposed to be played." Or like when a referee throws a personal foul flag after a big second quarter completion to sophomore Brett Huffman that negates the big gain, throws the Massillon crowd into offended chants of protest, and draws a shrug and a they're-out-to-get-us smile from Coach, who turns to his similarly offended sideline full of players and coaches and warns, "Don't say a word," which they don't. But at halftime, he says, "If these officials are smart, they'll stop throwin' the flag. Then we'll ease up and play a respectful game. Until then, we're goin' after them."

And Lashawn—the Big Gulp himself—goes after them midway through the second quarter in an instance that underlines the way the Tigers play football on this night. Coach has signaled in a "93 Y Screen Right" which calls for Lawshawn to make a phantom block at his tackle position, and then rumble out toward the sideline where one of his smaller and swifter mates is waiting to haul in Steve's short pass before heading upfield with Lashawn and Vince Volpe as his burly escorts. Lashawn's job is simple—wait for the receiver's "Go" call and then move upfield, intent on taking out the first defender that provides resistance. On this play, it is usually an outside linebacker who offers up the first challenge, and sure enough, here comes one flying at Lashawn. But Lashawn doesn't hit him, because Lashawn surmises the position of this converging linebacker, and he won't make the tackle, and so shuns him in favor of the safeties and cornerbacks that are shooting back from downfield like Tyger-orange meteorites.

"Yeah, I saw him," Lashawn says post-game as he stands in the shadow of the concrete bleachers enjoying a hot dog and Coke. "We're taught if they don't pose no threat, let 'em go. He wasn't no threat, and there was other guys to go after."

A few feet away, Coach is surrounded by the customary onslaught of reporters. In response to the first question he says, "There have been no distractions from the Phillips situation. It was well-handled by the superintendent. We have moved on." The next question concerns the contest's lopsided score, and Coach says, "They've got a new coach here at Mansfield. They're going to have a good program once they get on track." Then it is on to the darkened bus with his boys where *Swordfish* is the movie of choice for the ride home. Palma tosses the videotape to Coach, who juggles it before it lands on the floor with a crash. He picks up the tape and inserts it into the VCR. But then, when he presses "Play," nothing happens, and he shakes his head and says, "The fumble cost us." But Palma puts his videotape knowledge to work, and before the bus is out of the Mansfield city limits the opening credits are rolling.

It's after midnight by the time the bus arrives back at Massillon and the players and coaches make their way toward their locker room in the dark stadium. The team's victory celebration is over and it's time to start thinking about tomorrow morning's JV game, and next Saturday's varsity trip to play St. Ignatius, the big Jesuit school that Massillon has never beaten. Some coaches will spend tomorrow with the junior varsity players, many of whom saw action in the fourth quarter of tonight's big win. Other coaches will break down film or scout St. Ignatius's game at McKinley or, like receivers coach Ramir Martin, will travel with a Tiger player to take in a college game. No one will have the day off.

As for Coach, there's the groundhog hunt after his radio appearance, and, while he and Bill Caples, who is the "Voice of the Tigers," fill the hour-long show with plaudits all around concerning last night's success and the general success of the program, Brian Blosser slides into a back booth, along with his strapping eighth-grade son, Justin. Blosser played at Canton McKinley twenty-five years ago, but has it in his mind that he's going to move his family back to this area so his boy can play, not at his alma mater, which is about eight miles from where he is seated in the Rockne's bar, but right here at Massillon Washington for Coach Shepas. He's going to give up his business and sell his house and make the move and today is all part of that process. After the radio show, he and Justin are going to wander around town to check things out and maybe do a little preliminary house-hunting. But first, he'd like to meet Coach, and maybe give him the opportunity to get a look at his son, who has the solid build and steely gaze of an honest-to-god football player.

A question is lobbed from one of the bar tables where the thirty or so gathered Faithful eat egg burritos and sip coffee: "Coach, do you think we can beat St. Ignatius?" Coach repeats the question into the microphone, and then says, "If I didn't, then why even try playin' 'em." He responds to a few more questions and then it is time for Mr. Caples to wrap up the show for another week. Coach takes off the headphones like he might have taken off a helmet in his playing days and says, "I'm a go shoot me some groundhogs."

As friends and fans converge on Coach for a handshake or a word or even a nod of the head, Blosser continues to outline his Massillon plan at the back booth, saying, "This is the place ... this is the place. I'm tellin' ya, this is the place." Then he grips his son's shoulder and heaves his own thick body up from the Naugahyde seat. "Well," he says. "We better say hello to Coach." But by the time Blosser and son wade into the dissipating crowd, intent on meeting the man, Coach is gone—out of the bar, out of the asphalt lot, out of the town—and on the road to his day in the woods.

# Week Eight—Practice Like You Play

## Bettendorf High School Bulldogs: Bettendorf, Iowa

**F**OR RANDY SCOTT, the head coach of the Bettendorf Varsity Bulldogs, Tuesday morning before the school day begins is given over to his weekly Bible Study group. He arrives at Happy Joe's Café in the pre-dawn to sit with his bible and a glass of grapefruit juice and wait for the arrival of the five or six other men, who since 1976 have considered this morning a time of sacred fellowship. As Coach skims through today's lesson, the guy who's in charge of leading it, Merv Habenicht, squeezes him on the shoulder and has a seat across the table with his coffee and bagel and bible. Coach and Merv go back a ways. The same year this Tuesday morning ritual began, Merv took over the Bettendorf football team and hired Coach as an assistant in charge of the offensive line. For the next twenty-four years, Merv headed up the program and Coach toiled away with his linemen, quietly building up a reputation as the finest teacher at his position in the state of Iowa. And also for those many years, after a 4–5 record in their initial season, the Bulldogs compiled an at least winning record in every season and brought five state titles back to the Bettendorf campus. Merv retired from his teaching and coaching jobs a couple years back, and last year, in his first as head coach at "The Bett," Coach led the Bulldogs to the state title game, where they came up just short of bringing home another championship trophy. Merv was pleased for Coach and his troops, but he also couldn't stand to sit out and watch, so he has thrown his hat into the ring once again, this time as the offensive coordinator at Davenport North. Merv hired on there with the new head coach, Skip Eckhart, and the two of them are working together to rebuild a team that was in disarray. So far this season, the Davenport North Wildcats have compiled a record of 2–1, which is an exact match to Bettendorf's record to date. Both teams are feeling okay about their seasons' start going into this week, but one of them will slide back to .500 after Friday's game because the Bulldogs and the Wildcats will be squaring off against each other under the lights of Davenport's A. R. TouVelle Stadium.

But nobody would ever guess this showdown looms on the horizon, as more men—all coaches—waltz up to the table with their coffee and bibles. There is Reggie Speak, who started this whole affair way back when, and who offers up the weekly pre-game prayer for the Bulldogs. There is Tom Freeman, who himself coached at The Bett for twenty-six years, and now in his retirement, works as an assistant with St. Ambrose College. There is Mark Brooks, the Bettendorf athletic director. And there is Coach Eckhart, who, along with Merv, has already spent countless hours studying ways to use North's superior speed and athleticism to defeat a Bulldog team that starts seven juniors on defense and eight juniors on offense. Right now, though, after handshakes and "good mornings" all around, the talk is not about football, but about these men's relationship with their God and their families and their little bit of this world. Merv directs the crew to open their books to James V, glances around the table at this small fraternity of teachers and coaches, and says, "This lesson probably won't apply to most of you because it's about rich people."

Coach knows, all too well, the dichotomy between teaching and coaching and the amassing of wealth. He earns a few extra thousand dollars a year heading up the Bettendorf program on top of his salary as a P.E. teacher at the school, and his assistants earn somewhat less than that. For this extracurricular investment, the school district gets about a thousand hours of work out of each of these fellows, and it would be difficult to find a program in the state that is more focused on helping its players and its team be the best they can be. Take New Year's Day, for instance, or the Fourth of July. On both of these days, the Bettendorf players are down at school early in the morning, lifting weights and running sprints. Says defensive coordinator Aaron Wiley, "We have 'em in here at seven a.m. on those days for the toughest workout we do so we can say, 'The other guy is in bed right now while you're out here working your ass off. You deserve to win. You've earned it. You're earning it.'"

And the off-season training regimen does sound like an awful lot of work. The team is in the weight room every day except Sunday for at least a couple of hours, and then they are out on the stadium track afterward for their two-and-a-half mile "rusty run" on Monday. On Tuesday it is over to the steep hills that form a bowl around their practice fields for what the players like to call a "hill party," a series of full-speed, leg-churning burns up and down the slopes. Wednesday means back to the stadium to run sets of "bleachers" on the stadium benches. Thursday is several sets of "40-yard dashes" using "high knees" and "deer bounds" and "side-steps" and "full-speed" among other approaches to the age-old sprint distance. Friday almost seems like a day off, as the entire team—maybe a hundred kids—engages in a no-holds-barred Bulldog version of two-hand touch football. Finally, Saturday means a series of stretching, leg lifts, and plyometrics. Everyone who thinks they might want to play football for the Black and Gold in the fall makes it a point to participate in these workouts.

The mastermind behind this out-of-season grind is assistant coach and standout member of The Bett's first-ever state title team, Kevin Freking. He arrives at the high school every day from his forklift job at the Honda warehouse over in Davenport ready to challenge his recruits to "take it" and get better. "I don't want to hear about how you're tired. You're in shape. Take the pain." And they do.

Coach says of Freking, "He doesn't teach here, but he gets everything out of these kids. They listen to him, and they have a relationship with him different from what the rest of us have."

And whatever this relationship is based on, it's not subtlety. As he runs another line drill that the Bulldogs affectionately call a "pig fight," which is basically a test of wills and brute force between an offensive and a defensive down lineman. Freking makes sure that each set of participants knows where they stand. "Offense, you're the loser," he announces, after a young guard gets pummeled into the dying grass. Then, as two boys crash into each other like bighorn sheep and no one can get the upper hand, Freking says, "Stalemate. Both of you are losers."

Coach feels strongly that his team had better be ready before Friday night comes, so, beginning on Monday morning, when the offensive and defensive squads meet in the locker room and coaches' offices, he and his staff familiarize them on exactly what it is they're up against with these newly energized Davenport North Wildcats. "This is our biggest game so far," says Coach to his offensive squad. "We've got to be better in the 'Red Zone.' We have to get better at blocking. We must eliminate penalties." And it's not just their own improved play the Bulldogs need to worry about. "The Wildcats have team speed like we haven't seen before," says Coach. "Overton is impressive as a kick returner and punt returner.

He's a live wire that you gotta commend. He's very elusive … very dangerous. When we kick, we want to kick away from him."

Back in the coaches' film room, Wiley's defenders slouch in desks and overstuffed chairs and on the floor as he tells them, "The basis of any defense is gap control. This is a big offensive line we're facing this week. We've got to communicate and we've got to get off the ball and to our gap responsibilities … and we've got to be quick about it."

Another window of opportunity that Coach is anxious for his team to improve upon is their usual propensity for blocking punts that seems to have escaped them so far this season. "Last year at this time we had three punts blocked," says Coach. "This year we have zero."

As they work on the kicking game out at practice, Wiley says, "We must, must, must, must be better on punt return. They rest on special teams and that's where we outwork them and beat them. This is a crucial phase of our game that's got to be better. We are emphasizing this." And so, the front line of the punt return team devotes the next several minutes to practicing "getting skinny," which means that anyone "heads up" with an offensive blocker on the interior of the line does everything he can to slither through the six-inch-wide gaps that exist along the line, while the guys on the "edge," or ends of the interior line, practice taking off at the center's snap like a rifle shot, and then flying (literally flying as they near the punter and leave their feet in a swimmer's-dive attempt to block the kick) toward the mind's-eye spot where the ball should make contact with the punter's foot. As much as Wiley is convinced that one of his "edge" players will be uncovered this week, and free to take an unhindered shot at a punt block, he still wants his inside guys to find the gaps and burrow through them. "Make yourselves skinny!" he calls out from his post behind their positions.

But, as they continue to work at "Bettendorf Punt Block," Freking, who cannot get their recent failures to block a punt off his mind, and who sees before him now more of the same frustrating inadequacies, explodes with, "If you do not get skinny … if you do not use your hands … you will do up-downs!" Mark Wallace, a junior down lineman, takes heed of this warning on the next play and scrapes and scraps and crawls and wriggles his 220-pound way through the six-inch gap, and Freking says, "That's the way to get off the ball, like you're a rocket."

What makes the Bulldogs' inability to block a punt even more baffling is the fact that their two bookend edge guys are Jake Carter and Sean Rizzo, whom offensive coordinator Brian Barquist refers to as "Stan and Larry, those two crash-test dummies in the commercials who get slammed into the wall, fall to pieces, get pieced back together, and then get thrown into another wall."

Both Jake and Sean are frequent customers at the school's "best-in-the-state" training room, so when Eric "Dr. Death" Knudson and Paul "Dr. Gloom" Flynn, the team's two full-time trainers, walk down from the fieldhouse, they wince every time Jake spins or feints or dives into a pile on his bad ankles that are wrapped in boxy braces that resemble something Gene Simmons might wear onstage.

"He goes about 8,000 miles an hour, and he'll hit you in the mouth every time," says Dr. Death of Jake and his throw-caution-to-the-wind style of play. "He's one of those kids that doesn't really care about his body now, and we have to worry about his future health." He has a similar analysis of Sean, who is continuously aggravating a hip contusion by making dive after full-body dive into the practice field turf. Says Knudson, "I see a lot of poor decisions by the kids where their bodies are concerned, a lot of injuries that go unreported because they don't want to give up playing time.

As athletic trainers, we want to help these coaches keep the kids healthy and playing. But we also want to make sure they're healthy after their football-playing career is over."

One player who Dr. Death and Dr. Gloom don't have to worry about putting his health in jeopardy is junior placekicker Chris Mahoski. Problems far short of serious injury make him a wild-card for practices and games. Problems like the one before the season started, when he found out that part of donning the Bulldog varsity uniform means wearing knee-high socks. He approached Freking in dismay and said, "I've never kicked in long socks before. I don't know what I'll do."

As Freking recounts this tale he says, "You don't even want to know what I told him."

This week, though, it's an actual injury, or at least the early warning signs of one, that weighs heavily on Chris's mind. As he and the team's punter, Donnie Conner, warm up their legs with some pre-practice boots, he feels an ache in his kicking leg, and so wanders over to the sideline to tell Pete Ivanic, a local radio personality and a former kicker himself. "I think I pulled a muscle," says Chris.

"What are the signs?" asks Pete.

"Well, it hurts," replies Chris. "I think the problem is that I felt a twinge and kept kicking."

"Oh," says Pete. "Well you should have stopped when you felt something." This analysis goes quite a ways with Chris, who hobbles off to track down Coach. It also makes an impression on Coach, who listens to Chris's prognosis, points to Donnie and says, "You're kicking this week. I want you working on low, short line drives and keeping it away from Overton." Coach jogs off to check on his linemen; Chris limps up toward the fieldhouse to pay a visit to Dr. Death; and Donnie, who is weakened by a bout with the flu, starts hammering footballs high and far toward his downfield returners. "I'll be kicking 'em into the end zone on Friday," he says. "Coach doesn't think I can kick 'em deep because he watched me yesterday when I was kicking bad. I'll be kicking 'em deep on Friday." Unlike most kickers, who prefer to sport a more open facemask on their helmets, Donnie wears a mask that has a thick bar that bisects his nose and gives him the appearance more of a down-sized fullback than a guy who spends the majority of a game on the sideline trying to stay warm until it's time to trot onto the field and apply foot to ball. "Ahh," says Donnie. "I don't care what it looks like. I just grab any helmet." But then he pauses to reconsider and says, "Well, actually, I want people to think I play another position."

One of Donnie's fans on the team is Ryan Fick, the Bulldogs' junior quarterback. He beat out a senior for the job before the season began, and, as soon as this older kid got an idea of how his final football year might scroll out before him, he quit. This added to Ryan's job security, but it also may have created even more pressure on him to be better than good, as he is already drawing comparisons to his father, who played quarterback for the University in Iowa City.

"People are expecting a lot out of him," says Barquist of his young signal caller. As Donnie continues to boom kicks toward the far end zone, Ryan moves off to where his receivers are lining up to catch some specialty period passes. Ryan is nursing a bit of a banged-up throwing hand, courtesy of an opponent's helmet, and as he limbers up his arm, Barquist asks, "How's your finger today, Pumpkin?"

Ryan gives it a shake and a glance, and says, "It'll be all right." He starts his receivers out with short hitches and comebacks and slants and quick outs, but then eventually works up to the deeper fade route where he says, "Now we're pushing for the outside shoulder today, just like we have all season, right?"

Barquist stands back to watch his quarterback toss spiral after high, lazy spiral, and seems almost mesmerized by the arc of the ball. He's a guy in his early thirties who wears the rounded-frame glasses and carries the shoulder-strapped messenger bag and has that steady, clear-eyed way of talking that says, without adornment or disguise, "Hey, I'm a teacher. That's what I do, that's what I like to do, and I want to keep doing it." But he's also a coach and a "student of the game" and of an age and intensity that might be leaning toward something more than running the offense in a program where the head guy doesn't spend too much time telling him or Wiley or any of the other assistants what to do. In fact, Coach himself says proudly, "When someone gets hired on at Bettendorf, he knows he's gonna coach." But is this enough?

As Ryan continues to throw his rainbow spirals, and whippet-thin kids like Euseph Messiah and Chris Ivory continue to gallop downfield to haul them in, Barquist has a chance to think about it. "When I first started, that was absolutely my goal—to be a head coach. But now I don't know. I'm the offensive coordinator and I get to be in charge of that and call the plays, and I'm happy with that." He pauses a moment to motion toward Coach, who is over at the equipment shed tossing out blocking bags toward the practice field. "But it'd be hard to put up with what he has to put up with ... and then you see what he goes through, and what it does to him ... I don't know."

One thing Coach went through before the season even started was a tough decision concerning one of his standout players. He was a kid that the Bulldogs were counting on heavily for this, year, after he recorded twelve quarterback sacks last season and was named to the All-Conference team. "He's quite a player," says Coach. "There's a strong chance that he would have been included on the All-State team this year." But that's not going to happen because, as good a player as he is supposed to be, he wasn't a good leader for the team. "He was late for practice," says Coach. "He had a poor work ethic, and that attitude of, 'I'm good, and I don't have to do all this.'" The Bett has a phrase for this type of approach and it's called, "Conduct Unbecoming a Bulldog." And this program also has a way of dealing with it. "Kids at this age," Coach says, "you gotta have rules. Here's my simple rule on excuses: I deal with excuses before the fact. I don't deal with them after the fact." That standout kid ran through his excuses and Coach told him not to show up for his senior season. "We are accountable for what we do in life," Coach continues, "and, sooner or later, you'll be held accountable."

This "star" player's lack of accountability and subsequent dismissal from the team doesn't leave the Bulldog coaching staff scratching their heads and wondering, "What do we do next?" Rather, it gives players like senior Parker Quail—kids who are accountable and who are, as Drinkall says, "in there bleeding and sweating"—an opportunity to step up and shine. Parker is the kid who stood in to fill the All-Conference shoes, and thus far, he has done so more than ably. Freking has done some tinkering with his defensive front for this game that includes a shift for Parker from his outside defensive end spot to a place on the interior of the line to play heads-up with North's offensive tackle, and Coach is curious about why. "The reason I moved Parker down there," says Freking, "is because he'll be lined up against a sophomore and he'll knock the hell out of him." Another wrinkle that Freking and Wiley have added is what they call their "nickel rush package" for this week, which means that, beside the four down linemen, one of the three linebackers will—against the pass, and on a predetermined sideline call—fling himself pell-mell across the line of scrimmage in pursuit of the quarterback. Freking is excited and can't help but envision

Jake "Stan" Carter on a blitz call from his outside linebacker post. "If he hits the quarterback, he'll kill him," says Freking, "And if he hits him from the blind side, he'll murder him."

Conventional football wisdom seems to dictate that a team show as little as they can in the weeks leading up to a big game to hold onto the element of surprise, but Barquist doesn't buy this approach. "I want 'em to have to prepare for as many different things as we can," he says. "The more time they have to spend figuring out what we do, the less time they have to get better at what they do." No matter who they're playing next Friday—or this Friday—the Bulldogs try to add at least one new trick play every week, and this week it is a variation on the "draw" play that has been around and in popular use since the days of the leather helmet and no facemask. Instead of running the traditional draw, the Bulldogs begin, this week, to perfect a draw with a twist that is so new to them that they haven't come up with a name for it yet. The deviation in this remodeled draw, which senior fullback Tom Langford suggests be christened "The T-Nasty Express," is that, instead of executing the classic deep pass drop, the quarterback "rolls" at a forty-five degree angle to his right—or left, depending on the play-side call: "T-Nasty Right," "T-Nasty Left"—and then, as he passes behind his running back, who is crouched in the blocking stance that is a signature staple of the original draw play, he slides the ball under his outside arm and into his gut in a reverse-pickpocket move before continuing on toward the sideline and executing a melodramatically mimed toss downfield. Once he has the ball safely tucked away, the runner gives the cursory pause and then starts searching for daylight at and beyond the line of scrimmage. While Barquist takes a few moments to describe the intricacies of this draw derivative, offensive assistant Kevin Wojtkiewicz turns to Sean "Larry" Rizzo as he gets ready to step in at running back and says, "You know what's so scary about this whole play is we're counting on you to be sneaky, Rizzo. You might get the ball and be crouched down there and forget it's there." But it is Tom Langford who seems truly infatuated with this fresh page in the playbook. He steps in at halfback to get his "wraparound" hand-off from Ryan Fick, holds his position for a count or two, and then darts through the line and up the field. As he trots back to the huddle, he can't resist a wide grin as he cries out in elated disbelief, "I sold the fake! I sold the fake! Did you see me sell the fake?"

While Tom sings the praises of this week's new bit of razzle-dazzle, the coaches fret over Davenport North and their fastback, Overton, who doesn't need much sleight of hand to make his way to the end zone. Even though his usual offensive position is split out along the line of scrimmage in a slot, Wiley can't drive home the point enough that crafty Merv Habenicht will find ways to get Overton the ball. "They'll try and throw it to him downfield at least once," says Wiley, "and they'll toss him some hitches to try and get him one-on-one with you guys. But they want him running it, too. They think he's their hero. They want to get him the ball. They think he's going Division I."

Coach has the same concerns about this speedster on special teams. "Now Donnie," he reiterates to his kickoff artist, "what I don't want is the middle man catching the ball on the fly. That's Overton. We want to kick away from him."

And to underscore the gravity of the Bulldog kickoff coverage, Freking mutters to Greg Reckman, who is lined up and awaiting Donnie's line-drive boot, "Anybody walking, I want you to punch 'em in the mouth." Reckman nods in complicity and then joins his cohorts as they sprint like greyhounds in the wake of Donnie's skittering kick. Later on, when the team lines up for Donnie's regular fourth down duty, Coach says, "The big thing with punt is keeping the ball away from Overton. If you don't keep it away from him, you're going to have to cover him. But you can't let him get started. That's how you stop a good back, don't let him get started." And Overton isn't only an offensive and special teams threat. He is also someone that Barquist has to plan for on the Wildcat defense. When Coach asks him, "How do North's defensive backs look?" Barquist replies, "Overton scares me."

But as respectful as the coaches are of Overton's raw speed and possible Division I moves, they cannot help but feel confident about this latest game in a series with Davenport North that The Bett has dominated over the years. They have lost maybe once or twice in the twenty-plus times the two teams have faced off, and the coaches and their players know it. "They have fast guys … but we have fast guys too," says Barquist to the gathered squad. "Friday night, we're the show."

Wojtkiewicz says, "We'll be looking to make big plays on Friday. It's big plays that deflate the opposition."

It's the team's newest addition, though, that gets the final say on this gloriously bright Thursday afternoon at Bulldog Stadium. And, in reality, he's not new to the program at all, having been a teammate of Freking's on that first-ever state championship team in 1981. The team's new "special assistant" draws whoops and cheers and slaps on the back from coaches and kids as he's introduced by Coach in his new job capacity. Steve Lampe is outfitted today in his sweater and socks and black Bulldog ball cap, the same uniform he sported for the team's title run during his senior year, and he guides his hand-controlled electric wheelchair to settle into the middle of the crowd next to Freking. He himself doesn't have a whole lot to say unless you count the nonstop grins and full-throated laughs that he has to offer this crew of his. But he did type a few words that Freking picks up off the chair's chest tray.

"Talk is cheap," Freking reads. "Make every single play count out there tomorrow night." Freking looks up, Lampe grins, the team roars, and now it's almost time to start doing damage to Davenport North.

The coaches, though, aren't quite ready to leave the stadium. Coach Lampe is here and Coach has to remind him of the '81 title game and its aftermath when it was Lampe's turn to hold the trophy. "So I hand it to you, and what do you do?" says Coach as he shakes his head, and Freking shakes his head, and Lampe shakes his head, and the three of them are smiling as they peer back through all those years. "You've got it in your hands, Coach Lampe. That trophy. And what do you do but drop it … drop the damn thing on the ground. And there it is, broken to pieces, scattered all over. How could you, Coach Lampe? How could you do it?"

Nic Palczynski asks this same question of a few offensive linemates who plan on paying their six dollars to join Freking and assistant Matt Drinkall at the Hy-Vee supermarket dining tables for a little more team time and a lot of pretty much anything they want to eat—pizza, pork chops, spaghetti, fried chicken, and salad. "How could you do it?" Nic asks in disgust. "Hy-Vee has the exact same flavor in all their food."

"It tastes good to me," one kid says as he sits on the concrete bench in front of his locker.

"That's right," chimes in another O-line pal. "We're all fat, but we can still call each other fat … and we can still show up."

And this hefty crew does show up, along with many of their teammates, to sit and eat and talk and enjoy themselves. Freking has a bite to eat, and so does Drinkall, and as they sit at ease and watching these young men that they spend so much time with and devote so much time to, Drinkall talks some about Coach. "He's one guy you just don't want to disappoint, and the reason why you don't want to disappoint him is that everyone, and especially you, respects him. If you do something really wrong, in school say, when Coach confronts you about it, he'll stand in front of you, take a grip on your upper arm with that thick paw of his, like you're caught in a vice, and just stare at you in total disappointment and anger. When he does that you feel about that small."

As Drinkall and Freking continue to talk and eat, the kids bus their trays, then walk up to the coaches' table to offer up a "thank you" and a handshake and a "see you tomorrow," and then walk out the supermarket door. After all the kids have made their way outside, the coaches themselves push away from their plates to find their way home.

•  •  •

FRIDAY OFFERS UP its share of big moments but none of them really involve the Davenport North Wildcats. In the early afternoon, Coach's son, Garrett, watches his junior high team's day-old victory on the office VCR while his dad relaxes in an office chair, alternately studying his "play sheets" and gazing around the room. Matt Speak, the Tuesday morning founder, leans back in another chair with his black felt cowboy hat on his knee as he descends into contemplation about this evening's team prayer. Wiley is here, and so is Wojtkiewicz, both settled in at their desks and both with an array of notes and formations fanned out before them. Barquist will be back from home in a few minutes, and Freking is also on his way. And here's Chris Mahoski, the once and future kicker, fresh back from the doctor's office and peeking into Coach's doorway. "The doctor is happy with the progress," he says.

"Well that's good," says Coach.

"Should I take some practice kicks tonight?" asks young Chris.

"Absolutely not," says Coach. "You're our emergency kicker tonight."

Chris says, "Okay, Coach. It's supposed to be better next week."

And then there is the training room and Dr. Death, who's got Carter on a table with ice on one ankle and fluid draining out of the other, and Rizzo with some electric current and a cold gel pack on his bad hip, and the invaluable junior linebacker Pat Angerer, who hits like his name and who has fluid draining out of his knee. Matt Gowan is here as well, getting his ankles taped, when Jack Smith shows up out of breath at this third floor office space. He is worn out from huffing up the stairs under Freking's orders to "drag Gowan's ass back down here" for the defensive meeting. Jack wears a black eye patch and this is his first day back with the team since undergoing surgery to repair damage done by a waywardly flicked penny. He spends this afternoon and evening running errands like this one, and handing out water to his teammates, and reveling in the "Ay, mateys!" and "Shiver me timbers!" that they jubilantly offer up to show how much they missed him.

There's also Coach, whose breath mists out of his pulled-over hood, pacing, his fists stuffed in his pockets, he looks the picture of a football coach. And, he looks even more like a coach after he says to his team at halftime of this blowout affair, "Good teams finish teams off. I want you to come out with the same intensity we started the game with. Smell the blood. Get in a frenzy," and then the offense comes out for the third quarter with their 33–0 lead and goes flat. It's three and out on their first possession. So Coach gathers them around him on the sideline in a wide circle and they are on their bellies and their feet, their bellies and their feet, pounding away, doing up-downs, and Coach is snarling, "You're going to humiliate me? I'll humiliate you. You're still in the locker room!"

And where is that Davenport North speed? Where is Overton? Where is the test that this Wildcat team was supposed to provide … or at least some measure of resistance? Tonight it's not there.

So the Bulldogs win this one going away. And even though the Wildcats try to laugh and joke with them as the two teams shake hands at midfield after the game, the kids from The Bett are already thinking about next week, thinking about the Assumption Knights. "Go out there and take your practice level higher," says Freking as the team gathers in its own locker room after the bus ride back. "I can almost assure you victory."

But before that chance at victory, in their own Bulldog Stadium where they have lost maybe ten times in twenty years, they've got a team workout early tomorrow morning where they'll run and lift in the first real chill of autumn, and they'll wish Coach a happy birthday in rousing song. And Coach will watch these boys, his young team, gaining in confidence and experience and momentum, in their tours around the stadium track, and he'll breathe in a deep draught of this frost-tinged air, and say, "Now this—this—is just starting to be my kind of weather. I'm starting to feel it."

And what will it be like on Friday in that full-house stadium under the lights, even deeper into fall and with the white-uniformed Knights mustered and anxious on their sideline, to look up the hill in the gathering darkness, toward the chants and yells and exhorted shouts of a black-clad horde, sprung loose and thundering down, ready for battle?

# Week Nine—Stoke the Fire

## Valentine Rural High School Badgers: Valentine, Nebraska

**S**UNDAY AFTERNOON IN Valentine means flag football at Badger Stadium across the asphalt parking lot from the rural high school. It means a bunch of preteen kids—mostly boys, but a few girls also—sprinting and shaking and juking their way up and down the same field where the Badger varsity performs on Friday nights. It means Dahn Hagge, who runs the whole show, striding from sideline to bleachers to brick-built concession stand, bearing clipboards, ice packs, bun bags, footballs, neon orange cones, armloads of flag belts, and an unshakable resolve to keep this six-year-old youth league going and growing in this isolated Nebraska Sandhills community.

And it means Dahn's husband, Mark, the high school head coach, standing on the black-tarred running track that loops around the stadium field. He's got sunglasses wrapped around his ruddy face, and his shielded gaze is fixed on the field of play where youngsters continue to charge at and around one another. As he watches these small bodies scuttle across the still-green grass, Coach does not see them as the preadolescents in untucked shirts and ripped-knee Wranglers that they are, but rather as what he hopes they will be in a few years—rope-muscled teenagers in shoulder pads and helmets "bustin' concrete" for the Badger Nation on a breezy Friday night.

Because as fine a day as it is, and as wonderful an opportunity for these youngsters to be running around out here with their gaggle of volunteer coaches hollering out instructions from the sidelines, and great as it might be to get parents and friends together on this weekend afternoon to watch their kids play ball, to Coach, these boys and girls on this field mean a whole lot more than that. This is where the fire starts, where these same children out here today are on the other side of the chain-link fence on Friday nights pointing at his guys—at Brad Arnold and Timber Burge and Paul Itaaehau and Johnny Kolessa—and saying, "That's me." These kids are his foundation, his future, and the future of this Valentine program that it is Coach's dream to build into a Nebraska small-school state powerhouse. He wants these youngsters thinking football and dreaming themselves of one day being a Badger, and he wants his boys, who represent the school and the town in their red and white jerseys, to know that "these kids absolutely idolize you." Coach wants "tradition" and he knows that its building blocks are scurrying around on this Sunday afternoon flag football field.

But it isn't quite enough just to want it, and only to imagine these kids and what they might end up becoming a few years from now isn't going to get the job done. So Coach watches a little more of this elementary school action and then hustles home. He uses a length of railroad tie and a short section of chain-link fence to rig up a cultivator to the back of the family's ATV in hopes of getting started on the grass lawn they have planned on their creek-side lot before he has to get back down to school. As he works to lift the wood chunk and secure it to the fence piece with baling wire, he winces in sincere pain from the shoulder he dislocated last week while he was "working with the kids." What he did to aggravate this old and oft-repeated football injury was jump into the middle of a full-pads blocking drill in his sweatpants and red pullover to demonstrate "how it's done." Besides accomplishing that with his linemen, he was also able to show them what happens when unprotected human flesh and sinew and joint meet plastic shoulder pad in full-force contact, and to reiterate just how badly he wants them to succeed as a team. "Sometimes," says Coach, "I get a little too worked up out there." But he doesn't have much time to reflect on this injury; it's almost five o'clock, which means it's time to head back to school to meet with his varsity team and staff.

At this point, almost midway through the season and heading into their Homecoming game against the Cozad Haymakers, Coach's Badgers are sitting pretty well. They're 4–0, with their last victory coming in Friday night's three-hour road trip to Hershey, where Coach says, "I was content to hammer it right at them, 'cause they were playin' like a dirty football team."

And he's got the tools to hammer people with, starting with his 245-pound Tongan fullback, Paul Itaahau. On Monday afternoon between the day's last period classes and practice, Coach calls Paul into his office inside the team locker room for a little talk. Coach is short and stocky with a set of Rocky Mountain shoulders that, even in his pained condition, are formidable. As he stands face to face with Paul, though, a lot of his square build disappears next to the sheer mass of this senior captain's thighs and chest and neck. "Now, Paul," says Coach, "I know I haven't lost you. But starting today ... starting right now ... it's time to pick it up out there at practice. We need you to lead out there. We need you to run full speed when it's time to run, and we need you to work harder. Your team needs that from you."

Paul stands in this office with its short row of lockers and TV and overstuffed couch and couple of played-out recliners and bags of balls and tape and towels and extra cleats, and he's wearing his practice pants and no shoes or socks or shirt, and he's a man standing there with his sloping muscles and thick calves and his furrowed brow. But then he smiles his big innocent smile that hasn't been out into the world, hasn't really seen anything yet, and he's a boy again who says, "Okay, Coach," before he turns back toward his own locker and his laughing, joking buddies.

"Well," says Coach, "we'll see how that goes."

Coach can relate, at least a little, to Paul's less-than-enthusiastic approach to practice. It isn't that Coach has ever had trouble getting excited to go out there and play or practice or coach football. It's just that, in his earlier years, football, and any other pursuit that held even the thread of a promise of similar adrenalin-pumping excitement, were the only things that could garner his attention. Academics really weren't for him during the years that he played linebacker at Omaha's Creighton Prep, and maybe the one thing that kept him going to class was the back-of-his-mind dream of attending the state university in Lincoln and trying out as a walk-on for Tom Osbourne's Cornhusker football team. As he sits in his white vinyl office recliner, thinking about what got him to the University of Nebraska instead of pounding nails or cutting hay full time, Coach says with a tobacco-flecked grin, "I wanted to play football … I wanted to be a Husker." And he did both, along with earning his college degree and coming to the realization that teaching and coaching high school football might be a good thing to do in this life.

The University of Nebraska has claimed its share of conference and national championships; and its "Husker Nation," which envelopes the entire region in its red shadow, is unmatched in our country in terms of the devotion this state focuses on its one major athletic team. But, as much as anything else, in football circles at least, the Cornhuskers are famous for their walk-on Nebraska football players, the in-state, non-scholarship guys who are supposedly too small and too slow to play anywhere else. But that doesn't matter because they don't want to play anywhere else for any scholarship or any kind of money. The only thing they want to do, like Coach, is be a Husker. And Coach became just that, achieving the dream of his youth, and gaining, in Coach Osbourne, a man he could look up to as a bona fide role model and also seek out—along with the hundreds of other Nebraska Cornhuskers who played for Osbourne—for counsel and honest help. "Coach Osbourne got me my first coaching job," says Coach. "I was interested in applying for the position at Superior, Nebraska, and so I called him about it. He gets on the phone and says, 'Be in my office at six o'clock tomorrow morning.' He was familiar with my tendency toward wildness and maybe that was a concern, so, when I got to his office and sat down, he says, 'Are you prepared to be a teacher, coach, and role model?' I told him, 'Yessir, I am,' and the next thing you know I had my family moved out to Superior and I was a high school football coach."

Much of what Coach brought with him to that first job, and then here to Valentine, was instilled in him by his college coach. "Coach Osbourne cares about his players and that comes through." Right now, Coach is thinking of one particular player that his college coach cared about, Lawrence Phillips, a rough kid from a rough neighborhood, who almost nobody understood, and whose only chance in life may have involved football.

He played for Nebraska in the mid-1990s, the best in a gifted stable of Husker running backs that also included Ahman Greene, who is now an All-Pro performer with the Green Bay Packers. As good as he was, though, Lawrence just couldn't seem to connect with people and he couldn't seem to stay out of trouble. He was arrested at the end of his senior regular season as the team prepared to play for the national championship in the Sugar Bowl, and the charges were that he attacked his ex-girlfriend in her apartment and dragged her by her hair down a flight of stairs. There was a media outcry for justice in the case above and beyond what "the system" was prepared to investigate and mete out, and for Coach Osbourne to pursue disciplinary action against this wayward player, who was besmirching the good name of the team, the university, and college football. But instead of banishing Lawrence from the team, Coach Osbourne stuck by this young man and kept him a part of things and playing while the justice system went about its task of determining his guilt or innocence, which prompted a firestorm of outrage in the media over this perceived double standard. "They had all those good runners," says Coach. "And you think he was just trying to win a football game? The fact is, he couldn't turn his back on Lawrence Phillips. He stood his ground and did what he thought was best for the kid. I take that from him. I want to develop these kids physically and have them on the muscle. But we want to develop them spiritually and intellectually as well."

One kid that Coach has stuck by and believes in is his senior quarterback, Brad Arnold. "He's a follower," says Coach. "But his sophomore year he started for us at linebacker and we had a strong senior class with good leadership for him to follow, and he thrived on that. His junior year was different. The senior class was weak and there were a lot of troublemakers. As long as football season was going on, he listened to me, followed along, and kept giving it his best shot. But once the season was over, he got wild and got into trouble and got kicked off the wrestling team, and the whole rest of the year was pretty rough for him." Now this, his senior year, has again started off differently for him. "He looks around now and there's no one to follow, so he's become a leader himself. He plays hard, and he pays attention, and he's not afraid to get a hold of the younger guys to say, 'This is how we do things here.' You think that's not gratifying to see him blossom like that?"

And there's something else. "We're working at getting him to go to college, to get an education and play football … and he wants to go. It never even occurred to him until this year that he could go. But a couple weeks ago, he came up to me and said, 'Coach, I think I want to be a teacher and a football coach.'"

These long-term goals are a fine thing for Brad to consider, but right now, in the heat of this season that has started perfectly, the thing that's most on his mind is winning football games and playing in the Memorial Stadium of Coach's college days, where the state title game is held. "That would be ultra," says Coach, as he considers the possibility of bringing his team to the same field of dreams where he was a part of so many Cornhusker triumphs as a player. Two years ago, they came close, losing in the semi-finals in a game where maybe one or two crucial plays decided the outcome. Then, the following week, as part of Coach's annual ritual of loading up a couple of vans with whoever wants to make the five-hour drive, they had to sit in the November chill of Memorial Stadium and watch the team that beat them go on to capture the state crown.

The next season saw most of the talent that had taken Valentine deep into the playoffs the year before returning, and so hopes were high all over Cherry County. But things didn't work out. "Last year should have been the year we closed the deal," says Coach. "But there was no senior leadership." This year is different though. There is a bit of a drop-off talent-wise from the athletic graduates who just couldn't seem to blend all of their individual abilities into one unstoppable unit, and instead succeeded mainly in frustrating their coach and disappointing themselves and their anxious followers. "But," says Coach, "this year the kids are responding and taking some coaching," and that seems to make all the difference.

Besides this renewal of the idea of "team," the Badgers are getting help from some unexpected places—like the cross-country squad, where Joe Hesse, one of the school's swiftest runners, decided last spring as he was trotting around Badger Stadium in the heights of track and field season, that he might like to give football a try. He conferred with Coach, and the two formulated a plan in which Joe, whose father, Rick, is the school's athletic director, and whose mother, Kim, paints the bright red Badger head at midfield for home games, would accompany the team to the state-wide summer football camp they planned to attend, which would give him a chance to decide whether or not football was for him. "He was afraid he wouldn't be good enough," says Coach. "And I think he was a little intimidated by the contact." This fear and intimidation factor dissipated pretty fast, and so Joe just kept hanging around and hanging around, and by August he had engineered a full-fledged defection from running the area's sand hills in the fall to chasing wide receivers around a flat-planed, white-lined grass field. In this, his first season as a starter, or as a football player for that matter, he leads the state with his five interceptions, and Coach is beginning to look for ways to get him in on the offensive side of the ball as well.

Then there is the team's kicking situation. During summer practice Coach devoted a lot of time to fretting over who might handle the kicking duties this season, and he scheduled several minutes of each practice session toward giving a number of different kids the chance to try their foot at directing the ball through the white-painted uprights. A whole slew of kids tried with success rates varying from limited to cover-your-eyes bad. Then the school year started up, and Martem Perrilla, the new Brazilian foreign exchange student wandered up to Coach in the hallway and said he would like to give American football a shot. So out to the practice field he came, and when Coach handed him a ball and a tee, he promptly started soaring fifty-yard field goals through the posts and powering kick-offs into the opposing end zone. "Here," thought Coach with a thankful glance toward the cloud-streaked sky, "is our kicker."

It turns out, though, that Coach was somewhat premature in his assessment. After an initial practice period where Martem boomed his kicks and Brad Arnold lofted up lazy passes to his backs and ends, and the linemen sort of sat around, taking it all in, Timber Burge, a junior offensive guard, pushed himself up from his blocking bag lounge chair, snapped up his chin strap, and called out, "Hey fat asses, over here," to his fellow linemen. Now it was time for the Brazilian kicker to see the other side of this American game, which, after Timber and his mates got situated in their blocking practice lines, included a copious amount of big bodies slamming into one another.

The next day is when Martem began wondering aloud about aches and pains in his kicking leg and saying that maybe he should rest it instead of rushing right into the full pads uniform that is a big part of practicing and playing for the Badgers. "No problem," said Coach. "Rest your leg. Make sure you're feeling okay before you try and kick again." Then Coach renewed his search for a kicker, a search that continues on through this week, as Martem continues to come out to practice in his jersey and shorts and sometimes carrying his helmet, where he stands off to the side, twirling a football on his fingertips and wondering exactly what a full-speed collision with Brad Arnold or Paul Itaaehau might feel like.

At practice, someone might say to him, "Martem, let's see you kick one."

But he only shakes his head, kneads his thigh, and offers up a tentative grin, as he replies, "My leg," and then goes back to spinning the ball and thinking, like he's a boy perched on a forty-foot cliff over water.

Andrew, one of Martem's friends, has his own cliff where he's got his own tenuous foothold, and at the forty-foot bottom of it is a sea of drugs and alcohol where a lot of people are trying to keep him from drowning. Like his sideline-mate, Martem, he's new to northern Nebraska, having moved from Iowa this summer when his legal guardian, Bill Tuma, accepted the position of Valentine Rural School District superintendent. Andrew is a friendly, 300-pound block of a kid who, in full football pads and with a little training, could inspire the kind of awe that a coach dreams of when he thinks about offensive linemen. "He's going through some difficult times," says assistant coach Kevin Pettigrew. "And they're looking at maybe a rehab option for him. At least staying with Mr. Tuma has given him a more stable home environment," says Pettigrew. "And it keeps him away from the physical and mental abuse dished out by his father."

After three straight missing-in-action days, Andrew is on the sideline for Thursday's practice. He wears his red game jersey, just like his teammates who are out on the field going through their pre-game run-through, and, as he stands next to his man Martem, and, even though he's not exactly smiling, he's feeling a lot better than he has in a while. It does look as if he'll soon be heading to enter a treatment center in Omaha or Grand Island, and, even though he's pretty nervous about it, he's mostly hopeful that it will make a difference in his life. "I want them counselors to help me understand why I make the bad decisions that I make sometimes," says Andrew. And he's hoping that he might get fixed up enough by Thanksgiving to travel back to Iowa, where his mom and eleven-year-old sister still live. "I want to hug them," he says. "I want to help my sister make the right decisions, and we can look at my right and wrong choices to help her do it."

Andrew is a reader, and he has spent quite a bit of his time in Valentine at the town library. "Sometimes when a friend calls and wants me to go do something, I don't. I just sit home and read, and

I like it. Of course, I've only done that about two times. The other times I went along with my friends and made some bad choices."

Andrew interrupts himself to turn toward Martem, who wears his own red game jersey as he continues to twirl a football along his spindly fingers and to bounce it off his knees and feet in a personal game that reminds him of home. "Hey, Martem," Andrew says, "you ought to kick a few." Martem instinctively reaches for his leg, but Andrew keeps on with his suggestions and finally his Brazilian teammate simply cannot resist the urge to jog out with ball and tee to the vacant end of the stadium field. Martem settles himself into position and starts swinging his leg in an easy sweeping motion that seems almost genetically programmed. While he watches this natural-born kicker in his isolated machinations, and listens to the claps and whistles and pad splats of his team's last-day preparations, Andrew thinks about the future that, at least right now on this sunny Thursday afternoon, he is determined to make for himself. He hopes to be back out here next season as a junior, playing football for the Badgers.

Andrew isn't alone in his struggle to make the right choices. Coach says that when he arrived here, there was a problem of drug and alcohol use among young people. Although it hasn't vanished, things have improved. Coach asks his players to pledge abstinence, and, in support, he himself avoids alcohol during the season. "My guys are on top of it, too," says Coach. "If they see my pickup parked down in front of the Peppermill for a Huskers' game, they'll stop in to make sure I'm drinkin' my water. It's important to them … and to me." This pact is especially apparent on a Thursday evening after the downtown Homecoming parade and pep rally, when Coach accompanies Pettigrew and Tom Scott over to the Peppermill to check out the college games on the big screen and to wind down a little before Friday's onslaught. When the three coaches have a seat at a backroom table in this steakhouse and bar, they are engulfed by friends and well-wishers and recent parade viewers who all want to know how the team is looking this week, and who all want to buy them a drink. That sounds pretty good and damned harmless—a beer with friends to relax a little and to raise a glass to tomorrow night's success in revenging last year's game that Coach Scott says, "still leaves me with a bad taste in my mouth." But this isn't for Coach, even with friends, and even with maybe his best friend in town Jim Quigley, who is mad because the closed-off parade route forced him to walk across the street from his law office instead of drive, and who says, "Dammit, I'm buyin' you one, Hagge."

But once Coach has his glass of water and everyone is situated around this round expanse of a table, it is time for "Quig" to talk a little about Coach, who he has known almost as a son since the summers of Coach's youth when each year his own father would send him from Omaha to stay with Quigley and work cutting the sand hill hay that spreads out from Valentine and from the narrow Niobrara River Valley like an ocean. It is difficult for Quig—who had a big hand in clearing the road for Coach to move out here—to downplay the difference he's made to this town and this team, but he tries … sort of. Quig has lived here his entire life, except for his military stint and his time in college and law school, and, he says, "The attitude, disposition, and mentality of this team is better now than it's ever been. These kids like him, and that's about ninety percent of it right there."

But as much weight as it carries for Jim Quigley to say of Coach, "He's the right man for this job. He's gonna get us to Lincoln. He's gonna keep these boys moving forward," one must also look to the town, to the streets where only an hour ago the parade had the pavement teeming with people. A few years back, this wasn't the case.

"When they first started this deal, it was like a ghost town out here," says Scott, who moved from Lincoln to Valentine a couple years ago to get his foot in the teaching and coaching door. Tonight, though, as the sun settles behind the carved-brick oxen mural on the First National Bank building, there's not a place to park along Main Street—even for Quig—as ranch trucks and Blazers, with tailgates down, doors open, and radios blaring, crowd into curbside spaces. Every sidewalk window along the strip is splashed with red and white painted murals, and with rallying slogans like "Bale the Haymakers" and "Burn the Bales." When the varsity Badgers finally round the corner past the "Sweetheart Cove" to turn onto Main Street in their red and white jerseys, and with their chests puffed out and heads held high, the crowd really gets going. There is a swell of applause and shouted wishes that rolls with the team in its slow promenade up Main, and as they pass, the crowd falls in behind to congregate at the flatbed trailer rallying spot, where Coach takes the microphone to say to the gathered faithful as they mob around him, "It's not enough to see the mountain. You've got to move it." And as he talks—almost whispers really, in that soft voice of his that makes you want to lower your shoulder and start pushing—you can see that he believes it, and that his players do, too, and that these folks who weren't out here five years ago but are here now, well, they're starting to believe it as well.

If Quig isn't enough, or all those people at the Rally, how about Boyd Powell, who has taught biology and coached wrestling and football here for almost twenty-nine years, and who says, "Things are pretty good here these days."

Or look at the Isom twins, Jacob and James, Valentine's bookend offensive tackles, whose combined bulk can't hide their still shaky confidence, and who both carry a brass key in their pockets that Coach gave them to keep as a reminder that, "You are the key to our offense."

Coach keeps the twins after practice to work on their technique and "just to let them know that their blocking is critical to our success." They drive into each other like young bulls just starting to realize their strength. Over and over they hit and repeat, hit and repeat, and Coach is right there, saying, "Get your head acrost, Jacob," and, "You got to commit to improve, James," and coaxing it out of them like a piccolo player sitting cross-legged beside a wicker basket, and he tells these quiet giants, "We're working for perfection here … but I'll settle for great."

On Monday, Coach is working with this week's kicking prospect, Clay Robinson, who can't find the goal post with his close-range attempts, but who has Coach by his side as he hooks ball after ball toward the pine trees that ring the practice field. The only thing holding Clay's black shoes together is a wrap of athletic tape, and there's Martem watching intently from the sideline, but Coach just keeps whispering, "Stroke it through, Clay. Relax, and stroke it through," and when he does clear the uprights his team is right behind him saying, "'Atta' boy, Clay," and, "Power it up," and, "That a way to hit it," and this continues all week, beginning with a new pair of used cleats on Tuesday, and Coach saying, "Stroke it through," and, "Those shoes make a difference," and moving Clay back five yards at a time with each made attempt, and his buddies saying, "Keep it up," and, "Lookin' good," and by Thursday's practice he's starting to look like a kicker.

After that Thursday practice, Coach gathers his team around him and they're all on a knee and looking up at him, and Coach can already see tomorrow night. He can see Paul blast through rag doll defenders and Brad hurdle over the wreckage; he can see Johnny and Amos and Brogan and Joe, all charging up the field, all elbows and pads and whirling legs and hell for leather to the end zone; there's Clay Robinson as he moves toward the ball and strokes it high and end over end, almost suspended in the night sky; and there's the Isom boys who have their keys tucked into knee-high socks and they're moving mountains. They're all there, and the stadium is awash in red, it's red everywhere, like a flood in the midst of these dry-land hills.

But right now they're here in front of him gazing up into the sunlight, listening and expectant, so Coach says in his calm and even and cajoling voice, "Tomorrow night I want you to come out on the field and absolutely explode. This is our important game where we begin to make our mark in the state. Give us just a little more tomorrow night. We want just a little more passion, a little more energy, fire, aggression, and commitment. We want to show them who's boss." With this, it's off the ground and all hands up into the middle, and Coach and Pettigrew and Scott and Powell stand back to watch this swaying, leaping scrum of red and white that breaks up for the day with a ringing call of "Boss!"

Friday night Cozad calls to say their bus broke down and can the game be pushed back an hour, in a ploy that Coach thinks is more psychological than mechanical. So Coach gathers everyone in the locker room and says, "You linemen, get off your asses, and drive people down the field. Backs, I want speed and attitude. Quarterback, good decisions with the football. Defense, we got to get it goin' up front. You defensive backs, read your keys. Linebackers, fly to the ball. PAT, you block your rules, nobody gets acrost your face, nobody steps inside you, and we go through it like a walk in the park," and then it's everyone packed in at the front of the room, with Coach almost backed up to the grease-penciled whiteboard, and saying in that soothing whisper, "The key from here on out is stoking that fire," and he's building it in his mind and in their minds, and he's got his lips pursed and he's blowing soft breath and saying, "Stoke that fire," and he exhales another soft puff of breath. "Bring that passion to every second you're out there, fellas ... forty-eight minutes. Nobody let down their intensity, and not only will you have a chance to win, you will win. Refuse to get beat," and this is when all heads go down and eyes get shut, and there's a little moment of prayer, and then this roomful of boys and men says as one body, "Day by day, we get better and better. The team that won't get beat, can't get beat!" After this they're out the door and across the asphalt lot and storming onto the field to the whoops and roars of this red-dyed town that packs the stands and spills onto the track and lines the chain-link fence, and they play this game so all-out that Coach has to say on Mike Burge's next-morning radio program, "Our boys absolutely wore out the Haymakers. Cozad knows they were in a football game."

And maybe best of all, better than the Main Street parade or rousing pep rally, or Clay Robinson's good kicks, or Andrew on the sideline with his water bottles and little-kids grin, or Martem in full pads and booting the final kickoff into the end zone to the wild cheers of his teammates, or Coach yelling out directives to Brad on the field and Brad saying, "Coach, I got you," and then turning back toward his team to handle his business, or the way people in the crowd can't stop saying, "Now there's a leader"—maybe better than any of this is the game's end, after the handshakes and the cheers and this ever-so-big win, and you can stand out on the field and look up into the bleachers, and say to yourself, "Here they come," because they are pouring out of their seats and toward mid-field, students and parents and all those flag football kids, and teachers and cheer squad and band, and there they all are, surrounding their undefeated team, and with Coach in the middle of it all, in the heart of this Badger Nation, talking about the fire, talking about the mountain, and saying, "It's not how we start this thing, it's how we finish."

# Week Ten—You Have to Play

## Sheridan High School Broncs: Sheridan, Wyoming

**A**T FIVE O'CLOCK Sunday evening, the Sheridan Broncs' coaching staff is gathered in their high school office with a Formica table full of brownies and chips and pop, and the wood-grain big-screen TV ready to replay their team's Friday night road game against archrival Gillette. Head coach Bob Simpson presses "Play" on the VCR's remote control and the white and blue and gold of the Broncs' pre-game huddle begins to flicker on the screen. Defensive coordinator Mark Elliot, headphones molded around his ball cap and play sheet rolled up in his fist, barks out instructions to the kickoff team and then retreats to the sideline while his players fan out across the field. As he watches the wide-screen version of his sideline self watching his specialty team, Elliot sinks deeper into his cushioned seat on the floral-print couch and says, "Just what I want to see: a picture of myself getting sick."

It has been that kind of year for the varsity Broncs. They have beaten Laramie and Cody and lost to everyone else, including this Gillette squad, in a game like so many others this season, where the coaches are still not certain on this Sunday night that their team really showed up to play. As their defense gets run over and around on the game's first series of downs, the staff starts up a mini-debate over one play that they rewind over and over again just

157

to make certain that their eyes see what they think they see. It is a simple "sweep" call by the Gillette offense, where the quarterback takes the snap and then pitches to his tailback, who heads with the ball toward the left sideline for a solid eight yards before he's forced out of bounds by a Bronc defender. The coaches are trying to decide whether or not their "play-side" defensive end was "cut," or blocked below the waist on the play. A few more times through the sequence reveals that it was legal to block him so low because it took place inside the imagined "box" along the line of scrimmage, and not on the perimeter or up the field where it would have been deemed illegal. But just as they are about to agree that this was the important block for the Gillette gain, consider the mystery solved, and go on to the next play, one final look shows them the difficult truth that this cut block was no more than a final insult to their defensive end, who chose an inside route, thus taking himself out of position to make contact with this outside runner. Says Bronc assistant Bill Ryan, "It's pretty hard to get cut when you're already beat around the end on the play."

On the next defensive series, a Sheridan defender looks almost as if he's waving to a Gillette ball carrier as he darts through the line of scrimmage gap and on up the field for another big chunk of yardage. "He could have slapped him five," says Chuck Flickinger, another Bronc assistant. "He could have given him five and said, 'Have a nice run.'" Then the Gillette quarterback goes to the air again, but this time a Sheridan defensive back is there to intercept the ball. As he falls to the ground, he loosens his grip and the ball squirts out to result in nothing more spectacular than an incomplete pass.

"Look at us. This is so bad," says Coach. "He tries to soften his fall instead of taking the harder fall and holding onto the ball." The other coaches are in agreement about their poor defensive showing as well, and the only thing they don't understand is how the Gillette quarterback came within one vote last year of making the All-State team.

"He threw for seventy-one yards," says assistant coach Jim Friessen. "Eleven for nineteen. If he really was Division I caliber like everyone says he is, he'd of picked us apart." They also notice that, in some instances, the referees seem to be providing better pass coverage than their own defensive backs. Even when a Bronc defender does something okay, like when their left tackle takes on a double-team by the offensive tackle and tight end, something else goes amiss to cancel out the effort. "Now that's a good play from our tackle," says Coach. "But the end gets pushed downfield. If the tackle got doubled, the end should have made the play. Kyle should have just killed that one."

Things are no better for the Broncs on the offensive side of the ball. Their junior quarterback, Joe Evers, is recently returned from a broken collarbone, and memory of the injury, combined with the several weeks of missed practices and games, are having an adverse effect on his play. Coach watches Joe's tentative execution of the "veer option" play, where the quarterback fakes a hand-off into the line and then continues down the line of scrimmage toward the defensive end, either to draw in the end and pitch to his trailing back, or to turn upfield himself if the end doesn't attack him aggressively. But the Gillette defensive end can't really be aggressive because Joe is moving down the line so slowly that the play develops almost without him. "What's he doing there?" asks Coach. "If he runs downhill and pitches, we got a first down at least." Running downhill, or at full speed, is a lot to ask of Joe in this game where, even on tape, it seems to be rushing by his rusty reflexes in a blur. His discomfort is even more apparent on the occasions when he drops back to attempt a pass. As they watch the tape, the coaches can feel him feeling the pressure. The offense tries a screen pass that ends up as nothing but an incomplete throw at the receiver's feet, and Coach says, "If Joe could have waited another second, we might have had something there." Or when he does manage to get a wobbly throw off, the ball sails far over the head of a receiver who had made his break a second before and was already headed out of bounds anyhow. "I don't think he has any idea where his receivers are," says Coach. "He's so pre-occupied with the rush that he's not even looking for them. We're doing a good job of forming a pocket for him to throw out of, but all night he's running scared out of it."

The game is out of reach for the Broncs by the fourth quarter, so Coach keeps Joe on the sideline, replacing him with Zach Wheeler, the team's fullback, punter, and All-State linebacker who took over the quarterback duties during the weeks of Joe's absence. Zach is an odd-looking presence on the grainy screen because, when he takes the snap and retreats back to pass, he does so in his oversized defensive pads and neck roll, and when he winds up to heave the ball downfield, it is with the obvious strain of trying to overcome these monstrous humps on his shoulders. But somehow, two of these awkward passes drop like unexpected rain out of the north-east Wyoming sky and into the arms of Bronc receivers to set up the one Sheridan touchdown of the evening.

This brief sequence of good fortune and good results does little to improve the coaches' critical eye toward this game, where even the Sheridan student doing the film work has a bad night. First, there is the one play early in the game where Joe does set up tall and con-fident in his throwing pocket and finds a receiver who has gotten behind the Gillette defense. The camera does a fine job of tracing the arc of the ball into the receiver's hands, but, as he bobbles and then drops this one perfect pass of the night, the big-screen pic-ture goes into a spasm of jerks and shakes and shimmies that startles the coaches like a scene from *The Blair Witch Project* and upsets them even more than the bumbled reception, until they realize that it was their own Coach Ryan who had jarred the camera in his Friday night press box reaction to the dropped pass. After this spastic moment, the camera work becomes a collection of missed shots and off angles for the remainder of the contest. The coaches are treated to long panning shots of their team's offensive huddle, followed by a view of the crowd instead of the play they need to see. Or a Gillette fake hand-off will fool the camera like it is supposed to fool the Bronc defense, and so, while the ball stays with the quarterback, the camera follows the fullback as he makes a harmless punch into the line.

These coaches are upset at every aspect of their team's performance, including the camera work, but there are still two more games remaining in the season, and if the Broncs can manage to win one of them, they will qualify for Wyoming's large-school playoffs, even with their dismal record. So there is work to be done, and they have thought up a few avenues of exploration to try and make their team better for this final stretch of a disappointing season. First on their list is Joe Evers, who, at 6'4" and 200 pounds, is the classic picture of a "drop-back" quarterback. But his wide eyes and "happy" feet on this Gillette videotape offer up a different picture for the Sheridan staff, one of a kid whose confidence is rattled by a lack of practice repetitions and the heavy weight of responsibility he bears to make the right decision fast. And the coaches don't really have the luxury of keeping him on the sideline to learn because Joe is pretty much all they've got. So, how to make him better and more comfortable back there in the pocket? "Joe is 'Mr. Indecision,'" says Ryan. "We need to draw up some passing plays where he doesn't have to think, where we can say, 'Throw to that guy.'"

Coach agrees, but he is also certain that Joe's problem is more than a lack of focus on which receiver should get the ball. "I don't think he sees 'em," he says. "He had good protection—six seconds in the pocket—and then he'd flush himself."

As Friessen listens to this exchange, he starts to formulate a plan that might help their gun-shy quarterback to "see 'em" better. "How about when we go 'group' tomorrow, we get a full offense out there against a defensive line, and with no linebackers or defensive backs?" he suggests. "That way he can feel the pressure, but also see where his receivers are running their routes."

Coach leans forward in his plastic chair and taps the remote control on the snack table. "That's something to consider," he says. "Let's do this 'live,' with halfway decent guys on defense."

"Yeah," says Friessen. "We want him to feel that pressure, but work at stepping up into it to release the ball."

"No defensive backs," says Coach. "It'll be like the chuck and duck—three-step drop and throw it to a pre-selected man, because this week that six-second pocket won't be there." He pushes his compact frame up from his chair to demonstrate what he wants Joe to work on with this newly constructed drill. "He'll have time for the snap and the fullback fake," and then get rid of it now."

Coach ejects the Gillette video, inserts another tape in the machine, and he and his staff are confronted with the color film version of the Natrona Mustangs, Sheridan's Homecoming opponent this week and the top-ranked team in the state. "They have forty-five seniors," says Coach, "and forty of them are 'players,'" and watching them on film is a reaffirmation of why people are calling the 2003 Mustangs "the best team in Wyoming in several years." The first Natrona tape that the coaches watch is their game a few weeks back against Riverton, and the first play is a Riverton kickoff deep and to the opposite corner of the field from the Mustangs' all-everything senior running back, J. C. Navarro. This is a solid strategy on Riverton's part—keep the ball away from Navarro. But his response is to hustle across the field, pick up the football, and sprint up the sideline for a touchdown. "Is that legal?" asks assistant Terry Burgess.

But as elusive and dangerous as Navarro is, he's only one guy, and, after his opening-play end zone run and the subsequent Natrona kickoff, the Sheridan staff gets their first look at the eleven guys on the Mustang defense. The sight is unnerving because, as they watch play after dominant play in search of maybe that one soft spot, that one place, the coaches are coming up with next to nothing.

They continue to watch in near-amazement, and the office settles into an appreciative hush until Burgess says, "They consistently have three out of their four guys in the backfield, so we've succeeded in finding the weak link."

"So that's what we do," says Coach. "Run right at 53. Don't deviate a foot in either direction." The coaches watch another play where the Riverton offense does just that and is rewarded with a two-yard gain.

"See," says Burgess, "53 held back and made the tackle there."

"Yeah," replies Coach. "He'd be a superstar with our team. With them, he's the weak link."

The coaches have no more luck in their search for a weakness to exploit on Natrona's offense, where J. C. Navarro is hardly their one explosive weapon. "What number's Cogdill?" Ryan asks as he looks for a Mustang receiver who is supposed to be half a second faster than the fastest kid on the Broncs' squad.

As a black jersey streaks toward the end zone, Friessen says, "He's the one who's running so fast that you can't see his number." But he's not motoring so fast that Collier, his running mate, can't join him for the final twenty yards of his jaunt, and for the two receivers to joyfully exchange high fives on their way to the goal line.

The Mustangs have had quite a bit of practice at celebrating in a season where they lead the state in rushing, passing, scoring, and penalties for the excessive pleasure they take in their ability to accomplish all of these things. But they seem to do everything so fast and so well that the Sheridan staff almost can't blame them for thumping on their chests and saying, "Look how good we are." And their speed and explosiveness isn't limited to Navarro and his backfield mates.

"Look at 58," Coach says as he watches Natrona's right guard. "He's so quick, he's got enough time to scratch his ass as he pulls out and goes around the corner."

But Burgess isn't sure about Coach's observation. "No," he says. "He's signaling to Navarro, 'Cut off my left cheek.'" Coach and Burgess argue their contrasting perspectives as Navarro cuts upfield, offers up a shake of the hips to an air-grasping linebacker, and slices into the secondary for another big gain.

On the next play, though, Riverton finds a way to bull-rush its way across the line of scrimmage and corral the elusive back for a rare loss. "That's the way to do it," says Ryan. "Get him before he gets to Jukeville."

Ryan is right on with his observation. The way to at least slow down Navarro is to pack the defense up on the line of scrimmage and fill every gap aggressively from sideline to sideline, in the same manner Riverton used in this one successful defensive stop. Natrona is primarily a running team and this is the way to stop the run. But this is also the way that Natrona finds itself leading the state in passing yardage, not with a bunch of short-yardage ball-control completions, but with six or seven throws each game catapulted over the top of defenses stacked at the line of scrimmage. And Cogdill and Collier don't make their high-fiving way to the end zone via fancy crossing routes or intricate "flood" patterns.

What they use is their unparalleled speed and leaping ability to run almost nonstop fade routes past overmatched single-coverage cornerbacks, and then to haul in the high, arcing throws that their quarterback, Russell, has mastered as his special contribution to this offensive behemoth.

As Natrona's demolition derby treatment of Riverton winds down on the big TV, the coaches slouch in their plastic desk chairs and sprawl across the flower-fabric couch, tired of watching the Mustangs sprint exuberantly up and down the field and drained from imagining their own beleaguered squad trying to keep up with this combination of Olympic-style track meet panache and WWF Battle Royale bravado that will be parading onto Homer Scott Field in a matter of days. There is a bright side to the video-taped beat-down that the Mustangs have just administered to this hapless Riverton team, and that is that Sheridan will be playing them next week in the final, playoff-saving game of the season, if the Broncs can find a way to survive the Natrona storm on Friday night. "I say we hunker down and save the equipment," Ryan suggests as he thinks about Sheridan's already thinned and banged-up ranks. "Then we'll try and beat Riverton next week." So, the next thing you know, Coach is standing at the whiteboard with grease pencil in hand, everyone else is sitting forward in their seats, and they're all working together to try and figure out how to make a game of it against Natrona.

Coach has the idea to try an old play called "The Tucker," and he draws out the Xs and Os to show off what he's thinking about. After having watched Riverton gain their scant offensive yardage against Natrona primarily through breakneck outside running plays, he is convinced that "The Tucker" (a play where the quarterback pitches to the tailback, and then leads all hands in a hard angular push to the sideline in the hopes of knocking down a defender or two and turning the corner upfield) might give the Broncs a chance to make some headway against the indomitable Mustang defense. "This is a reliable play that we can dust off for this game," says Coach. "We use our best players, and it's our quickness against their quickness. We can hope for three or four yards."

This doesn't sound like a lot of real estate, especially when it's only a gain the Broncs can "hope" to earn, but any three or four yards they can steal away from Natrona will be a victory, and Coach thinks that, if they can find a way to string enough of those together, it could make a difference on Friday night. These short power runs will keep the clock moving and keep the ball out of Natrona's offensive hands. Besides "The Tucker," Coach wants to use the short pass and "take what the defense gives us." He is betting that the Natrona cornerbacks will play loose against his receivers, thus opening up the field to quick slants and short hitches. "If we can hit a few of those and get them to tighten up, our outside receivers can try to beat them on a fade, and our slot guys can run a quick out underneath that," says Coach. But he doesn't have any illusions concerning pass protection or his quarterback's tremulous psyche. "No matter what we throw, it's gonna be three steps and release, and we're gonna pre-select where he'll throw it. I don't want him to have to try and think out there, and I don't want him getting killed by 76 or one of those other guys." Ryan suggests that maybe an offensive lineman could hold up No. 76, and then a back could come up and cut him. But Coach shakes his head at this and says only half-jokingly, "His leg would separate our back's shoulder … either that or a concussion." He is serious though about using these short, pre-determined throws almost like extended hand-offs to loosen up the Mustang defense, and maybe even slow them down and get them thinking just a little bit. "You want to work on that in 'group' this week?" asks Coach.

"We're going to be needing 'group' after the game," replies Ryan. "Group therapy."

Defensively, Elliot's primary hope is that Coach and his offense can keep the Mustang offense off the field for the longest possible stretches of time because, says Coach, "As good as the Natrona defense is, their offense is the thing that is really scary and explosive." There is also the possibility of adverse conditions on Friday night that could slow the game—and the Mustangs' scoring drives—in dramatic fashion. "Nothing equalizes talent like Mother Nature," says Friessen.

Elliot doesn't have any special gimmicks or dusted-off plays like Coach's "Tucker" that he wants to use this week. He foresees utilizing primarily the 5–3 defense that the team already has in place, with two cornerbacks to play loose against Cogdill and Collier at their wide receiver positions, and then the one safety-man, who'll look to help out against the Natrona deep ball and then come up pseudo-recklessly on the vast majority of plays when the Mustangs opt to run. So the Broncs will crowd the line of scrimmage, trying to keep Navarro from making his way to "Jukeville," and, says Coach, "forcing them to beat us with the deep throw." He predicts that, no matter what, Natrona will go deep at least six times. But he believes that playing his cornerbacks ten yards off the line of scrimmage will go at least some ways toward preventing anything too bad from happening. "I don't even care how many hitches they run in front of us," he says, "as long as we can keep their pass gains under ten yards. If they have to march the ball down the field, they're not used to that, and the more plays they have to run, the more chance there is of something going wrong—overthrow, underthrow, dropped ball, interception, fumble, penalty. We have to count on these things to help us out. But we also have to do our part by slowing them down. If we don't do that, then forget it."

Coach will add a few quirks offensively and depend on his personnel and their ability to respond to this challenge. Elliot will "go base" defensively, keeping everything simple and straightforward, working hard all week on technique—covering gaps, reading "pass" versus "run," being positioned correctly to take on a block, refining pursuit angles, getting to the ball, and tackling, tackling, tackling—and he'll rely on his players' ability and desire to use these basic techniques that they have been learning since grade school to make plays. And on Wednesday, in a moment of frustration that Coach refers to as "some vociferous coaching," which turns yet another lackluster Broncs afternoon into what Burgess calls "the best practice we've had in weeks," Elliot explodes at his guys in his own almost despairing attempt to say that, ultimately, they are responsible. "Freelancing does not work," he begins, as he watches yet another linebacker take yet another wrong angle to the football. "When you do your job, things can go pretty good. When you don't, things can get ugly." Then he steps back so the scouts—or "All-Scars," as Coach likes to call them—can run the play again, and his defense can go through the motions of stopping them again, this time using the correct lanes that he has repeated for them … again. But as he stands at his vigilant post, behind his defensive backs, Elliot sees his defensive starters moving lethargically back to their own pre-play positions, just like so many other times in this practice and so many others, and this, finally, is just too much. "When are you gonna get sick and tired of gettin' your ass beat down?" he yells. "When are you gonna say, 'Enough,' and get after it? Maybe it's you. Maybe it's your generation. I don't know. You gotta stay on each other and make each other do your job! It's not gonna be my fault! I'm gonna get my job done! From this point on, it's unacceptable to be the weak link! Find the fire!" Elliot is breathing hard, and he stalks back to his post and he's mad and ready for his defense to play some football—to really play—and, for the rest of this practice at least, they do just that.

. . .

SHERIDAN IS A proud football program that has won more state titles—twenty-two—than any other team in Wyoming. They play on a game field and work out in a $1.8 million dollar on-campus fitness center financed mainly by Homer Scott, who was a Sheridan Bronc on the championship teams of the early 1950s, and who used to watch the Friday night games as a boy, when they were played at Central Field, where the stadium was built into a hill and where the raucous screams of the capacity crowd echoed off the high brick walls of the old high school so deafeningly that a visiting team couldn't hear themselves think. "Nineteen-forty-six," says the man whom everyone calls "Scotty." "That was my team." He is sitting at the Perkins' Restaurant that he owns, having just ordered the chicken tender lunch and mentioned to the waitress, "You know, if you were to put an extra dab of apple sauce on there, it wouldn't go to waste." And he is dreaming. "I remember walking up to the stadium in the evening and the thing I liked most was watching the lights shine off the helmets."

The stadium lights still glint off the gold and blue Bronc head-gear, but the crowds have thinned since the team moved up the valley to its new field at the new high school. And the cheers no longer ring in the ears of Sheridan opponents. It was back in 1995 when the Broncs claimed their last championship. Since then, the high school that was already shrinking has only gotten smaller. Wyoming's methane gas boom has skipped over Sheridan. This is great for the view and the crystalline air, but not so great for the high school that this year has seven hundred kids attending in grades ten through twelve, while many of their peers have moved to places like Gillette and Rock Springs, where their parents have found work in the mines and the factories—the "dirty industries"—that haven't gained a foothold here. This drop in schoolwide population—twenty-five percent, or about two hundred kids, since 1995—has a tangible effect on the varsity football team in the form of fifteen or so guys who just aren't there anymore, four or five of whom might be real "players," and maybe one or two who might be that 280-pound athletically gifted lineman or the silky-smooth running back with 4.5 speed that could make all the difference for this high school team. So these days the Broncs go into a game against a place like Gillette or one of the Casper schools—places that double or triple them in students—and they "hope." They don't know if their guys can stand up to these big schools, but they can hope.

And this is where the intangibles of this week's match-up come in, the seemingly uncontrollable variables that an underdog likes to believe he can at least hope to count on, and a heavy favorite dreads because there is nothing that all the talent and hard work and preparation in the football world can do to combat them. "Anything could happen," says Friessen. "It could rain or snow. Natrona could have six turnovers. They could come out 'flat.' They could play really bad and we could play really great. You just never know." Coach can't help but agree with these possible scenarios. "They could come out flat," he says, "or have a bad week of practice, which isn't uncommon in high school. They could overlook us and already be thinking about the playoffs. And," he adds, "our guys haven't been in a game yet where they've played like they're capable of playing." On the school bus ride home from Gillette, he asked his kids, in the darkened bus, after this doleful loss, in the middle of this forgettable season, and with Natrona looming ahead like some irresistible force of nature, "What do you think?" And each one of them, as he made his way back along the vinyl-seated rows, said, "I believe we can win." "So," says Coach, "I've got to believe, too." And you never know. Homecoming can be tough on a superior team on either side of the stadium. "If it's yours and you're better than your opponent, there's a good chance that overconfidence and the hype of the week can make you play flat and make you have to struggle to win," says Coach. "Whereas, if you're playing a tougher team, you have a tendency to be more focused on winning because who wants to lose their Homecoming game?" These things can happen. These things can make a difference. And Coach knows it as he says, "That's why you have to play the game."

You have to hope, you have to believe, and you have to play, and that's why Casey Temple, a sportswriter for *The Sheridan Press*, tells Coach, "I look forward to writing the upset story," after their weekly Wednesday interview session, and why Coach relates his "Upset Formula" to Trevor Jackson in a Thursday afternoon radio interview. "The favored team under-prepares and underestimates the underdog," he says. "And the underdog believes it can win and prepares to win." It's why Coach says to his rangy quarterback, "Joe, you gotta play with courage. You gotta lotta pads on ya. If ya need more, I'll give 'em to ya," and why, even after Monday's full-rush, no-defensive-backs practice where Joe connects on only seven of his twenty throws and responds with a bewildered, "I don't know," when Coach asks him why he stepped right up into the defensive pressure, and where Coach turns in disgust to Ryan to ask, "Have you seen any good mechanics yet? 'Cause I haven't," Coach sticks with him and watches him stand taller and throw with more authority in each successive practice, just like everyone on the field knows he can do, so that Coach is moved to say in Thursday's radio talk, "This week Joe has worked to find his accuracy, and he's found it, and that's exciting." It's why Friessen says that a week before summer football practice started he was in the middle of remodeling his kitchen and building a greenhouse, and he didn't want football to begin so he could get those things done. But a half hour into that first morning practice he was saying to himself that he would way rather be out there than working on the house. "The kitchen is done, but the greenhouse isn't even started," he says. "And I don't even care, because this is where I want to be—out here with the kids." It's why Sam Simpson, Sheridan's ASB president and starting left guard, and Coach's son, closes out the Wednesday night bonfire rally with his let's-beat-Natrona take on MLK's "I Have a Dream" speech to roars of approval from his gathered schoolmates. And it's also why Coach says to the team in their Friday pre-game meeting, with everyone seated and anxious in the gymnasium bleachers, "How often do you have the chance to go out there and play the best, to beat the best? No one is giving you a chance. You've got nothing to lose. Play football like you've been taught. Every guy's got ahold of the rope. One guy takes a play off, and the rope slips. If you play your asses off for forty-eight minutes, leave everything on the field—hellacious effort—then you've got nothing to be ashamed of. You can hold your heads high."

But in the midst of these dreams and beliefs and these careful preparations in the hopes that anything might happen, there is also cold reality. And on Thursday night, after the team's pre-game walkthrough and Coach's admonition that, "These plays we've got for you on both sides of the ball work. Now it's up to you to make them work;" when the staff adjourns to "The Equestrian Center" for their own weekly ritual of buffalo wings and bar talk, someone asks Elliot, a fellow who has devoted much of his young life to playing, teaching, and coaching Wyoming football, "Do the Broncs have a chance to win it tomorrow night?" Elliot takes a contemplative sip of his draught beer, then sets down his glass, steadies his gaze, and says, "No."

And he's right. For the first few moments of this final home game where the temperature drops below freezing, there is the slightest glimmer that maybe, after all, this could be Sheridan's night. The Broncs challenge Natrona's No. 76 with two straight runs right at him, and then Joe drops back on third down, settles into his crumbling pocket, and drills a beautifully spiraled throw to Kyle Kansala that squirts through his freezing hands, clanks off his facemask, and dribbles to the frost-dimpled turf. And the rope starts to slip. The defense, though, weathers a first play long-ball from Russell to Cogdill that falls harmlessly incomplete, and then, with Zach Wheeler leading the charge, stuffs Navarro on two straight runs to put the ball back into the Broncs' offensive hands. But after Joe stands tall again to deliver another tough third down throw to Kansala, who this time holds on for a juggling, acrobatic reception, a quarterback sack for a forty-yard loss by No. 76 and company further loosens Sheridan's grip, and, by a minute into the second quarter, Navarro has run wild, the Mustangs lead by three touchdowns, and things are ready to get worse. Not so bad that Natrona's Russell can't say to his mates on the halftime walk down to the gym, "C'mon guys, we gotta play a better half than that," but bad enough for Coach to say to his beleaguered squad, "You're not rising to the challenge. You're not making plays. Why are you so afraid of success? Isn't that why you play the game, to make plays?"

But it's tough to make plays against a team as dominant as Natrona is this year, and so tonight it's going to have to be enough that the Broncs hang in there, maybe staggering some, but never lying down to say, "Stop. Please. We give."

For Joe Evers, who still has next year to think about, it's a night where he gets beaten down again and again. But back he comes, standing erect, eyes narrowed and surveying the field, still looking to strike, even as he's pulled under in a swirl of black and white.

## HOMETOWN HEROES

For Zach, though, this is it, his last home game of his last year, and late in the game, there he is—All-State, All-Everything at Sheridan—plunging forward, fighting for those inches, getting caught up and bent double, stretched back hard over his own legs. But he bounces up off the pile, hobbled and hurting and ready for the next play. He's smiling, still caught up in the game, and you can almost hear him say, "Let's finish this, guys. Let's finish this right."

# Week Eleven—Strap 'Em Up

## Charles M. Russell High School Rustlers:
## Great Falls, Montana

I N THE DEEP pine forest of the Bob Marshall Wilderness, up near the Continental Divide, there's an abandoned rough-board shed that is a fine place to build a warming fire and eat lunch and then lie back on a nylon groundsheet and listen to an autumn mountain wind skip and clatter across the rusted tin roof. This is Jack and Rosann Johnson's spot. Their horses are hobbled outside browsing on the rich grama grass of this backwoods meadow, their Ford diesel pickup and gooseneck trailer are parked back at the Gibson Lake Trailhead, and seventy miles down the mountain is their hometown of Great Falls, and the coaches' office, weight room, and football practice fields of C. M. Russell High School.

For most of their thirty-one years in Great Falls, this first visit to "The Bob Marshall" doesn't come until late in the fall, after one of CMR's deep runs into the playoffs that have culminated eleven times in state championships—the most for any coach in Montana's high school football history. But this year, says Coach, "It looks like hunting season's gonna come early," because the Rustlers chances of making the state playoffs are slim, and Coach is faced with the tough possibility of his first losing season ever after Friday night's loss to Kallispell put their record at 3–5 with two games remaining on the schedule—this week's match-up with the winless Butte Bulldogs, and the season finale against cross-town rival Great Falls High, a team that has emerged this year as one of the state's large-school powerhouses. So when the coaching staff arrives in the black dark of this mid-October Sunday morning to climb the stairs up to the second floor of the CMR fieldhouse, it is with the knowledge that they are on the cusp of Jack Johnson–era history, and not the kind of history that he or they or the kids who step out onto the field on Friday nights are any too pleased with. But they also know that there isn't a whole lot they can do about this predicament except begin the preparations that will help ready their young team to face the Bulldogs this week.

Assistant coach Brian Greenwell says simply, "We don't get too emotional about things around here. We just do our jobs. Business as usual."

The main business right now is to try and figure out ways to jump-start an anemic Rustler offense that hasn't scored a touchdown in more than ten quarters. When Gary Lowry, who coaches the receivers and backs, is asked about the primary goals for Butte this week he says, "Score."

Coach echoes this sentiment, saying, "We got to get our guys into the end zone."

It is no real mystery to these coaches why their team is having such difficulty putting points on the board this year: In a state where varsity football is a senior-dominated sport, the Rustlers go into the Butte game starting eight juniors on offense—far and away the most ever during Coach's tenure—and counting on Drew Savage, a sophomore who has already seen time at varsity tailback, to be available in case Ryan Bagley, the senior starter, gets bogged down by the arthroscopic surgery he underwent a few weeks ago to repair the meniscus in his knee.

And Ryan himself, who is hearing from a number of Pac Ten and Big Sky schools and will more than likely be playing football at one of them next year, is far from comfortable at this tailback position where he was inserted at the beginning of the year because the Rustlers simply don't have anyone else.

Ryan's discomfort and inexperience at this new position has been apparent all season, and as Lowry and offensive line coach Scott Hartman sit in the upstairs foyer of the gymnasium watching the replay of the Kalispell game on this Sunday morning, they find a play that sums up the frustrations they have felt all season with Ryan at this new position and with a junior-dominated offensive line trying to create running space for him. The formation that they have run out of in this second quarter sequence is called Twins Left Ted. The play call is "GF Counter Sweep Right," the "GF" meaning the left guard and the fullback will lead the blocking on the play and the "Counter Sweep Right" indicating that all of the post-snap motion will start to flow left, but then, once the deep tailback gets the ball, he and his blockers will veer to the right side of the field. And this is what happens on this particular play at this particular moment of the Kalispell game, or at least it's almost what happens because the ball is snapped and the fullback starts left as the quarterback reverse-pivots out in his direction, and the left guard pulls to lead the sweep up the right hash-mark in conjunction with the fullback reversing his direction to follow in the guard's wake in a ploy that, along with the right offensive tackle, forms a V-shaped blocking chute for Ryan, the deep tailback who has just been handed the ball, to run through. But Ryan, once he's got the ball tucked firmly in his gut, instead of heading expediently toward this blocking alley, hesitates for an instant and then angles straight toward the line of scrimmage and a mob of black Kalispell jerseys that have been momentarily fooled by the "counter-action" of this play. By the time Ryan adjusts his angle to run outside and through the tunnel created by the fullback-left guard-right tackle triumvirate, the defensive hoard has also adjusted their path and they meet Ryan a couple yards upfield to allow only a minimal gain on a play that could have gone for much more if only the tailback had "hit the hole right now" instead of hesitating.

As Lowry and Harts watch the play four or five times in succession, their concentrated facial expressions never change. They simply bend their heads down to their notepads to record what happened at each offensive position during the four seconds it took to run this play. Then they take a moment before moving on to the next sequence to talk about why it failed.

"Ryan's just not familiar with the position," says Lowry.

"Yeah," agrees Harts. "That, and his knee, and maybe he's not quite sure what the line is gonna do." And it's right there on film, that instant of hesitation, where Ryan isn't confident that the block he needs will be there. It is there, but Ryan sees it too late, and so it's another missed opportunity for the youthful Rustler offense and another game quarter without a touchdown.

Then a few plays later in this Kalispell reel, the Rustlers find themselves in a passing situation. The plan is that both receivers will run short hitch routes where each takes three hard steps upfield and then turns back toward Kyle Johnson, the junior quarterback, ready to receive the bullet-like throw that should already be headed to one of them, which he'll snatch out of the air, tuck under his arm, and then spin back upfield to scramble for yardage until he's dragged down.

Besides bearing the responsibility of choosing a receiver, Kyle also has to decide whether or not the hitch is the appropriate route for his two receivers to run on this play, which has a built-in "audible," where Kyle can change the play-call at the line of scrimmage if the defense is lined up differently than expected. On this play it is, and Kyle recognizes it. As he jogs up to the line of scrimmage, he notices that the two cornerbacks who are responsible for covering his wide-split receivers have crept up to crowd the line of scrimmage, thus making the hitch pattern obsolete.

The hitch is effective when the defensive backs are playing at least seven yards off the line of scrimmage where they create a cushion to guard against a long pass, but also opens up the offensive opportunity for something underneath. Now, though, with the defensive backs playing up, there is only one course of action to take, and so Kyle shifts a half-step back from his position under center, turns to his right to give his facemask a firm tug, and then pivots to the left to repeat this signal that tells his two receivers to forget the hitch and instead run the fade route that will take advantage of this tight coverage with those three hard steps that it shares with the hitch, and then the bow out toward the sideline, and the wall that the receiver creates between the defensive back and the ball that should drop out of the sky, over his outside shoulder, and into his waiting arms. Even better for the Rustlers is the personnel mismatch on the right side of the field where they have a 6'4" receiver lined up against a 5'8" Kalispell defensive back, and so Kyle, before he takes the snap from center, has already made the decision to throw to this receiver whose basketball height and breakaway speed make him perfect to complete this play. In the twenty-five seconds since the referee's whistle blew to signal the end of the last play—after the teams hustled back to their huddles and then broke for the line of scrimmage, after Kyle made his yeoman-like survey of the field and signaled the necessary adjustments to his receivers, after he settled under center, and barked out his crisp cadence, and took the snap, and made his picture-perfect three-step drop behind the offensive line and running backs and their pocket protection—after all of this that has been carried out so flawlessly by these eight juniors and three seniors, the Rustlers are ready to make something good happen. But all the positives that should come out of this play begin to unravel the instant the football leaves Kyle's hand because, instead of the high, lazy spiral that floats like a pillow over the outside shoulder and into the hands of the tall, fast receiver, the ball is released on a low line more toward the center of the field, forcing the receiver to dive back under the defender's outstretched arms in an attempt to make an impossible catch that results in a football that dribbles harmlessly to a halt on the turf and one more instance when the difference between success and failure for this CMR offense is measured by split seconds and inches.

. . .

ALMOST FIFTY YEARS after he was introduced to the game, Coach knows what's going on with his team this season, and he knows there's not a lot that can be done about it. Maybe that's why Rosann is able to say of her husband, "All things considered, I think he's taking things pretty well … probably better than me."

But that doesn't mean that Coach doesn't want to find ways to win. He knows that, as tough a time as these juniors are having this year against more experienced schools like Helena Capital and Billings West, their buddies on the junior varsity team are undefeated, and this combined crew will be a difficult team to beat next year if they can make it through these final two games with team morale intact.

Times have changed since Coach first took over the program and borrowed $500 on his own name so he could purchase the weight equipment that would help institute his year-round conditioning regimen that laid the foundation for the Rustlers' first state title two years later. That 1975 championship team was the beginning of a ten-year run where CMR failed to participate in the state title game only once. This unprecedented success also brought about a dramatic change in the way football is practiced and played at the large-school level in the state of Montana.

Coach was the first to institute a weight-training program, which he began in 1973 with three students. Today, he runs five full classes during the school day and two other teachers are responsible for weight-training classes as well. And then there are the afternoon practices that are held out on "Pride Field," where players and coaches run from drill to drill in a non-stop choreography of predesigned individual, group, and team periods that are controlled by a game clock overlooking the field. A coach's Monday practice sheet might read: 3:50 Pre-practice, 4:00 Cal/Run/Agility, 4:05 Team Go, 4:10 Indi/Group, 4:45 Swap, 4:55 #H's vs. #I's, 5:00 Ice, 5:05 KO & KOR, 5:10 Skelly, 5:20 2-minute, 5:25 Team, 5:45 "Chicken Fight" JV Fronts, H-H Meet, Kick. Within each of these practice periods, announced by the squawk of a team manager–controlled loudspeaker, a visitor might watch Harts lead his offensive linemen in a full-throttle charge against Coach's defensive linemen for a pass block/pass rush segment; or a "Pass Skeleton" segment where one of Coach Mike Henneberg's embattled defensive backs, who have given up more than nine hundred yards of passing in the last three games, gets in a good "pop" on a Lowry wide-out, and prompts Coach to say, "I knew we'd tune up these sissy wide receivers."

Near the end of practice, the team prepares for today's "Chicken Fight" competition, where everyone circles up to create a mini-arena for five green-jerseyed offensive linemen and five gold-jerseyed defensive linemen to knee-walk at each other and then engage in a no-holds-barred wrestling clash that is a cross between *Braveheart* and *Animal House*, and where the last man kneeling wins his side of the ball an exemption from post-practice wind sprints.

After those sprints, Coach brings the team together with a gravelly call of, "Awright. Let's circle the wagons," and that concludes with a hearty chant of "Rah, rah, Rustlers!"

To watch the team practice—the speed, and the focus, and the way a back-up quarterback like junior Matt Schoonover takes command of the scout team offense, from play-calling to substitutions to keeping up a constant tempo that will ensure the first team defense "gets a look" at everything the Butte Bulldogs might throw their way on Friday night—and then to think about the team's 3–5 record, is one way to form an idea of just how good high school football in this state is, and also how much the fellow running this Rustler practice has to do with making it that way.

It's not a gang of Supermen blocking and tackling and running full-tilt pass patterns out here on this wind-whipped autumn afternoon, but neither were the kids who first set foot on Pride Field back in 1973. When Coach showed up here, Montana high school football was a game dominated by the biggest, the fastest, and the toughest, and, if your program didn't have a gross of kids who could fit that bill, then you could forget about enjoying any kind of gridiron success. Coach showed the Rustlers, and the rest of the state, that you could take a bunch of kids with little more than the desire to play, and through disciplined and directed hard work, mold them into a championship-caliber football team. CMR has had its share of standout athletes and the walls in the coaches' office are lined with pictures of the dozens of players, including Lowry, Harts, and Henneberg, who have left Great Falls to compete on the collegiate level. But, by and large, it is "regular" kids who populate this program and bring back all those championship trophies.

Maybe that's what makes it so difficult for Duff Mahoney, a defensive assistant and another Rustler graduate, when a group of players approaches him in the fieldhouse to ask, "Are we Coach's worst team ever?" Duff is struck dumb by this question, perhaps because a glance at this team's record compared with all those other squads makes the answer seem so painfully obvious. He might be thinking about his own years in the CMR uniform, when those bigger, faster teams were still trying to catch up to the Rustlers and their college-grade approach to football. Or he might be looking at this earnest bunch of undersized overachievers and realizing that those days are over, that a lot of these other teams have studied Coach for so long, have watched the Rustlers and "how they do things," have adopted many of their ways, and have gone in search of some of their own "new" ways, so that now, instead of working hard to dominate, like the Rustlers have done in so many of Coach's years here, including last year, when they played in the state title game, CMR has to work hard to compete and wait patiently for those "special" players who can give them the boost they need to reach the heights that they've grown so accustomed to here.

But this knot of kids is still gathered around Duff, in their school clothes and clutching book bags, not quite ready to head down to the locker room and wanting to know, "Are we the worst?" But Duff just stands there with them and shrugs his shoulders and says, "C'mon, guys. Let's get ready to practice." And as they drift downstairs to get iced and get taped and get ready to step onto Pride Field, Duff sort of staggers into the coaches' office and he's numb and shaking his head as he takes a seat on a low stool. "Them askin' me that. I didn't know what to say. It was making me tear up, the way they were lookin' at me, like they already knew; but they still wanted to know." Duff takes his practice script out of his green jacket pocket and tries to study it. "What was I supposed to say?" he asks.

And what is Coach supposed to say when Travis Hartman, a senior team captain, comes up to his office on Tuesday morning with all his gear to tell Coach that he's quitting? Coach steps away from his desk and his paperwork to stand in the doorway with Travis, a kid who throughout his CMR career has been asked to switch positions from quarterback to wide receiver, and now, just this week, to defensive back, where Henneberg's ranks are thin and shell-shocked.

"What's the matter, Travis?" asks Coach.

"I don't like that you want me to play DB," says Travis. He's looking at the cement floor and slapping his gear-stuffed mesh bag against his trouser leg, and he says, "I can't learn the position and I'm not being treated with the respect that I deserve."

"Well Travis, when I talked with you about the switch, you said, 'Okay.' You said you thought you could give it a try," says Coach.

"That's not what I think now," replies Travis.

"We're depleted back there," says Coach. "We could use your help."

Travis shakes his head. "I can't learn it, and I won't learn it."

"Well," says Coach, "you can 'man' somebody up and play it that way, can't you?"

But Travis won't look up and he won't budge, and he won't say anything else except, "No."

So Coach says, "Maybe it's for the best. Be true to thine own self rather than the team." So Travis deposits his mesh bag against the office door and turns to trudge back down the stairs. Coach walks over to his depth chart board, finds the aluminum-edged green card that says "Travis Hartman," slides it off its gold hook, crumples it in the palm of his rope-scarred hand, and deposits it in the plastic-lined trash can. Then he sits back down at his desk to keep figuring out how to get the rest of his team into the end zone.

That afternoon, after the staff has trickled up to the office, Coach relates to them this puzzling exchange and resignation of one of his team captains, and he does the same thing at the end of practice when the team has "circled the wagons" around him. "I don't know," says Coach. "I told him a couple days ago that we needed him on defense, and he seemed happy with it. Yesterday, after he had a chance to try it out, he said, 'This is fun.' But I guess he changed his mind today."

Coach, though, isn't so sure that it was Travis who changed his mind, and, back up in the office, with a Yankees–Red Sox playoff game flickering across the muted TV, he says as much to Harts, who, besides his responsibilities with the offensive line, also bears the distinction of being Travis's uncle. "That deal about 'not getting the respect I deserve,' that sounds like his mother talking," says Coach.

Harts can only shake his head in agreement and misery and say, "I know," because he does know, and because he is also aware of whose job it will be to deliver to his brother's house the clear plastic trash bag full of socks and books and letter jacket that Coach cleaned out of Travis's locker this morning.

This situation with his nephew feels almost like "piling on" to Harts. This has not been his year, and as he blows out a resigned breath and heaves up from his stool to mope his way out of the office and toward home in his pickup, all the while trying to figure out how he'll deal with his brother and sister-in-law and their son, who is no longer a Rustler, but is still his nephew, Coach looks after him and says, "Harts is havin' kind of a tough week."

First, there is his young offensive line and the kidding he takes from Lowry and company about how they are the weak link on the offense. On Tuesday, as he stands with Lowry in the sunshine and cold breeze of Pride Field waiting for practice to begin, Harts is thinking, picturing his young linemen and how things could be better for them, and, consequently, him, and he turns to Lowry, his friend of so many years, to share these thoughts of his that he's been turning over in his agitated mind. "I've got to think it's the backs' fault we can't move the ball," he says. "My guys get in those one-on-one drills with the D-line, and we kick ass. But then when we go Team, the D does it to us. That's it. I'm not takin' the blame. It's the backs, not the line."

For his part, Lowry can only shake his head and laugh because he knows he was the one who got Harts thinking even more about his offensive line misery when he walked into the coaches' office a couple days earlier to find Harts seated at the long table with a state-issued hunting map spread out in front of him. Harts has secured a special tag permit, and he was poring over this map in a rare moment of pure pleasure, trying to decide where he stands the most chance of using it. He was picturing himself horseback, with his shotgun slung in its scabbard, and his Carhartt coat buttoned up tight around his chin, and that cold mountain air cascading into his lungs, and this image was maybe his own personal way of making it through a few moments of this season, until Lowry peered over his shoulder at his cartography work, and then said to Greenwell, "Maybe there's some correlation between Harts's deer aspirations and how lousy the O-line is playin'."

But no matter, because his thoughts of the hunt are clouded by a struggle with his weight that has bothered him since he graduated in the late 1980s from his offensive line job at the University in Missoula, where he followed a few years behind Lowry. He wants to get down to horseback size for hunting season. Two years ago, he was able to drop a hundred pounds and mount up, but he has since gained the weight back. This year, he is giving it another go, but not with the same fervor. "He's lost about twenty pounds," says Lowry, "which would put him at about three hundred," and puts him out of contention to saddle one of Rosann's horses for his hunting trek into the wild.

There is one bright light for Harts this week, and it comes courtesy of Coach, who makes a visit downtown, past the Charlie Russell Manor and the Stein Haus and over to Hoglund's Western Wear to get his palm leaf cowboy hat re-shaped and to pick out a set of new down vests for his staff. But he's worried because the Rustler-green style he wants to order only goes to Double-X. So he mentions to Harts, "Hey, why don't you drop by Hoglund's to see if those vests fit the big boys?" Coach is rewarded the next day because, as he pulls into the school lot, back from home and checking on Fancy, his sick colt, there is Harts, driving up to the building himself, and he is smiling that smile where no one else is around and you're feeling good.

Except Coach *is* around, and he sits in his own pickup, and waits for Harts to park and notice his big gray truck, and to stroll over, still with that kid's half-grin on his face, and Coach rolls down his electric window and Harts peers in to say, "The Double-X fits," and, in this season, that is a pretty good thing to think about.

It's family here at CMR where they can give Harts a hard time because if they can't kid him around, who else then? It's where school has been out this week for the last two days due to a teachers' conference, and so Harts and Greenwell get in the truck Thursday morning to "go drivin'" up around Greenwell's family ranch in the Belt Mountains and to scout out where Harts will shoot his big buck; where Rosann drops off cinnamon rolls at the Sunday morning meetings, and shows up on Saturday mornings with Coach and Henneberg to grade tape and count tackles and update the individual and team charts that line the upstairs football foyer in the gym. It's where Coach Henneberg played on the '92 title team with Mark, the Johnson's son, and where Kelly, their daughter, kept the team stats before heading off to college in Missoula. And it's where a plaque hangs outside the office door, honoring Kelly for her contributions to the team and the school and the world before she died in a 1991 accident that changed Coach's and Rosann's and everyone else's lives for good.

It's a place where Coach can look toward the conclusion of his thirty-plus-year career and point to Lowry and say, "He'll be taking over when I'm done."

This is a place where the coaches can lounge together on the Pride Field grass in the Friday afternoon goal-post shade to watch their sophomore team run roughshod over the Butte "sophies" and where Coach can tell his team on the pre-game bus about one thing he wants them to do at the stadium for this Parent Night and final home game. "When we get over there, after we kick and punt for 'specialties,' you're going to go over to the sideline and greet your parents, give them a hug, shake your dad's hand, and then come back over for calisthenics." And it's the kind of place where, when it comes time to follow these instructions, you can get a pretty clear picture in your mind of exactly what happens.

But C. M. Russell High School is also a place where they like to win football games, so when the staff gathers in that upstairs office before they break up to "chalk" with their respective position players, Coach stands in their midst to say, "If we can't shut these Dogs down with our basic 'D' then we better get 'em the hell off our schedule, 'cause they're just too good for us." Then he slaps his green game cap against his thigh. "Let's coach 'em up, boys, and draw a hard line. If we control their run, we win the game ... that's what I say."

When the running backs gather for their pre-bus meeting, Ryan Bagley speaks up to say, "Guys, we may have only three more practices. I don't want it to be over. We've got to step it up so we can keep playing."

Lowry is there with his greenboard and piece of chalk, and later he says of Ryan's plea, "The other kids were doing the open-mouthed nodding, and who knows what that could mean. Maybe this'll be the night that the eight juniors look around the offensive huddle and realize it's up to them and they have a chance to do something to make history."

So let's just say that this CMR team does make some measure of history on Friday night with the most-ever juniors to line the top row of Coach's depth chart, digging deep to shut down the Bulldog runners; Henneberg's defensive backs dust off their hip pads to hang in there; Harts's offensive line gains just enough leverage for Ryan to run behind them and for Kyle to throw over them, and the Rustlers win. They are able to walk off the Memorial Stadium field more relieved than happy; but these days, a win is a win, and Coach knows it when he tells the Great Falls reporters, "Helluva effort tonight. We wanted the kids to play hard, and they did it."

But how about if we step back some to outside the fieldhouse before the game, when it was still light out, and Coach sits alone on a concrete-block bench surrounded by piles of helmets and shoulder pads and green home jerseys, head down, elbows on knees, until the team musters around him, buckling up pads and tucking in jerseys, and then it gets quiet, and Coach says, "Awright, Regulators. Let's mount 'em up," and it's across the dirt grade to load up the buses before making the drive over the Missouri River and to the stadium.

When the bus swings onto Second Avenue and the wings of the cement stadium come into view, there is a call from the back of the bus, a senior leader sitting erect in his seat says, "Awright, boys! Strap 'em up!" as a pure matter of fact.

## HOMETOWN HEROES

The click of chinstraps snapped to these Rustler helmets echoes through the metal bus like a pre-infantry charge, and then there are more voices, calling, "Let's go, dammit! Let's get up!" And they are up, all of them, and out of their seats, jostling in the bus aisle in their green and gold, with their pads and helmets clacking together, and the buses pull up next to the stadium curb, and the coaches climb down, and then here they come, pouring out the doors, not in lines or rows or any kind of genteel order, but like warriors come to conquer. They are everywhere, clattering through the trees and up the sidewalk, over the asphalt lot and through the chain-link gates. And Coach can watch all of this from the tree-lined street—watch them bound into the stadium, young and determined and anxious to do well. And he can maybe give himself just a moment to think, "Okay now. This is really something."

# Week Twelve—The Next Play

## Kamiakin High School Braves: Kennewick, Washington

**THE MINER'S DRIVE-IN** restaurant is one of those hamburger stands and fried food emporiums that call like Mecca to men with large appetites. So, when the Kamiakin Braves board their two school buses on Friday afternoon to make the hour and twenty minute drive northwest to Yakima, there is added incentive to ruin the Homecoming festivities at Eisenhower High School because "win or tie" those same two buses will pull into Miner's First Street parking lot before making the dark drive down Interstate 82 toward home. And they won't be alone because, when they arrive, there are already rows of yellow buses here from Wenatchee and Prosser and Cle Elum and Richland, and the vinyl-boothed, brown-tiled dining room already has an Ellis Island look, with players and parents and fans and friends all heaving forward and calling out orders for french fries and double burgers and malted shakes, and these folks are cold and hungry and desperate for a place to sit and a bite to eat.

There is another world here at Miner's, though, and Kamiakin head coach Craig Beverlin maybe knows it better than anyone. So when the Braves' buses pull under the orange halogen lights that surround the restaurant, he springs out of his front bench seat to say to his varsity players, "Remember that you're representing our high school and you need to comport yourselves as such," and then he hops down the bus steps to head toward a meal that he has been thinking about since the previous Saturday morning. He marches across the parking lot and through the double-glass doors, wades through the massed bodies huddled in the restaurant's fire code–tilting main room, and then flings open the kitchen door to find his seat at the long clothed table that awaits his arrival. "Every year," Coach says, "we look forward to coming up here to beat one of these Yakima teams, and then we get to go to Miner's and brag about it."

That table the coaches have bellied up to is loaded down with heaping plastic-mesh baskets of fried shrimp, fried scallops, fried fish, fried chicken, fried potatoes, and anything else that can be dipped in batter and dunked in a vat of boiling grease for three minutes and then set in front of these high school football coaches for whom this is about as good as it gets at eleven o'clock on an autumn Friday night. After the strain of the week, the breaking down film, plotting out defenses, and sketching pass schemes, the only real worries in this coaches-only oasis are how much to eat and where's the ketchup.

And so, all week, in the midst of their plotting to beat "Ike," there has been another kind of strategy discussion going on among Coach and his veteran staff: "What is the best way to go about ordering the post-game feast at Miner's?" "There's no question," says offensive line coach Kevin McAfee. "You got to go with the double prawns."

Receivers coach Jeff Young nods his head and says, "Yeah, that's a given, the prawns ... but what then? Do you get more prawns, or do you expand from there?" Dennis Rose, who coaches the basketball team along with his football responsibilities says, "I go with the double prawns. You got to have them for the base. But then it's the Miner Burger and a chocolate malt."

Tim Maher, the team's defensive coordinator is impressed with this combination. "Ah," he says. "An aristocrat … and you're right about the prawns."

And Coach likes the idea as well, but he says, "You know, last time my wife got the prawns, but she went with onion rings instead of fries. Now that was a good idea."

"Onion rings," muses defensive backs coach Ron Redden. "Interesting change of pace, so long as you've got the prawns."

"Definitely, fried prawns," agrees Chad Potter, the junior member of the staff.

And defensive ends coach Jim Chesterfield adds, "Prawns. Preferably the double prawns."

"Hey," says running back coach Rick Kirsch, "don't they have a salad?"

Despite the gastronomical debate going on, in the back of every coach's mind is the question of how they are going to beat Ike without further damaging their already injury-depleted squad as they look forward to next week's showdown with cross-river rival Pasco, a team that is big and bad and, along with the Braves, one of the handful of teams that has a legitimate shot at winning the Washington State 4A Title. Kamiakin began the season as the No. 1–ranked school in the state and solidified its position with an opening game thrashing of western state powerhouse Snohomish at Seahawk Stadium in Seattle. Even with the injuries that have plagued this senior-laden team, they have suffered only one loss going into the Ike game, in a contest at Lake City, Idaho.

But it's not their conference-leading offensive and defensive statistics that dominate the conversation at their post-church Sunday morning meeting in Coach's locker room office. It's the rash of injuries the team has suffered that are fueling a strong discussion about what options the team has for these last three weeks leading up to the playoffs. Before they can talk, everyone sits back in their swivel chairs and listens to this week's installment of the injury report, which is long, distinguished, and sobering, and dates back to the first half of the first game against Snohomish, when Tyler Opitz blew out a knee and ended his season. But he's not alone. There is also Evan Ruud, a senior offensive and defensive lineman and team captain, who continues to suffer from a "subluxation," or near-dislocation of his shoulder, which continues to worsen to the point that it now requires a serious tape job and a specially prescribed $200 brace, and still, according to team trainer Leo Combs, "It pops out maybe every other play of every game and he has to come off the field so I can pop it back in and determine whether or not he can go back in. And it'll keep doin' it until he has surgery and maybe even after that."

There is Nick Genatone, another team captain as well as a starting linebacker and running back, who had surgery this summer to repair a torn rotator cuff that he re-injured Friday night on a hard, clean hit from his defensive spot that simultaneously brought the ball carrier to a grinding halt and popped Nick's damaged ligament off his shoulder bone. There is starting senior wide receiver and defensive back Brett Stephens, who, Coach says, "has been carried off the field at least four times this season," and who is working his way back from a knee injured two weeks ago.

And there is Ryan Sutton, of whom Maher says of his on-field demeanor, "He's the psycho of all psychos. I feel like he's like Don Zimmer and has a metal plate in his head." Ryan suffered a concussion two weeks ago, and also what Leo first feared was a broken jaw, but which later turned out to be a broken tooth and a bruised jaw, in Friday night's game.

There is also Cody Roberts, who experienced what Leo calls "one of the worst injuries in a high school setting" three weeks ago in the Lake City game and hasn't played or practiced since. He took a hard shot to the leg that, according to Leo, "We had to wait several days to rule out a fracture or a broken bone." Now that they have determined that there is no break, Leo has been able to start treating Cody for the deep thigh bruise that injured all of his muscles down to the bone. League-leading quarterback Steve Davis has played all season with a pair of twisted ankles. Scarier than any of these is junior offensive lineman Ben Salsbury, who doesn't make the list until he collapses in Monday's practice. Leo has to hustle across the field from the post-concussion tests he's administering to Ryan so he can have a look at Ben, who is stretched out in the grass with his head cradled in Coach's thick arms.

Besides taking Leo away from his concussion ministrations, this emergency distracts Coach from an offensive team practice that includes senior guard Brent Rushin and his painful lower back contusion, and sophomore Brad Satchel, who is filling in at the other guard even though he's got a hole cut in his shoe to relieve some of the pain of a foot infection that started several weeks ago when he stepped barefoot on a wooden stick. Missing from the practice lineup is a starting linebacker who filled in Friday night at running back for Ryan Sutton in a performance that inspires Coach to say during Monday afternoon's pre-practice offensive film session, "Kyle Kopp, whatever you ate that day, I want you to eat it every Friday. You are running here like you're possessed." Kyle's not running anywhere today, because he's at the doctor seeking treatment for bone spurs in his heel.

On Wednesday, Coach walks up to Kyle and says, "If you're not walking tomorrow, you won't play." A pause. "So what am I saying?" "Make it all better?" ventures Kyle.

"That's right," says Coach.

In all, the Braves go into Ike week with backups at nine starting positions and prepared to start seven sophomores against the

Cadets. And some of Coach's favorite things to say this week are, "Don't tell me how many sophomores we're starting," and, "I don't even want to think about how many sophomores we're starting." What makes things even tougher on him and his staff is that this is *the* team, this group of seniors that they've been following since the fifth grade, knowing they could win it all.

So on Sunday morning, before the coaches break off into their offensive and defensive units to start putting their game plans together, they have to talk about the next three weeks and the games against Ike, Pasco, and Wenatchee that are their gateway into the playoffs, and they have to take a look at their guys and decide who's going to play, and when. There's no question with most of these players that they'll be in the lineup this week and every other week, unless something worse happens to prevent them from suiting up. This group includes Steve Davis, who has been dealing with his tender ankles since the beginning of the season, and who can't expect them to properly heal up without several weeks of rest. So sitting him out at this juncture of his high school playing career isn't even a thought in the back of his or his coaches' minds. Leo will just keep unwrapping rolls of athletic tape and Steve will keep playing. The same premise holds true for Josh Bond, Brent Rushin, and Brad Satchel, whose pain is enough to keep them wincing, but not enough to keep them off the field where their team desperately needs them. Ryan Sutton will be back after he gets his broken tooth crowned, and will stay back as long as he continues to pass Leo's battery of concussion tests and can tell Coach how many fingers he's holding up. The same goes for Brett and Kyle. If they're walking with any amount of competence by Thursday's walk-through practice, they'll be suiting up Friday. With Ben Salsbury, things are a little touchier because Leo isn't exactly certain what is causing his game and practice collapses.

So Ben is headed to the doctor this week for a string of tests to discover not just if he's healthy for football, but if there's something life-threatening that needs immediate attention.

Then there's Evan Ruud and Nick Genatone, two guys who are getting used to all the attention they are garnering from a number of Big Sky Conference universities. These two seniors, along with Steve Davis, are the very core of a team that Coach thinks can win Kamiakin's first-ever state title. With them, there's a good chance of this happening. Without them, there's virtually no chance because the Braves just don't have the beef to combat the cross-river giants at Pasco. So, as they lean forward in their office chairs on the Sunday morning leading into Ike week, it's not really Ike they're thinking about. The big Pasco boys are haunting these coaches' minds as they peer up at the long roster of wounded players on the office whiteboard. Neither Ruud's nor Genatone's shoulder injuries will heal up without surgery, and there's no way either boy will be going under the knife before the conclusion of football season. The doctors have told both young men that there's flexibility and strength in their hurt shoulders, and, if they can handle the pain, they can play. So the big debate is when to bring them back. The longer they can hold Evan and Nick out, the better chance there'll be of them staying on the field for as long as the Braves are in the playoffs, which, with them in both the offensive and defensive line-ups, could be a long time. But, with three games remaining on the regular season schedule, Kamiakin needs to win one of them even to make it into the playoffs, and the best chance for a win comes this first week against Ike.

"The Ike game is huge," says Coach, "because if we stumble against Pasco and Wenatchee we could be on the outside."

But Maher responds, "We're not gonna lose against Ike."

So Coach says, "Ruud and Genatone won't play."

Then there's next week's game with Pasco, their bitter rival, that will be played in front of 12,000 howling fans. With Evan and Nick suited up, Kamiakin can win, but without them, they probably won't. "Second place will only hurt our pride," says Coach.

"That's right," agrees Chesterfield. "And we'll get 'em again in the playoffs."

And so it's agreed by this veteran staff that these two big guns won't see the field again until the playoffs, unless something goes dramatically wrong against Ike, and their presence becomes necessary for the Braves' post-season survival.

One other kid who won't be seeing the field against Ike, or any other team for that matter, is Jeremy Kimball. This normally staid senior lineman exploded on Friday night in a profanity-laced torrent that carried over to the Kennewick locker room entrance, where he nearly succeeded in taunting the cross-town Lions into a post-game brawl. Even though this was an uncharacteristic outburst by Jeremy, and even though the school's discipline office has given the incident its immediate attention, Coach vows to do everything he can to get him to quit the team. "My wife heard his 'F-Bomb Attack' clear up in the stands," says Coach. "And behavior like that will absolutely not be tolerated. He's never been like this before. But that's no matter because he will not step foot on the playing field again. We could be up a hundred to nothing and he won't play. A cheerleader will get in before he does."

While Jeremy languishes on the sideline, there are plenty of other kids who will hardly come off the field at all. One of them is senior wide receiver/defensive back Ryan Anderson, a preternaturally gifted athlete who is so unconsciously good that sometimes Coach wants to shake him and say, "What are you thinking? You have so much talent!" One of those instances occurred on Kamiakin's first offensive play of the Kennewick game and, as the coaches watch their Sunday morning replay of this incipient moment, they can't help but collectively cringe once again just as they did Friday night when it happened, and when Anderson's immense talent and on-the-field ingenuousness collided to create disastrous results.

The play is a simple one where Steve Davis retreats in the pocket and, after scanning downfield at an array of covered receivers, he dumps the ball off to Sutton, who has planted himself out in the "flats" as a safety valve for just this type of occasion where the downfield receivers are unable to get open and the defensive hordes are starting to close in on the Braves' fleet-footed quarterback. One of those downfield receivers is Ryan Anderson and when he sees the pass go to Sutton and sees Sutton begin to motor up the sideline, he turns back from his route to help clear the path—which is what he is supposed to do. When he spots his man, the Lions' middle linebacker and best player, he dives into him in a below-the-waist, illegal cut block that knocks the blindsided Kennewick defender out of the play, breaks his leg, and ends his season. All of this happens with no penalty flag and with a referee standing three yards away. The coaches rewind this sequence over and over again—Ryan's swim-race dive, followed by the defender's agonized crumple to the turf, followed by Sutton's uninhibited progress up the field, followed by the Kennewick kid writhing in pain on the white-striped sideline, followed by a break in the film and another Kamiakin offensive sequence—and these middle-aged men are struck silent because their guy did something cheap, and he got away with it. Although they know that he is wrong, they also know that he is one of those kids that, a lot of the time, has no idea how or why he does something. When Coach asks him about the play during Monday's film session, Ryan shrugs his shoulders as if he's seeing the play for the first time and says, "I don't know. He was pretty big. I guess I didn't realize I was that low."

Luckily for anyone who might have to face him on the football field, though, Ryan's gridiron days will be over when this season draws to a close because the sport that he really loves, and where he and his coaches and parents see his true athletic future, is baseball. And this is the week where, on Tuesday evening, representatives from the University of Washington make a formal visit to his house, and where he commits to accepting a baseball scholarship offer that will cover most of his tuition and expenses once he begins classes at the Seattle campus next fall. His baseball coach, Rex Easley, shares office space with Coach, and Wednesday morning he is ebullient with the news of Ryan's big night.

Another senior for whom football comes in no better than second place but who is also a major contributor on special teams and at his defensive cornerback position is Jason Hatcher. Friday night is for football, but then Saturday morning he's up before first light to get in the car with his dad and make the four-hour drive to Seattle, where he devotes the weekend to playing soccer with his club team. "It's tiring, but worth it," he says as he describes what it's like to spend the long drive home on Sunday night trying to cram in all his homework for the week. Like Ryan, he can see the conclusion of his football life drawing near, which, for him, only means that much more time he'll be able to dedicate to soccer. "When I'm playing football, that's all I'm thinking about," says Jason. "But when I'm playing soccer, that's *really* all I'm thinking about."

This single-minded focus that Jason has is what Coach Maher devotes much of his energy to bringing out in his defensive players. And on the videotape of the Friday night Kennewick game, there is a moment that crystallizes everything he lives for in his football coaching existence. It's the second half and Nick Genatone is already hurt and on the sidelines. His replacement is Steve Davis, who, in order to take over Nick's job, needed only to slide over one slot from his own regular linebacking position, and also to assume the responsibility of translating for the defensive huddle the instructions that Maher signals in from the sidelines. He's in charge now, on offense and defense.

Even before this big play, Maher is pleased with the way his defensive unit handles themselves after the departure of Genatone, their usual defensive leader, and in the absence of Evan Ruud, who is on the sideline in his game jersey and blue jeans, and he makes them aware of this when they gather in his social science classroom during Monday's lunch period to watch their Friday night performance. "Overall men, helluva game," he says. "Effort through adversity. It really hurt when I saw Nick go down but I'm proud of the way you fought through it. And I got to say that watching you pull together was almost as exciting for me as Nick's injury was painful."

Then Steve's defensive moment in the sun arrives and Maher starts out by saying, even before it has flickered across the screen, "This is a great play, Steve. A guy makes a play like that after three years in the program, and it makes you feel like somethin's goin' right." And then the sequence arrives, and all twenty or so of the kids in the room ignore their sack lunches for a minute and sit up a little straighter in their seats to take notice. Maher, he can hardly contain himself as he stands, erect and proud and eyes shining, at the front of this noontime school-day meeting, in the dark of his own classroom, gazing intently at a video screen that shows a Kennewick back running a simple "wheel" route where he vacates his spot behind the quarterback at the snap of the ball to run toward the sideline in a flat bell pattern where he bows back behind his original spot and then wheels up toward the line of scrimmage as he approaches the sideline; and it is here, as his momentum starts to take him upfield, that he should catch the sideways soft pass from his quarterback and turn his attention toward a healthy upfield run. But, on the other side of the ball, and in clear view of the camera's lenses, as the Kennewick back performs his wheel route, Steve Davis, at his new linebacker spot, is reading what is taking place in the Lions' backfield, and he's reacting to it in some kind of lethal combination of Maher's teachings and his own athletic instinct that results in a three-way physics equation of man and ball and man as the Kennewick back and the football and Steve Davis arrive simultaneously at a perimeter line of scrimmage location in a fearful collision that leaves the runner flat on his back, the ball dribbling to the sideline, Steve returning triumphant to his defensive huddle, and Maher brimming with empathetic awe. "Let's take some time to talk about that hit," he says to his defensive crew. "That's the kind of play that can change a team. Watch the next seven or eight plays, and the way our guys attack. Davis's hit set the tone for that."

But as fine a performance as Steve and his defensive and offensive units delivered on Friday night, it doesn't keep Coach from noticing all week how practice isn't quite moving along with the snap and hum of a team that is marching toward a state championship. And Thursday morning during weight training class, Coach calls Jason and Evan over from their leg press station to talk about it. "We've got seniors who aren't practicing hard and are taking practice for granted," he says. "Practice was ugly yesterday. Our kids are not recognizing the corner we're in. I have never made five seniors run to the pump house before in my life, but yesterday I did."

The two senior leaders nod their heads and say, "Yes, Coach," and walk back to their workout, and as Coach watches them, he's got a half-grimace, half-smile on his face. But underneath it is a nervous energy that, even though this should be a "get well" week against Ike, he just can't seem to shake.

He tries to page through his grade book, but there's no way that's going to take his mind off the game, and so he closes it, slaps it against his leg, and says, "We've got seven sophomores starting tomorrow and this week is reminding me too much of the Lake City week when we showed up flat and overly impressed with ourselves. We walk around like King Kong and don't have to work in practice. That's gonna change tonight; you get an animal cornered, it fights back. Well, we're cornered. But we're not acting like it."

Coach does start to detect a change at the Thursday afternoon practice, which he starts off by calling the troops together and offering up a dose of his earlier weight room talk. The team is bunched around him on the practice field grass. Their helmets are off and they've taken a knee and Coach says, "I know the coaches are uptight. I'm not sure the seniors are uptight enough. We are in a dogfight tomorrow. We need captains, seniors, juniors, and sophomores to show that you love this sport. Our backs are against the wall. We need this game tomorrow … we win and the pressure's off for the next two weeks. We're in the playoffs and our hurt guys'll have a chance to get healthy."

And even though today is supposed to be nothing more than a walk-through, this battered team comes to life in a convincing demonstration that they do love this sport. During "Team D," Steve hustles up from his linebacker spot to knock down a scout team wheel pass, and then jumps around some in a mock celebration of his feat and says, "Aw yeah, now that's coverage."

Then, Coach Young's sophomore son, Jared, who is filling in this week at cornerback, makes an acrobatic leap to bat away another scout team pass. Maher can hardly hide his glee at the thought of this youngster stepping up tomorrow night as he says, "The kid is faster and better looking than the old man, and therefore we don't know if he is his."

Ben Salsbury arrives with news that his blood tests are back and there's no diabetes and no heart troubles and he's clear to play tomorrow night. This takes some of the heat off McAfee and his offensive line shuffle, but he still says to Ben, "You'll play maybe a series or two tomorrow, but no more." And then the good fortune continues on into "Team O" where Steve has things moving crisp and efficient, even when they go "Geronimo," which is their term for their "Two-Minute Offense."

Salsbury is now one of those guys standing in street clothes behind the offense without an ice-wrapped thigh or a bandaged shoulder, but with a semi-giddy sense of relief over his doctor's visit, and he's smiling as he watches his teammates move up and down the field. "Kennewick ran Geronimo against us in the first half to try and tire us out," he says. "It didn't work. It tired them out." Ben is one of only a handful of juniors on the team and the coaching staff is already fretting about next year, when they'll be playing against these same mostly tough teams without much of the natural talent and experience that has carried them through this injury-riddled season. But the juniors don't seem nearly as concerned, as Scott Gerken sidles up to Salsbury to point out their buddy, Scott Schlender, who is walking around practice with a broken facemask that he can lift up like a garage door. "He's about as dumb as they come," says Gerken. "We don't have very many smart juniors. Duncan and Bond are the smart ones and they come up with the ideas, and whatever they say, we just follow along."

According to Coach Easley, though, these juniors aren't alone in some of their intellectual missteps. To counterbalance the football expertise that helped him take over a Kamiakin program that had lost eighteen straight games before his arrival and to transform it into a consistent winner, Coach has Schlender's Disease when it comes to any kind of mechanical expertise. "I can't fix a flat tire," he says.

Easley, Coach's office confidante, is quick to support his asser-
tion of mechanical ineptitude. "He had a new riding lawnmower
that he couldn't get to work," says Easley. "He'd start it up, and it'd
run for ten feet, and then die. He'd start it up again, and it'd run for
ten feet, and then die. He'd start it up, and the same thing would
happen. So he takes it to the mechanic, and it turns out he was out
of gas. So a few weeks later he buys a gas-powered trimmer and the
salesman sells him a hundred-foot power cord to go with it."

It is Coach's good fortune that out here on the practice field
there's a maintenance crew to cut the grass, and it's only his job
to get his teenage players to run around on it fast and with a high
semblance of order. And as he watches them head toward the locker
room on Thursday, Coach says, "That was a big improvement over
yesterday … but I'm not done spanking 'em yet."

Once everyone is gathered in the locker room, though, there is
no "spanking," only plaudits, because it is time for this Thursday's
edition of "Brave Deeds," where each one of the position coaches
recognizes the outstanding achievements of his players with helmet
decals and words of praise. And there are a lot of kids to recog-
nize for things like a hard run, or a good block, or a head's-up
tackle, or being a good sport on the sideline, prepared and listening and supporting the team. And then there's Davis's big play on
the wheel route. When Maher steps forward to congratulate him,
he says, "You will never see a more pure form of art in your life."
But he's not done. He wants to talk about Nick and how much his
absence hurts, but also what it means to have Steve step in there to
look toward the sideline for his defensive calls. "There's something
magic in being out there and communicating with someone forty
or fifty yards away, and what you're talking about or communicating about is the most important thing in the world, and that's the
next football play."

And then "Brave Deeds" is done, and Maher steps aside to make way for Coach, who says, "Gentlemen, the key word is 'focus' tomorrow. It's Friday night. It's high school football. Enjoy it."

And what's not to enjoy? The bus ride up is like a "Ride America" slideshow with the Columbia and Yakima Rivers, and the Horse Heaven Hills and Rattlesnake Hills, and a carpet of vineyards and apple orchards and hayfields, all landscaped under a powder blue sky and puffs of billowing clouds and an Indian summer sun. Coach dozes off in his front bench seat, but not before he takes a look back at his players with their headphones, magazines, and sack lunches, and their quiet conversations. "Twenty years ago," he says, "I used to make 'em sit quiet on the bus to whatever game we were headed to, but that's unnatural. It's human nature to want to communicate, and so I eased up real quick. I realized that it's the team that practices better and plays better on Friday nights that wins games, not the team that's the quietest on the bus."

And this game holds true to Coach's hypothesis, just as McAfee predicts it would, as he stands in the same warming sun on the sideline of the afternoon freshman game and says, "If everything goes as it should, and both teams play as they should, I'll be real surprised if we don't beat 'em by at least three touchdowns. Even with our injuries, our team speed, and especially Davis and Ryan Anderson, should overwhelm them." That is pretty much what happens that night. Ike does have a few things going in its favor, like their "huge, but out of shape" offensive linemen, and the videotape they borrowed from Lake City to see how they beat Kamiakin, which a Cadet coach mistakenly returns to Kirsch. That tape gets the wheels spinning in Coach's head about how Ike, in the midst of yet another one of their losing seasons, is preparing for this game a lot more than he thought, and how, "They'll hitch us to death after seeing that Lake City tape. That'll get their quarterback in a rhythm. We got to get the linebackers coming up on that."

Ike's best weapon is probably their quarterback, Brett Gordon, who, Maher predicts, "Will throw for three hundred yards on us, but what are you gonna do?"

But none of this is nearly enough, because, after Coach says, "This cinches the playoffs tonight," and after the Cadets score first with a flurry of hitches and slants and an exclamation point fade to the back corner of the end zone, the game belongs to Steve Davis scrambling around the pocket, and Ryan Anderson streaking up the sideline, and Kyle Kopp bulling over left tackle, and Ben Salsbury staying upright for his two offensive line series, and to Maher's defense getting tough and staying tough after that first score, and to Coach directing the offense from his press box perch. It belongs to all of them, and they're going to the playoffs, no matter what happens in the next couple of weeks, as they try to get well. But before that, and even before they start to think about Pasco or about heading back home down the dark highway, they're going to Miner's for some fried shrimp and french fries because when Coach strides into the post-game locker room in his tennis shoes and ball cap and red letterman's jacket to pat his boys on the back and to say, "Gentlemen, give yourselves a hand," he wears his gritted-teeth grin, and his who's-the-boss voice booms across the tile and tin room as he says, "Hope you brought your appetite. Because now the fun starts."

# Week Thirteen—Playing for Pride

## Waldport High School Fightin' Irish:
## Waldport, Oregon

**V**ARSITY FOOTBALL PRACTICE at Waldport High School can be a lonesome affair, especially on this drizzly Monday afternoon when the fourteen-member junior varsity team that usually joins in is up at Jefferson playing their final game of the season. Without these freshmen and sophomores and without Mick Bittick and Russ Dahl, the two assistants who have accompanied the JV on this trip, it's up to head coach Rod Losier, volunteer assistant Bill Naylor, and the eleven upperclassmen who make up the foundation of the varsity squad to begin preparations for Halloween night's season-ending road trip to Oakridge. And they know of no better way to kick off this final week than with a round of "eye-openers," the warm-up exercise that has begun pretty much every practice since the team started its two-a-day sessions back in August.

While the boys do that, Coach heads up to the school to borrow some footballs from the P.E. stash because the JV has taken the entire stock of team balls to their game. By the time Coach returns from his foraging mission, Naylor has the team broken up into blockers, tacklers, and ball carriers, and they have already begun to work out the bumps and bruises from Friday night's Homecoming victory and to shake off the accumulated rust of a couple weekend days without football. Jaymes Gallagher is lined up on one side of a tackling dummy chute facing sophomore lineman Anthony Catalfamo and, behind Anthony, cradling one of the puny rubber footballs, is senior lineman Dustin Phillips. It's Anthony's job to block, Dustin's job to run, and Jaymes's job to take on Anthony and tackle Dustin. At Naylor's "Hup!" all three boys spring forward, Anthony and Dustin in a straight, upfield line, and Jaymes in a sideways hop that helps him to brush past Anthony's bull-charge and then duck in to clip Dustin in the knees and topple him to the ground. As he springs up off the turf, Jaymes performs a bit of a dance to celebrate his deft defensive maneuver that Coach cuts short when he says, "Jaymes, you need to take on the blocker."

"Why?" asks Jaymes. "I went around him and still made the tackle."

"Because," says Coach, "you're not going to be facing an offensive lineman carrying the ball in a game like you are in this drill."

"Oh," says Jaymes as he strolls over to the offensive side so he can take his turn carrying the ball.

Jaymes may not be attacking the ball carrier in the way Coach has been trying to teach him and his teammates to do it over the last three months, but, with his dexterous sidestep and slashing tackle, he showed the signs of ingenuity and life that seem to remain dormant in most of the rest of the squad. Coach senses this and calls a halt to say, "So far, we're not having a very good this part of practice. Now let's get back into groups of three and get into it."

The boys look around to reconfirm that they can only form three full groups of three and so senior lineman Jesse Scarborough volunteers to switch back and forth between two groups to make up the difference. "Hey, this is the last week we get to hit each other," he says. "C'mon, let's hit somebody." But even this fails to generate much enthusiasm among the short-handed squad, so Coach sends them packing to the goal post. When they come slogging back, he calls for them to get into "hit" position with their knees bent, their shoulders hunched, their forearms up, their fists bunched, and their eyes wide and focused on him like hungry pups, and he says, "If we play half-hearted like we've practiced, then the ride home Friday night is gonna be longer than it already is."

Coach has reason to be concerned about Friday night's match-up with Oakridge because even though the Warriors' league record is only 2–2, compared with his own team's 1–3 mark to date, he has a hunch that this week's opponent is a lot better than that one-game margin indicates. The early warning signs start on Sunday morning when he meets with Dahl and Bittick and with his mentor, Gene Morrow, down at Bittick's portable classroom to begin preparing for the game. The scout tape they have of Oakridge is from a couple weeks ago when the Warriors played Central Linn, a team that beat Waldport earlier this season 33–6. Beginning with the first kickoff, the Warriors basically do whatever they want against Central Linn, and the Waldport coaches sit around the TV, watching it happen. By the end of the first half, Oakridge is up 40–7 and they have achieved much of their dominance by executing the Option, an offense that the Irish haven't faced all season. Bittick sums up the Warriors' first-half barrage when he says, "It looks like they run option, option, counter, option, option, option, counter."

Coach says, "Their quarterback can't throw very well, but he's a dandy runner."

But Dahl, who operates a waste management business and whose son, Blake, is Waldport's sophomore starting quarterback, is already formulating a solution to this Oakridge player that Coach is afraid might be close to unstoppable. "We need to get a big purple jersey, so every time our defensive ends see purple, they know to hit it." And everyone agrees with Dahl that the way to stop the Warriors is to attack their quarterback.

"We've got to put Bolin on the ground every time," says Bittick.

"That's right," continues Dahl. "We got to preach to our defensive ends to take this quarterback. We can actually stop this if we get our D-ends to do what they're supposed to do."

As Dahl imagines his defensive ends crashing down, seeing purple, and laying out the Warriors' No. 15 on play after play, the video version of Steffan Bolin continues to ramble across the screen in front of him, making hand-offs, faking hand-offs, tossing feathery pitches to his trailing backs, and, most dangerously, tucking the ball away and heading upfield himself. But the more the coaches study what at first appears to be a real display of option wizardry, the more they convince themselves that Bolin is not directing a true option attack, but is in fact following a "pre-call" formula sent in from the sideline coaches. The player who tips them off to this possibility is the Oakridge wingback who lines up a yard off the outside hip of their tight end and does one of two things when the Warriors run their option. When Bolin hands off to the "dive," or the fullback crashing straight into the line of scrimmage between the guard and tackle, the wingback loops upfield around the defensive. When Bolin fakes the dive and continues along the line of scrimmage, the wingback blocks the defensive end.

The coaches aren't certain how this tip-off will make a difference in their defensive strategy, but Morrow, for one, isn't surprised that Oakridge doesn't run a true option. "To option or not to option?" he muses. "That's the question. Very few people can run the Triple Option. You have to have a spectacular quarterback who can read that inside dive option. In all my years of coaching, I had one kid, one who could run it, and that was my son, Kory. You got to have a lot of time to teach it, coach it, and practice it."

Morrow spent forty-five years coaching fifteen miles up Highway 101 at Newport High School. Coach played for him in the early

1980s and worked as his assistant in the 1990s, and last season, when Coach took over at Waldport, Morrow came out of his two-year retirement from the game to fulfill a promise that he made several years back. "When I came back to Newport as an assistant," says Coach, "Gene said he'd be my assistant when I became a head coach." And so here he is, a man who has endured heart attacks, bladder cancer, by-pass surgery, and, earlier this season, a sideline collision that only compounds the health problems that cut into his time with the team.

So it's no surprise when he misses Monday's practice, and then hobbles up from the parking lot in the Tuesday afternoon damp. He's wearing his flannel shirt, black sweat pants, black tennis shoes, and a half-zipped rain slicker, and he has a Fightin' Irish ball cap pulled down over his white hair and thick glasses. "Anybody melt yet?" he asks as he makes his way onto the field.

"Not yet," says Coach. "How're you feeling, Gene?"

"Good. I'm feeling good. I always feel better after I've been to the doctor. She heats me up." Coach cracks a complicit grin and then turns his attention back to the offense that he is not only coaching, but also running because both of his quarterbacks are absent, even though the team's ranks have been bolstered by the junior varsity's return from Jefferson. No one knows why freshman Kevin Battles is missing, but Coach suspects that because the JV season is officially over, Kevin might be sitting in front of the TV instead of trudging around in the cold mud of this varsity football practice. As far as Blake, the team's starter, is concerned, Dahl can confirm that his son left school today to go the health clinic, but when he found out it was closed he went over to hang out in front of Chuck's Video, and now no one knows exactly where he is.

"I'll get him on the back of a garbage truck," says his father. "That'll straighten him out." And, to assuage Coach's concern that Blake might be ineligible for Friday's game due to this mostly unexplainable absence, Dahl pledges, "As a parent, I'll call him in 'Excused' if that'll help."

To counterbalance the absence of Dahl's son, Naylor has brought along Joseph, his own junior high–aged boy, and a buddy of his to hang out at today's practice. As Coach directs the offense, Joseph and his friend charge around behind the team huddle, tackling each other and rolling around in the mud and wet grass. Naylor interrupts his focus on the offense to say, "Boys, you want to be walking home?" Joseph and his pal shake their heads, and then nod when Naylor says, "Well, then I suggest you find something else to do, because I won't have those wet clothes in my truck."

The boys stand behind the huddle for about half a minute fidgeting and handing a football back and forth, and then Joseph glances longingly at the tackling dummies and he whispers to his pal, "How far is it to my house?"

Another kid who shows up at practice is Ian Bucklin, and, even though he was absent yesterday, is late today, and arrives at the field in his shorts and ponytail and tie-dyed T-shirt instead of his practice uniform, the coaches are happy that he's here because they have big plans for him on Friday night. When they first started talking about the Oakridge game on Sunday and plotting out how they might stop the Warriors' option attack, Dahl mentioned that he was dissatisfied with Mark Young, one of their regular defensive ends, and said, "Maybe I'll put in Bucklin for Young if I don't see some improvement." But then later in the morning, Dahl had a sudden realization that he might have to back off his aspirations for his possible new defensive end. "You know, I'm thinking," Dahl said. "Bucklin made the comment that he won't be there Friday. He's got a family thing or something. And we could sure use him against this offense."

The potential "family thing" isn't a surprise to Coach, who has grown accustomed to Bucklin's spotty attendance. He and his family are new to Waldport, and, says Coach, "He's one of those kids who has the tendency to turn up missing on you. He seems kind of transient and who knows where he might be next year?"

But concerns about next year are put aside when Bucklin makes his appearance today and promises that he'll be available for Friday night. Coach pulls him immediately aside to tell him about his assignment. Mark Young, Dahl's sophomore question mark at defensive end, steps in for Coach at quarterback and Bucklin stands shivering in his thin T-shirt, as Coach explains that there is an immediate opening at strong safety and he is just the man to fill it. Max Alfano, another sophomore and the kid they were counting on to play that spot on Friday, took a helmet to the thigh, giving him a temporary limp that ended his season early.

"So," says Coach to Bucklin. "Do you think you'd like to try playing strong safety for us?"

Bucklin nods and says a soft "Yes" through his chattering teeth and Coach hands him over to Bittick to explain the specifics of the job and then goes back to the offense.

For his part, Max Alfano isn't quite ready to concede his Friday night position, though the odds of him playing were uncertain even before Monday's injury. He's in trouble with the discipline principal for a fight he got into at school last week, but, as his JV friends discuss his part in it, their attitude is, "What was he supposed to do?" They are standing behind Coach and his offense and listening to Max recollect the hit that sidelined him five minutes into yesterday's game.

"Yeah," says the skinny sophomore. "The guy rammed me with his helmet right in the femur. At first I thought it was just dead leg, but then I tried to walk it off for awhile, and then I sat down on the bench, and then, when I went to get up, it wouldn't bend, and it hurt a lot, and I heard it pop." The other kids nod their heads and then Max says, "But I'll be ready for Friday." When one of his buddies asks about the fight and what's going to happen with that, he says, "I don't know."

There are personal emergencies, like Max's fight or his injury that might be something more than "dead leg" or like Ian Bucklin's possible Friday "family thing," and then there are emergencies of a more community nature, and on Wednesday morning during his fourth period math class at Newport Middle School, Coach experiences one of these, or at least he and his seventh-grade students get the call over their intercom that they and the rest of the school, "will now be experiencing a 'Code Red'" and so Coach walks over to lock his classroom door and flick off the lights, and then returns to duck underneath his desk in complicity with his twenty-two students, who have already ducked under their tables in a drill designed to prepare them for the future possibility of an on-campus intruder. But you wouldn't know that there wasn't an actual intruder prowling the hallways right now because these kids take this drill seriously. And Coach, from his crouched position, says to them in his gentle and soothing voice, the kind of voice that you might hear from the hypnotist at the county fair, "I think this is only a drill."

Coach has worked at this Newport school for a dozen years where his wife, Nora, is also employed as an instructional aide, and, although it might be nice to transfer over to Waldport to teach at the same place where he coaches, he doesn't see himself attempting the move anytime soon. Oregon public education is in the midst of monstrous budget cuts and Coach doesn't want to risk the seniority he's established here because teachers are losing their jobs all over the state, and one of the first criterion "the people in charge" look at when they decide who stays and who goes is seniority. For his cautionary tale, Coach looks at his middle school vice principal, Steve Hartman, whose home is down in Roseburg, and who is in his first year on the job in Newport. He has rented an apartment in town where he stays during the week and then he makes the three-hour drive every Friday night to spend the weekend with his family. His new colleagues are always asking him if he'll permanently relocate his family up here and he always responds with, "Why? I've already had five jobs in five different places and I'll probably have another five before I'm through."

A couple years back, when Morrow announced his retirement, Coach applied for the head coaching position at his alma mater, which is right across the street from the middle school, and where he had been his old coach's defensive assistant for several years. But when another assistant got the job and offered him a demotion if he wanted to stick around, Coach resigned his spot to help out with the flag football program at his own school until the Waldport job opened up. So he coaches down there and teaches up here, and he holds his breath over his and his wife's jobs, while educators all around him are losing theirs.

It takes Ian Bucklin one day to lose his job as the new starting strong safety because he is nowhere to be found when the Wednesday afternoon practice gets under way. Coach misses the very start of practice also, as he does on many days, due to his commitments up in Newport and the winding ocean-road commute, and so Bittick gets the session under way with a few rounds of eye-openers that are a little more spirited than on the two previous days and that include Blake and Kevin, yesterday's missing signal-callers. Then Bittick sends the whole crew around the goal posts. They start off at a slow jog, but gradually increase their speed and enthusiasm for the warm-up trot in such a way that almost all of them are actively having to "put on the brakes" as they sprint their way back to Bittick at the end of the circuit. When they finish, Bittick says, "Let's move over to the field and wait for Coach."

When Coach pulls in, he strolls over to his gathered team, and says, "Where's Bucklin?"

Dahl has the same question when he arrives on the stadium field a few minutes later, and so discretion is impossible for Bucklin when he shows up across the school grounds to rattle the locked locker room door in frustration and then to disappear once again behind the wing of school buildings. Dahl watches this whole performance like he might watch a movie. He shakes his head and purses his lips as he notes Bucklin "late and not in uniform." Then he says, "He got his chance to play strong safety and it looks like he didn't want it, and now he's not gonna get it."

It turns out, though, that being AWOL from practice is the least of Bucklin's worries today because he took the opportunity at lunch to meet a couple of his friends over at the "Smokers' Hole," a little sidewalk grotto at the edge of campus that has a nice view of the Alsea Bay and is conveniently hidden from the prying eyes of school administrators and faculty members. Except that today is the day that Principal Von Taylor meanders on over to see who might be enjoying the view and discovers Bucklin and friends "mid-drag" and so, practice or no, Ian's days as a defensive specialist are over before they've had a chance to begin, at least for this season.

"Boy," says Dahl. "We're gonna be hurtin' at the strong safety." But to help remind him that there are other concerns in this world besides what happens between the painted white lines of a football field, the sky that has boiled over with storm clouds all week gets cracked open by a sliver of sun and Dahl and the little knot of players gathered around him at the edge of the offensive practice can feel even this tiny bit of light, and, to them, it makes a difference.

Another person missing today is Coach Morrow, and when he shows up for Thursday's walk-through practice, he stands back a ways from the team, his hands dug deep in his jacket pockets and his black sneakers toeing the damp turf. He's getting paid this year to help out, and Coach says that Morrow feels guilty about it because of all the time he misses for his doctor appointments, or because he's too tired or sick to leave his house. This week is especially tough both because he feels bad physically, and because Dee Andros, the legendary coach at Oregon State, where Morrow was a standout quarterback in the 1940s, died a few days ago. So when Coach ambles over to ask about how he's feeling, Morrow just shakes his head and says, "I'm feeling old."

There's a gang of skateboarders at the strip mall across the highway and watching them perform their jumps and tricks and skids on the skinned-up pavement while his own guys charge up and down the field for their kickoff practice is starting to make Naylor feel a little old himself. "You'd kill or die to have those skateboard kids out here or have some of our kids to have the mentality that they have," he says. "They'll do the 'loop-de-da-loop' or jumps and break their arms or sprain their ankles or scrape themselves up. But they don't want to do that stuff out here. They'd rather just hang out with their friends and do all that crazy stuff with their boards."

As Naylor continues to admire this display of concrete courage across the street, Coach calls for his first-team defense to spread out across the field and Max Alfano limps out to the empty strong safety position in his street clothes. Dahl watches Max's wooden-legged progress and then scans the thin sideline ranks for maybe another guy who could be a stopgap for this week. His eyes come to rest on 140-pound freshman Paul Corwin and so he calls out to Coach, "If Max can't move, what's he doing out there? Put

Corwin in there." But Corwin seems content where he is with his hands stuffed underneath his shoulder pads and jersey trying to stay warm, and Max has taken so long to wobble out to his centerfield spot that Coach decides to just let him stay there while he instructs the team on how they'll go about trying to stop the Oakridge option.

Last year when Oakridge traveled down out of the Cascade Range, across the Willamette Valley and over to the coast to face Waldport, the Irish actually found a way to stop their vaunted option attack and Coach still isn't sure how they did it. They still lost, but only by a point.

This loss wasn't an unusual experience for the Irish during Coach's first year in charge. With their four victories this year, they have already doubled last season's win total, and with only this final Oakridge game remaining, Coach feels good about his team's progress. This year's team has less natural ability than the bunch Coach started with last year, but Coach sees them as a group interested in helping him build a team atmosphere. "I spend a good bit of time worrying about how I coach the team and worrying that I don't yell enough," he says. "But the kids can see right through that, and you have to be yourself. And, with a team as small as ours, if you lose two or three kids because they think you're too tough on them, that could be a real problem." And so, on Tuesday, when he calls his JV squad together, before he sends them to the locker room where Dahl is waiting with a surprise pizza and soda party as an acknowledgment of their effort this season, Coach says, "I want to thank you for your hard work and for running all those scout plays to help the varsity guys. It's important that we look toward the future. We need to get those eighth-graders out, and more kids out total. That'll make it more fun. The more kids out, the more things we can do."

And later on, as the varsity concludes its work for the evening, Coach puts the seniors in charge of conditioning while he walks across the field to shut off the stadium lights. When he makes his way back across the field, the kids are laughing and running in the dark. Coach heads over to stand next to Morrow, his mentor and friend, and explains, "Captain Scarborough's in charge."

Morrow shakes his head. "You're a soft touch, aren't you?" he says as he turns to make his slow way toward the parking lot and his rusted pickup.

Coach says, "Goodnight, Gene. See you tomorrow," and then watches after him in silence until his small team concludes its sprints and then jogs over to gather around him in the twilight. "This week is our last game," Coach says once they've settled in to listen. "And some of you are looking ahead to basketball or wrestling. But they're not gonna come any quicker if you blow off this week. And if we don't do our best to get ready for Oakridge, Friday night will be long and humiliating." The boys stand in their wet undershirts, clutching their helmets and pads, and Coach says, "Now let's get an Irish break," which brings them in closer to shout, "One, two, three … Irish!" before they start the walk over to the gym.

Bittick hustles ahead to unlock the door, but Coach lingers for a moment to watch his platoon-sized unit dissolve in the dark. He stoops to collect the mesh ball bag and then squints into the night in search of any errant equipment that might be strewn on the field. He is thinking about his team's chances Friday night and he has at least a glimmer of confidence that they might be good. "On paper, they're way better than us," he says. "But we have a couple of things going in our favor. Our two-game win streak gives us a little momentum and Oakridge was expected to do a lot better this year. But instead, they're out of the playoff picture. They're playing for pride, just like us."

Coach swings the ball bag over his shoulder and walks across the dark pitch of grass that stretches between the stadium and the team's locker room. He moves with the lumbering grace that Coach Morrow noticed and counted on as far back as his sophomore year at Newport High. "There was an offensive tackle spot that opened up and I'd been working at taking it over," says Coach as he peers back twenty years into his past, "and I remember Gene was talking with Jack Wilkinson, my line coach, and Gene says, 'Do you think he can do it?' and Jack says, 'Yeah, he's not gonna hurt ya.' And then we went down to Reedsport and I played the whole game on offense and most of it on defense because someone got hurt and I was so worked up that I got sick after the game. But I also remember that it felt good to know that Gene believed in me, and he gave me that chance, and I was able to give it my best shot and not let him down."

To pull himself back into the present, Coach sets down his bag in the locker room that is now vacant of players but cluttered with many of the items that have helped them to get through the season. As he starts to shape up the room, Coach continues to talk about Morrow, a man he puts right up there with his parents when he thinks in terms of respect and wanting to count on somebody and knowing that you can. "It's been real touch and go with Gene this year. I'm hoping he'll be around next year. He helps players out, pulls them aside, and those little things add up quite a bit. When he was in charge, you always felt like you had a chance to win, and I think he's trying to help me instill that same belief in my teams."

· · ·

THE WEATHERMEN PREDICT record-cold temperatures on Halloween night all over Oregon, so when the team gets off the bus in Oakridge, at an altitude 2,500 feet higher than the sea level that they are accustomed to, there seems to be a lot more consideration toward staying warm than toward having a chance to win this football game. Kevin Battles and his fellow freshman, Will Petersen, stand over their travel bags in the locker room and start to layer themselves with sweatshirts, thermal underwear, and knit socks.

"Dude," says Kevin, "You're gonna be hot in that."

"I'd rather be hot than cold," replies Will.

While the team gets ready, only Coach, Dahl, and Bittick are here to run the show. Coach Morrow will be showing up later with his son, Luke. Naylor is working a shift tonight at the jail and has already said his goodbyes to the team … for the season and for good because, for him, this is it. Yesterday, when the team finished up their walk-through and gathered around Coach for their "Irish Break," Naylor stepped into the huddle in his rain slicker and said, "Point of observation. Last minute or so … this is it for me, so keep it together, gentlemen."

There was a silence to follow this pronouncement, which Coach broke when he said, "Any other words of advice for the team?"

Naylor thought a moment and said, "When you turn eighteen, you're old enough to die for your country, so live life large now."

Dahl is also considering a departure from the coaching ranks, maybe in a couple of years, after Blake concludes his senior season. Tonight, he walks up and down the rows of lockers in the Oakridge girls' P.E. room, shaking hands with each of the players, and saying, "Thanks for the season," and "It's been enjoyable," and "It's gonna be a pleasure missing you, Jaymes."

Before the team leaves the locker room in their cold-weather gear, they take a knee around Coach, who says, "Everyone is trusting that you'll do your best. It's all about trust. You do the hitting. You hit them … not the other way around."

And Dahl adds, "Seniors, have a game you won't forget." Then the whole crew is charging out the door, across the parking lot and city street and onto the already frost-speckled turf of the stadium field. Bittick and Dahl take up their spots on the sideline and Coach jogs across the field to the Oakridge bleachers, where he climbs up to the sheetwood press box that the game announcer tries to keep heated with a propane camp stove. The referee crew walks to the Waldport sideline where Dahl and Bittick greet them with handshakes and comments about how damn cold it is.

Then it's game time, and, in almost a flip-flop from last year, Waldport finds itself leading 7–6 after the first quarter. But, as good as Bolin is at quarterback for Oakridge, it turns out that he's not even their most lethal weapon because they've chosen tonight to bring back Jeremiah Fine, a senior running back with a still-healing broken arm that is entombed in a fully padded cast so he can play in this final game of his senior season. By halftime, the Irish are down by three touchdowns and Dahl looks to be seething mad as his players try to stamp some feeling back into their feet in the warmth of the locker room. "One question," he says. "Have we put 15 on his back all night? That's what I wanna know. Then we stop and let their whole team walk through the gate before us. When are we gonna get mean? That's what I wanna know." Then he yells, "I'm outta here!" and stalks outside, slamming the metal door closed behind him.

Then Coach gives it a shot. "We gotta get fired up," he says. "'Cause this game is emotional. You play hard, play smart, and have fun."

After they're back out on the frozen turf, Captain Scarborough calls them together to say, "Awright guys, this is the last game of my life and, as they say, 'It goes a lot quicker than you think.' Before you know it, it'll be you. So let's go, guys!" This elicits a burst of enthusiasm, with teammates jumping and slapping and shouting. But by the time Oakridge kicks off to renew the game, this energy is gone in most of the team as they settle in to watch the clock tick down the minutes until they can head back to the locker room to take a hot shower. Coach is up in the press box, eating sunflower seeds and saying to Bittick in their headphone communication, "It'd be nice if we could get a break, a big play or something." But this is not a night for breaks or big plays for the Irish. It's a night where Jaymes Gallagher starts motioning to freshmen on the sideline to substitute for him on his special teams duties, and where Anthony Catalfamo says, "Why do you guys always want to come out? It's pissin' me off!"

But there is also Blake Dahl, who collapses to his knees to pound the turf as he tries to cough away the croup that has plagued him for much of the season before he heads back to mid-field to call the team's next play. There is senior lineman Matt Robinson, who splits a crack in his black helmet, trades it with another kid on the sideline and breaks that helmet, and then finishes the game with a third set of headgear. There is Scarborough, who—even as the score mounts higher and higher against his team—plays like this is the last football game of his life, which it is. And there is Coach Morrow, who arrives on the sideline mid-way through the third quarter with his cup of coffee and his son, Luke, and who asks Kevin Battles, "So what have you learned from tonight?"

Even after the lopsided conclusion of this final game, Coach is feeling okay about the season and he tells his team as much when they gather around him for one final time in the locker room. "Look where we were last year," he says, "and where we are this year—twice as many wins. That gives us something to build on." Then he and Dahl and Bittick step back to let the boys thaw out in the hot steam of the showers. They feel relieved more than anything else to have made it to the end of another long season and this minutes-old loss is mostly forgotten as Bittick thinks about trying to get some rest before Monday's basketball practice. Coach turns his thoughts to next week's All-League meeting, to collecting the boys' equipment, and to the girls' basketball practice he'll be in charge of up at Newport High School starting in a few days. Dahl thinks for a moment about his halftime outburst that he had hoped would light a fire under the team, and says, "Oh well, it was worth a shot."

As the boys start to emerge from the showers, pack up their bags, and trickle out toward the parking lot, Coach says, "I better check on the bus." He pushes open the metal door and steps out into the cold night, and there is Jaymes Gallagher's father leaned up against the brick wall, waiting for him. "Hey, Coach," he says from underneath the brim of his baseball cap.

Coach stops to reply and this is when Mr. Gallagher pushes away from the wall to start shouting, "Why did you wait until the end of the game to give my boy the ball? This is something that's been going on all year! I want to know why! Why don't you tell me? He's the best runner you've got and it's not right that he's not getting the ball more! I'm tired of it! What do you have to say? I want to know! Why don't you tell me? What do you have to say?"

What *can* Coach say? What would you? It's the middle of the night and cold, and Coach has twenty-five boys he needs to get packed up and on the bus and fed at the Oakridge McDonald's, and then down out of these frozen mountains and home safe, and so he stands there in the dark outside the locker room door, and he takes it, until Mr. Gallagher can't say another time, "What do you have to say?" and then Coach buttons up his jacket, and he walks down the sidewalk and across the street to the warming bus that will carry him and his team back home.

# Week Fourteen—Making a Statement

## Sutter Union High School Huskies: Sutter, California

**W**HEN JASON LEWIS strips out of his jersey and pants and pads and picks up his towel and bar of soap after Monday's full-bore practice, it is the first time all season that a hot locker room shower has felt good. Until last Thursday's walk-through, the temperatures had been at least in the nineties and often more than one hundred degrees, but then, and finally, it started to cool down.

Then, on Friday night, the Huskies traveled up to Gridley to play in the rain and wind of the Bulldogs' "Bone Yard," but by the time they got back to Sutter after yet another in their long string of blow-out victories the main thought on Jason's mind was a trip to the Taco Bell in Yuba City before he got home to his shower and bed. Today, though, is the day. After an all-team meeting, Jason steps out onto the practice field to breathe in great mouthfuls of clear air. He can feel the cool that is only going to get better after he works up a bit of a sweat and after the sun sinks behind the walnut and almond orchards that stretch for endless miles to the west of Wayne Gadberry Stadium. So after a couple hours of nonstop defensive drills, a round of full-team conditioning, and a slow jog to the field-house, Jason can drape his beach towel over the tiled partition of the P.E. locker room, twist the spigot on, and relish the soothing hot stream that has been worth the wait of all these many months.

While Jason luxuriates underneath the hot water spray, head coach Scott Turner sits at his desk in his closet-sized office, poring over a statistics sheet that Craig Provancha, his freshman team coach, delivered to him earlier in the day. The "Frosh" squad has already concluded its season with a 7–1 record, which bodes well for next year's junior varsity team that goes into its Friday afternoon pre-varsity finale against Winters looking to extend its winning streak to twenty-two games. This gaudy succession of victories is only a little more impressive than Coach's success with his varsity, which was unbeatable two years ago, lost twice last year to one team, and is 9–0 this year and ranked fourth among small schools in the state as it goes into its own regular season–ending match-up. So, the future looks good. But when Spencer Rickertsen, the Huskies' 295-pound offensive tackle, steps into the office to peer over Coach's shoulder at the Frosh season summary, the future takes a backseat to memories of his own early days with the program.

"First day out there, and I didn't know anything about football," says the curly-headed senior. "Never played it. And Coach said, 'Who wants to play center?' and I said, 'What do you do?' and he said, 'Snap the ball, and go two steps right or two steps left,' and I said, 'Cool, I'll do that,' and I looked back and saw who else was going for it, and I thought, 'I'll be starting no problem,' and then I didn't even get to play half the year."

Even though Spencer is now a starter who knows his way around the football field, his senior season reflects his freshman year in terms of playing time because he and many of his fellow "A"-teamers spend the second half of most games on the sideline cheering on their younger "B" team backups due to the Huskies' habit of steamrolling their opponents. This creates an enviable dilemma for Coach and his staff, whose main game decision each week seems to be when to take the starters out to relieve some of the pressure on the other team and to give their own reserves a chance to get in and gain experience. And it's a problem that is made all the more difficult because Sutter operates a two-platoon system where, except for one or two players, everyone on the team plays either an offensive or defensive position for the entirety of his varsity career. So when Coach looks at someone like Dave Heckman, the senior linebacker who captains the "A" team defense that hasn't given up a point in more than a month, he has a difficult time yanking him out of a game where he may have only participated in a dozen or so ball-stifling defensive plays.

Coach is also trying hard to keep his guys from getting complacent and self-satisfied, and this can be a full-time job in a season where the only real competition they have faced is on the occasions in practice where the "A" offense and the "A" defense square off against each other. "That can get pretty intense," says Coach, who uses these scrimmages to wake his team up and keep them sharp, and to burn off a little of the boundless energy they still exhibit this late in the season. So on Tuesday he watches his offense run plays against air, and as he feels their enthusiasm wane Coach sends the call out from the main field over to the practice field, where defensive coordinator Ryan Reynolds has his guys going through their "Every Day Drills," that it's time to scrimmage.

So the A's line up across the ball from one another and the exhortations come from the sideline to "Blow 'em up!" and, "Let's go!" and, "Get some bugs on that shield!" Then there is the clash of flesh and plastic as the number one offense in the Northern Section and the number one defense in the Northern Section get after each other.

As good as the offense is (and line coach Pat Daddow likes to compare it to a NASCAR race), these scrimmages are usually a time for Heckman and his defensive mates to dominate, for no other reason than that they are so familiar with the "Wing T" that Coach installed several years ago and that is the signature formation that the Huskies use to move the ball. The only defense that seems able to stop it is their own. But today, junior quarterback Tony Wagner and his Wing T mates are moving the football, and it is starting to get to the normally staunch Husky defense.

When Coach calls across the ball to a defensive lineman to ask why he was such a terror on Friday night against Gridley but is getting pushed around so far here today, there is no reply until a backup defender on the sideline says, "Because Gridley sucks."

His fellow reserves look at him in feigned shock and he says, "It's true. Our B team was better than twice as good as their A team." And so it might have been Friday night. But today, after a few tentative plays that can't really be called victories for either side of the ball, Coach calls "30 Wedge," Tony Wagner relays the message to his offense, and suddenly, after the crisp huddle break and the rapid-fire snap of the football, this formerly "going through the motions" kind of practice comes to life. And it's all courtesy of junior fullback Jake Winship, who transforms the 30 Wedge— usually a short-yardage play—into a highlight reel–type explosion and an opportunity to show the defense that they might not be quite as invulnerable as they have come to believe. Coach does his part by making the call when the defense is spread out and not expecting it. Tony does his part by getting his sturdy fullback the ball. And the offensive line does its duty by getting a big push against a defensive front that is prepared for pretty much anything except for this Wedge.

"This is good stuff. You guys are gettin' after each other," says defensive line coach Chris Macon. And Coach busies himself with high fives all around for his linemen until Jake rejoins the huddle, breathing hard, but smiling big.

Then Coach says, "That's some smackin' goin' on there." He stands back to watch his guys continue their march down the field, and, a few plays later, into the end zone, to the teeth-gnashing anger of a defense that almost never lets something like this happen … on Tuesday afternoon or Friday night, or any other time for that matter. "Hey! Not bad," says Coach to his offense. "Eighty-yard drive right there … eighty-yard drive. That's what we need. Keep your heads up, and keep playing hard."

Heads are down over on the defensive side and Macon says to his guys, "If it was easy, everybody'd do it." But this whole crew is beyond consolation at the end of this Tuesday scrimmage, and as Macon walks away from them, he says, "They haven't been scored on in four weeks by anyone. The defensive guys are genuinely upset."

What makes today's offensive eruption even sweeter for the offense and tougher for the defense to take is Coach's sworn policy to try and put his best guys on the defensive side of the football, and to cobble together an offense with whomever he has left over. "The other team can't win if they don't score," says Coach of his personnel strategy, and he is committed to his split-squad system. When he considers the Huskies' Butte View League competition, he says, "It would be less fair if we put those guys on offense. But we want 'em on defense. As long as we can, we're going to go two-platoon."

Reynolds likes the way they go about things here as well, saying, "I'd way rather take a pretty good player and watch him get better and better at a position than have him sitting on the bench while the absolute best guys on the team play both ways."

After the players are gone for the night, Reynolds takes the chance to start lobbying to get more superior talent for his defense. It's him, Daddow, Macon, and Coach, all squeezed into the tiny office, along with Mike Ayotte and Rick Giovannoni, to talk about their

JVers and the three or four of them who they think maybe ought to be brought up for some varsity experience during the playoffs. Two sophomore linemen in particular keep surfacing in the discussion, Tyler Holt and Troy Robison, and the more Reynolds talks about them, the more his eyes shine as he says, "They'll be tough on defense next year."

"Well," says Coach, "bring 'em up. Coach 'em up."

This has Reynolds grinning, but Daddow, who is fresh off the field with his offensive linemen, many of whom are graduating, snaps to attention, saying, "Whoa, whoa, whoa … you either get Troy or Tyler. I got to have one 'a them boys over with us."

"But wouldn't you say that Troy and Tyler have that defensive mentality?" says Reynolds.

"That may be," says Daddow. "And I will say that that Troy's not intimidated by anybody."

"So," says Reynolds, "there's two defensive players right there."

"No," says Daddow. "There's one defensive player. You're not gettin' 'em both."

"I can try, though, can't I?" says Reynolds. "I'm a scavenger."

"You can try," says Daddow. "But my eyes are open."

Daddow's eyes were actually opened several years ago to what living, working, attending school, and being a part of the Sutter football program might mean to him and his family. They had just moved into a house that he had custom-built with earnings from his rice-trading business when his wife spent a day substitute teaching at Yuba City High School, an institution of almost four thousand kids. She got back to their brand new home and she was crying and saying it was like a zoo down there and there was no way their boys were going to go to school there. So they put their dream house up for sale and bought a place in the country outside of Sutter and they've been here ever since.

It's Tuesday night and his white pickup is parked at the edge of the grass waiting to carry him home to rest up for his rice-trading job that, he says, "I don't like and it's full of people who are always trying to get the best of you and I do it for no other reason than to make money."

But then there's this coaching deal, and he starts to try and explain what it means to him, but when the exact words don't come, he stops trying to explain. Instead, he holds up his hands in a surveying-my-domain kind of gesture that encompasses the classrooms and the locker room and the weight room and those yellow-grassed practice and playing fields and the almond and walnut orchards and the Sutter Buttes that are broken-toothed towers in this Sacramento Valley flatland and the deepening dark that is settling over it all, and, in this way, everything that he might want to say, but that appears in no known dictionary, is clear—in a world where all our lives are dedicated to trying to find a home, a place where we belong, he has found it.

Coach Macon thought he was ready to take a step back from the sidelines he called home, so he quit coaching after almost twenty years at Yuba City. He still loved the sport and loved working with the kids, but the bureaucracy and the "politics" and the headaches finally got to him. Still, the whole time he was getting fed up with things in the big city, he was also hearing about this burgeoning Sutter program about seven miles out in the country, and then he started running into Coach at the fitness club where they both had a membership, and one day he walked up to Coach and said, "I'd like to be a part of what you got goin' on there."

Coach agreed, so here he is, three years later, a fifty-year-old man who runs the team's calisthenics period, their conditioning period, and their defensive line, and who Reynolds says is "invaluable."

When Macon claps, the team claps. When he shouts and whoops, the team is right behind him bellowing and shouting out their support. And when he starts to move, which is the moment he hits the practice field every afternoon, then everyone else is moving too, and you better be also, because here they come, with Coach Macon leading the charge and saying, "Scoop and score! Scoop and score! Scoop and score!" and defensive bodies flying everywhere to do just that, and Macon knows he wasn't ready to call it quits for good.

For his part, Coach is pretty certain he knows when it'll be enough for him. His son, Dane, is a seventh grader this year, sinewy and blond and looking every bit like the Sutter running back that it's his destiny to become, and Coach can see his boy's senior season as his own final season.

His first few years here were bumpy at best, a continuation of the up and down seasons that were dictated mainly by either a wealth or dearth of big, fast, talented athletes, a cyclical fact that Sutter shared with all of the other small schools on their playing schedule. After a while, Coach came to the realization that he hated to lose and he wasn't going to wait for the talent to appear, so he set about discovering how he could avoid losing as much as possible. He searched out veteran coaches who had built up strong programs to find out their secrets, and, of all the many people he talked with and learned from, he credits his relationship with Randy Blankenship and Dave Humphers, the former and current coaches at Nevada Union, for helping him to find that golden path to consistent excellence. Their program, nestled up in the foothills of the Sierra Nevada mountains, depends on the same Wing T offense that Coach brought to the Huskies so many years ago, and it's an offense that, according to Coach, is perfect for any high school team that can't depend on a steady supply of talent to dominate games and seasons. "You're not always going to have that great back to stick back there in the I," he says. "And you're not always going to have that good quarterback to run the Spread. But you will always be able to find kids to put at spots in the Wing T."

So this is what they use, with their fullback lined up four yards behind the quarterback and two wingbacks flanked off the hips of the outside linemen and almost always someone in motion before the snap of the ball to initiate a succession of sleight-of-hand fakes and hand-offs and quarterback bootlegs. The Wing T relies less on strength or speed or football talent than it does on execution, and the way they achieve that execution at Nevada Union and at Sutter is via the old-fashioned route of repetition and practice. The boys at both schools start running the Wing T in their early days of grade school Pee Wee Football, so that, by the time they reach the varsity level, they are experts and getting better at the intricacies of this offense that relies on a full-speed approach. The Huskies jog back to the huddle at the conclusion of an offensive sequence and, by the time they get there, the next play call is usually in from the bench, and Tony Wagner is barking it out with barely enough time for them to get a break, charge up to the line of scrimmage, get set, and immediately fire off for the next play. "Our goal is to run as many offensive plays in a game as we can," says Coach. And the same goes for practice, where the tempo is always game speed. Coach watches his offense sprint from play to play, in endless and precise repetitions, tilts back his straw golf hat, and says, "I'd rather have a bad 'rep' than a good stand."

This year the Huskies haven't had too many bad reps on offense or defense, and it's not just thanks to a Wing T formation that helps them to compete in years when their talent isn't so great and to dominate when they are bigger and faster and stronger than their North State opponents. It also has to do with Reynolds' attacking defense where the coaches keep individual statistics on their players because, says Coach, "It's good motivation for the guys. If a guy is trying to get a 'stat' by making a tackle, that's good for him and for the team."

Even though he likes to emphasize statistics with the defense, he feels the opposite about his offense. "When you start posting stats, kids start looking at them and thinking about them and this starts to guide their play," says Coach. "They want the ball and when they don't have it maybe they don't block as hard or play as hard because they're busy saving up energy for the next time they get to carry the ball." As Coach explains this and sits back in his office swivel chair, Gary Collett, the senior running back who has carried the ball more times for more yards than anyone else on the team this season, pops his head into the doorway.

"Hey, Coach," he says. "Did you see I'm number one in the league in rushing and number four in the section?"

"Yeah, that's good," says Coach. "We can get you some more yards if you start blocking more when you don't have the ball. Then we'll get you more carries."

Gary gives Coach his best I-want-the-ball-but-I'll-try-to-block grin and says, "I'll get it, Coach. I'll get it," before he retreats back to his metal-mesh locker.

Coach is happy for Gary, but when he announces to the team that Gary has gone over a thousand yards for the season, Coach calls for a round of applause, not for the runner, but for the offensive line that opened up all those running lanes for him and for Tony and Jake and the rest of the backfield corps as well, and maybe that innocent office exchange with Gary offers a hint as to why Coach has his sights set on a retirement deadline six years down the road. And it's because, more than anything else, he's tired. He's tired of not being able to play a kid as much as he'd like, a kid who has worked hard and earned playing time, but who is backing up a better player. He is tired of dealing with parents who think their kids are better players than they actually are and who are always wondering and complaining about why their son isn't playing more or getting the ball more. He's tired of all that it takes to always be good and have everyone else around trying to knock you and your team off the mountaintop that you have worked so hard to ascend and where it requires so much energy to remain. "By the end of each season," says Coach, "I'm exhausted."

What's making Coach the most tired this week is his having to worry about Friday night's game at Winters, a team the Huskies should manhandle, but you never know. So all week he and Reynolds and the rest of the staff keep the pressure on because if Sutter somehow stumbles on Friday night, they'll be sharing the BVL crown with Winters and Coach tells his squad time and time again, "We don't want to share anything with Winters."

As the team huddles to conclude Monday's cool-weather practice, Reynolds steps into the middle of their ranks to say, "A couple of weeks ago, the Wheatland coach, after we gave 'em a good thumping, had enough energy left to say that he thought Winters would give us a good game. So that's what we're playing for … respect … that same old thing. And if they're not gonna give it to us, we're gonna hafta physically take it from them."

During Wednesday's pre-practice stretch, Coach pulls out a newspaper article from before last week's decisive thrashing of Gridley and he says, "Here's what other teams think of us. The Gridley coach says, 'I don't know if they've faced a complete team like us. Offensively, they're huge, but it's not like the old Sutter Wing T. You can see where they're going with the ball.'" Coach holds the faxed article over his head and says, "It's a good thing we didn't see that before we played 'em." Then later, as the offense performs rep after rep at their breakneck pace, Coach challenges them to do better, to fake better and run harder, and he says, "Our fakes have to be good enough so that we fool people. Gridley says they don't, and, even though we beat 'em 48–7, it still pisses me off."

Macon uses the Gridley slight as well when his defensive linemen go through their Every Day Drills, and he growls, "You don't think Winters got a copy of that fax? What are we gonna show 'em?"

Reynolds vows to his defense that Friday night, "We're gonna sell the farm. We're gonna use everything we got against 'em." He wants a show of force because he thinks Winters might end up in their playoff bracket, "And if they get all this thrown at them, it'll freak them out."

When these two teams met last year at Wayne Gadberry Field, it was Winters who tried to freak Sutter out when they opened up their first offensive series with a "swinging gate" formation where the center is lined up over the ball, the quarterback is lined up behind him, seven yards deep in the "shotgun," and the rest of the offensive contingent is lined up rugby-style next to one or the other sideline. Coach took one look at this weird but timeworn configuration and yanked off his headset and had his defensive captain call timeout, so the whole unit could gather around Reynolds and figure out how to combat this oddball tactic. "They tried to surprise us," says Coach. "But we adjusted pretty easy. And the best news was that I knew right away that Winters was nervous and scared and thought they had to do something crazy to compete."

What was even stranger about this Winters offensive strategy is that it is usually opposing defenses that totally change up their schemes to try and slow down the Huskies' potent offense. And as Coach watches the A and B units roll through their infinite offensive selections on Thursday afternoon, even he can't help himself from saying, "Damn we gotta lotta plays. But in case they take somethin' away, we gotta have somethin' to go to. Improvise and conquer." The B team is up and tight end Chad Ziegenmeyer plows upfield to lay a running play block against a phantom linebacker. He's going full-speed with his arms and legs pumping and that cool autumn air rifling in and out of his nose and mouth, and, as he's running, he really *looks* like he's running and Coach says, "Doesn't it sound like he's workin'?"

And maybe that's their secret here at Sutter. Maybe it's not their one-size-fits-all offense, or the hell-raising defense, or the flashy uniforms that they buy new every year, or even the simple joy these kids and coaches seem to get from running up and down a football field. Maybe it is just hard work that keeps them right there year after year, within an arm's reach of that ring that everyone else is grasping for as well. And there usually is someone else right there with them to try and wrestle it away, but it's always someone different. This year it's Lassen, a new team in the division, who last year ran over all the smaller schools in the North State and has moved up to try and do the same in their new classification.

At this late date in the season, the real challenge is to stay ready just in case someone pretends that they want to play with the Huskies. But until that time, they've got to rely on those Every Day Drills, and on the A on A scrimmages, where, says Daddow, "We usually go until things get too intense. Our guys really don't have the threat of getting hurt in an actual game because they're just better, and better prepared, and they play at a different speed, a different tempo. But the scrimmages scare me because you're playing along and the next thing you know, things heat up and someone gets hurt, and eventually, and it might not be until Lassen, we're going to need people to be healthy."

As he describes what it's like to coach a team where there's no real competition in sight, Daddow wants to get it right, so he says,

"Back in 1999 we didn't win a lot, but it was a great season to be a coach at Sutter because the talent was limited and the job was a challenge. When we were successful at giving them a chance to win, the feeling of accomplishment was a satisfying one. We had to coach hard and do a good job of coaching every day. Then you look at the 2001 season when we were really good. By the first day of school I was bored because there was really nothing else to do. They had it all down and they were so good that it didn't matter what they did, they were going to be successful at it. We could draw up something in the dirt, and it would work. It didn't matter. We were that good, and it got boring as a coach, and the only real challenge was to find ways to keep their enthusiasm up and their attention focused because no one could compete with us. And the challenge is the same this year."

So, it's not really an understatement when Coach says to his team on Thursday, "This is just another speed bump on the way to Taco Bell." But then he remembers himself and his team's ever-precarious place at the top and he says, "Play your game. Period. Winters has a lot to gain with a victory, and they don't give up. No lettin' up. Remember that article in the paper? That's what they think of you guys. Let's finish out the regular season 10–0. Slips count in a bear fight. No slips."

Then Daddow says, "Guys, this is where it is. Don't let Winters share the title with us. They don't believe in us, and I don't know why they don't believe in us."

Macon adds, "Hang half a hundred on 'em."

And then, before the coaches head toward the office, Coach can't help but add, "I predicted we'd be right where we're at right now. It's fun to stand on the sidelines and watch you mow over people."

With that, he and the staff leave the team to their captains, but they aren't quite out of earshot when Dave Heckman starts off today's players-only meeting with, "First of all, last Thursday was a bunch a crap. If you can't sacrifice ten or fifteen minutes for what we got to say, then leave. I'm tired of it."

Coach nods his head, and says as he continues on toward the school building, "That's one of the reasons we're so good. We got guys who can take care of business." The following night, just prior to their march into the Winters Warriors Stadium, Reynolds says, "Let's go, boys. Friday night lights. No one respects us. It's time to make a statement." Then the Huskies storm the field and play a first half that is like every first half they have played all season.

At halftime in the locker room, Reynolds looks at the team and says, "I was listenin' to them on the way in. They've quit already. When a team quits on us, that's when we step it up and play harder. That's when we put the boot to them."

These are some strong words, but what really are you supposed to do when the most taxing part of the first half was your jog back to the locker room? What the Huskies do is give their A-teamers one series in the second half, and then the coaches take off their headsets, Dave Heckman and Spencer Rickertsen and company take off their helmets, and Jason Lewis and his B-team crew get the run of the field for the rest of the game. It's a blowout game, not quite "half a hundred," but close, and yet another Husky shutout. And for the second half at least, there's no discerning the Warrior sideline from the Husky sideline, but for the fact that one is in their home red jerseys and the other wears their travel whites, because, on both sides, it's a bunch of guys standing around waiting for the clock to tick down to zero so they can get the hell out of there.

There is no real joy in Winters tonight. The Warriors have been soundly beaten in a game where they had no chance to win. As for Coach and his wrecking crew, well, they've got to content themselves with yet another BVL Title for now, but not get too contented in the two weeks until their first playoff game as they work at staying focused enough to play Winters or some other team that they have already "mowed over," on their way to the Thanksgiving Eve section title game. They'll maybe take a day or so to rest up, but next week it'll be back to the weights and the film and the drills and the reps and all the unending work that these Sutter Huskies put in to get good and stay good.

# Week Fifteen—Stay at Home

## Grant High School Pacers: Sacramento, California

**C**OACH MIKE ALBERGHINI swings his van off Grand Avenue and weaves through a Del Paso Heights neighborhood that is bright and quiet on this Saturday morning. Last night, his Grant Pacers dismantled yet another one of their Metro League opponents, and Al is on his way to Lynn Reed's house, where the varsity staff plans to watch the hours-old 54–0 victory over Sacramento High before they turn their attention to this week's regular season finale against Nevada Union, which is known as "The Game" in the Sacramento area. In a town where most varsity football games are sparsely attended, this match-up draws big crowds that are anxious to watch an epic battle between the two premier programs in the region.

Last year, Grant hosted The Game, which Nevada Union won 43–40 in a wild affair where the second half was played in a thick bank of fog, and where, says Reed, "If we'd'a scored one more damn touchdown, we'd'a won." His assessment of this near miss sums up both sides of a rivalry that has only intensified between these two schools in the twelve years since Coach Al moved from defensive coordinator to head man at Grant, and Dave Humphers took over the Nevada Union program. The heads-up record in that time span, including a couple of playoff match-ups, is seven wins for Grant, six for NU, and one tie.

When you throw in the under-the-surface antagonism between the two head coaches who attended the same Sacramento city high school at different times, and who, says Al, "aren't on the friendliest of terms, and at one time it could be said that we didn't like each other," and the on-the-surface contrasts between the two schools—inner-city poor and mostly minority for Grant; small-town affluent and mostly white for NU—and you have yourself the makings of an honest-to-goodness, full-blown rivalry. If you are searching for a "Big Game," it doesn't get much bigger than this Friday night when the Pacers take their 8–1 record up to Grass Valley to face the undefeated Miners.

Friday night seems a long way off, though, as Al parks along the curb and climbs out with his videotapes and a can of diet soda. When he steps up the front walk and into the Reeds' living room, he is greeted by a roomful of coaches who view his late arrival as an opportunity to say, "Where you been, Al? You holdin' up the progress." Al grins and takes a look around at his staff; at Lynn Reed, who played here in the 1970s and then went on to Oregon's Linnfield College, where he played football and earned his degree; at Lynn's son, Carl, who followed in his father's footsteps; at Thomas Henderson, a Portland, Oregon transplant, who is in his second year with the program; and at Reggie Harris, a Virginia native who moved out here with his wife last year. Coach settles in and the men get ready to watch the film.

But before Lynn can press "Play" on the VCR, his four-year-old son Ju-Ju comes bursting out of the back hallway in his pajamas, carrying a picture book that he's ready for someone to read to him. He approaches Carl, his half-brother, to show him the book. Carl takes a look at the cover and says, "Go-Bots. Damn! Tha's one'a my old books."

"You can tell," says Al. "It was never used." While Carl looks through the book, Ju-Ju bounces like a pinball around the room, until his mom takes him by the arm, gives him a smack on the bottom, and sets him down in front of the TV on his sleeping bag.

"I'm not a timeout person," she says. "I whip their ass and get it over with."

And this is pretty much what Grant did to Sac High last night, in a game where Al yanked G, the Pacers' star tailback, after the fifth play of the game for showboating. "He knows he's not supposed to act like that," says Al as he watches the taped replay of his senior captain tiptoeing toward the end zone. "And yet he still feels the need to do it."

Even though Al can't condone this type of behavior, he can understand why his players might do it, and it's not so much from an oversized ego as it is a battle against sheer boredom. This victory is the third week in a row where the opponent has failed to score and where Grant's starters have had minimal playing time because the game got out of hand so early. For seasoned veterans like G and his half-brother, Bully, this isn't such a bad thing because it helps them to avoid injuries and stay fresh for the playoff run to come. But for the younger starters, like the sophomore- and junior-dominated offensive line, competing against these inferior teams has halted the progress that Al is depending on for Friday night's match-up with Nevada Union. "They were maturing and peaking until the Yuba City and Sacramento games," says Al. "But all we needed to win was a minimal effort, and that's exactly what we got. I'm definitely concerned going into this game against a good team. But at least we have athletes to have concerns about. At some schools they have question marks and no one to fill the gaps."

The presence of physically gifted athletes never seems to be a question mark here at Grant, where they have two graduates in the

NFL and four current team members (G, Bully, Joaquin Martinson, and Syd Quan Thompson) who are all getting looks from Division I programs. In addition, they also have that young but gigantic offensive line that the coaches call the Milk Farm, and a whole supporting cast of big and strong and fast kids that cause most other teams to shudder in their cleats at their mere appearance.

But even in the midst of all this talent, it is Sammy, the third-string tailback, who steals the Sac High videotape show on this Saturday morning at the Reed house. Because of the lopsided nature of the Pacers' recent victories, Sammy has enjoyed a lot of playing time over the last three weeks. Last night's game was no different, where the running back position was his for the entirety of the fourth quarter, and where the hapless Sac High defense looked like superstars because the only direction Sammy headed was backward. This is good news for Carl Reed, who is Sammy's ride home after weekday practices and who placed a friendly wager with the 130-pound senior reserve, who, before he entered the game, vowed to his coach that he'd gain at least fifteen yards on six carries. "You're on," said Carl, who is now basking in the thought that Sammy owes him a fountain soda.

But at least as good as the soft drink he's supposed to provide for Carl next week is the show Sammy is providing for the entire staff with his fourth quarter performance. He's lined up really, really deep in the Pacers' "I" alignment, so deep that Al says, "That looks like punt formation." Then, every time he is handed the ball, he is immediately thrown for a loss.

As the coaches watch Sammy get tripped up far behind the line of scrimmage yet again, Reggie says, "Ouch! Sammy was gittin' killed."

"He says he wants to run behind the starting line," says Carl.

"He couldn't run behind the Green Bay Packers," Al replies.

Sure, these coaches can't help but give Sammy a hard time, but who can blame them? Because, as they recline on the chairs on this bleary-eyed Saturday morning, eating from the pizza and chicken wing spread that's laid out on the kitchen table, last night's game induces the same kind of ennui that led to G's early exit and to Carl's bet with a third-team running back, and at least "The Sammy Show" offers up a scrap of entertainment in a game where their guys came out flat and still scored eight touchdowns.

Once the Sac High game comes to a merciful conclusion and Al switches the VCR to a Nevada Union–Kennedy match-up, the mood in Lynn's living room abruptly changes. The snacks are forgotten and the whole crew of coaches leans forward in their chairs because, even though this game is no more hard-fought a contest than their own, the week's challenge has officially begun with the appearance on the screen of the Miners' "Wing T" offense that presents the ultimate frustration for Al. He knows how to stop it, and he's got the scheme and the athletes to do it. And there's no real mystery to what Nevada Union does, which is to line up their fullback a few yards behind the quarterback, and to line up two halfbacks flanked as "wings" at the ends of the offensive line, and then use motion and backfield cloverleaf patterns and sleight-of-hand fakes in a maddeningly similar yet infinite variety of combinations that cause Al to say, "The Wing T, when NU runs it, is like frikkin' Houdini."

So the same scene is playing out this morning in the Reed living room that has played out in some living room or classroom on this approximate mid-November date since Al began coaching the Grant defense, and that is Al watching a film of this Nevada Union Wing T, picturing in his mind the defensive scheme that will stop it, going through a mental checklist of the players he's got to populate that defensive scheme, and then convincing himself that those players are going to carry out the plan that he lays out for them to reduce this potentially lethal offense to a bunch of guys flailing around in the backfield for three straight plays, and then punting the football away so his own talented offense can get their hands on it. The foundation of his plan lies in covering gaps and getting his players to stop the NU run.

Coach is less worried about stopping the pass because the Pacers have Syd to rely on, a player who may be the most gifted kid on any field where he plays. So Al wants to know if they should start out their defensive backs in zone coverage or in man-to-man. "Do we put Syd on their split end right away?" he asks. "Or do we wait till they piss us off, and then do it?"

"We do it now," says Reggie, and it doesn't take him long to say it. "This is the game to see who got it, so I say we put him on that right now."

With that settled, Al can't keep himself from thinking about what Carl calls his "What-What Group"—What the hell are they doin' here, and what for?—of which dashing Sammy may be the unofficial chairman. But Sammy's not alone, and so, in the middle of this storm of scheming, Al has the What-Whats on his mind when he says, "I think we need to have Muffin somewhere because Muffin keeps the other team on the scoreboard." It's fun to imagine Muffin getting some playing time this week, just like he and Sammy and a whole gaggle of other reserves have gotten in most of the Pacers' games this season. But, in reality, and if this NU game is anything like almost every other game these two teams have played against each other, Muffin and Sammy will spend the entire evening on the sideline, while the big guns will man their regular posts for this most important engagement of the year.

Once the What-Whats are relegated back to the back of everyone's minds, Al springs up from his spongy spot on the couch to say, "Motivation's not gonna be a problem. They're gonna be jacked up for this game. With our kids, simple is better. Don't inundate our guys with too much. They'll snap the ball, and we'll still be talking. Let's line these guys heads-up. Their guards very seldom block heads-up. Let's slant our linemen, and teach our ends that we're not gonna get beat by 'counter' and 'buck sweep.' We're bigger than them, and we're sure as hell tougher, and this is the year we gotta beat 'em up."

And Al has a similar plan of attack for his offense, where it's no secret that he'll use his big, inexperienced line and his fast, experienced backs to run the ball right into the heart of the Nevada Union defense, which will be stacked up front to try and keep the Pacers from doing just that.

They've replaced the NU–Kennedy tape with a video of last year's NU–Grant match-up, and, as the first half starts to unfold, Al comes off his we'll-ram-it-down-their-throats offensive strategy just a bit because he notices a big Miner defender who doesn't normally play defense lined up directly over the Grant tight end. "But," says Al, "he's not playing the tight end. He's playing straight run." Al seems to be onto something. Every time this Nevada Union behemoth is lined up on the end of the line, when the ball is snapped he doesn't even pretend to look at the tight end, which leaves him free to concentrate on the football and where it might be headed, but also leaves the Pacer tight end all alone three or four yards up the field. If Nevada Union uses this same ploy again this year, Al's Tight End Arrow should work to not only gain the Pacers some much-needed passing yardage, but also to loosen up the Nevada Union run-oriented defense that will now have that Arrow pass in the back of its mind, and will have to either respect it, or continue to leave the tight end open for more catches and more yards.

Thinking about the play, Al starts to think about a way to run a variation on it, but then gets a picture in his mind of Peewee, his junior starting quarterback on whom the variation would rely, and this is enough for him to question this choice of plays, not only on Saturday afternoon, but also for the remainder of the week, leading all the way up to when Peewee steps out onto the field to take command of the Pacer offense on Friday night. "Peewee is a kid who can implode at any time," says Al. "He doesn't have a lot of confidence in himself." On one hand, the Tight End Arrow might be just the kind of wide-open, easy throw that could provide the confidence boost that Peewee needs to get through the game. "But I'm also afraid that if Peewee runs it, he'll call a timeout in the middle of the play and ruin the whole element of surprise," Al says.

For the first time all season though, Al has another option to his quarterback dilemma, in the form of Bobby Bunfill, Peewee's junior backup who has yet to play a down for the Pacers because he transferred in to Grant during the second week of this school year from Jesuit, where "the powers that be" refused to sign the eligibility forms that would have allowed him to begin playing immediately at his new school. "Eventually, Bobby's gonna play in his first game," says Al. "I just don't know if it should be this game. The thing is, he would probably already be our starter if he were eligible." Instead, Bobby has spent this first part of the school year at practice and on the bench and trying to get caught up at the third high school he's attended since his freshman year.

Bobby isn't the first Pacer player to have tested the waters at Jesuit before he came over to Grant. G and Bully spent their freshman season at the cross-town private school, but when things didn't quite work out the way the two brothers had expected, they came back ready to start their varsity career for the Pacers the next year. But their three years got cut down to two, when, in a move similar to Bobby's situation, the Jesuit administration decided not to sign the brothers' transfer paperwork; so, instead of making an immediate impact on the Pacers' varsity, G and Bully had to sleep-walk through their sophomore year with the school's junior varsity squad.

But varsity or no, and football or no, Al can sit in a broken-wheeled office chair at the door of Grant's rusted-out cavern of a weight room on a Thursday afternoon and look at these two kids as they laugh and joke with their teammates and lift the occasional weight, and he can smile to himself as he says, "They share a father, but they haven't spent too much time with him, and neither of them lives with his mother—G stays with his grandma and Bully lives at an uncle's house—and I'm trying to find an explanation as to why they're such 'good' kids, and I don't know why."

Perhaps Al could begin with himself and his coaching staff in his search for an explanation because, in a city that is rich with football talent and shaky at best in on-the-field football excellence, he has found a way to help his Grant kids stay in school and on the team in such a consistent fashion that, in his many years here, he's had only one player who made it through his program and failed to depart the high school with a diploma in hand. "These other schools around here have the athletes just like we do," says Al. "But you've got to work with your players and get along with them if you hope to get as much as you can out of them. You've got to make sure that your guys know that they're getting something out of the deal—a chance to graduate and maybe go on to college, a little help with schoolwork, some guidance in life matters, a ride home, maybe a meal at your house, or even something as small as someone who pays attention to him and shows a little interest— the chances of him responding to what you want him to do get a lot better."

And Al and his staff do all of those things here. They yell and scream and ridicule their players and each other with equal opportunity abundance that no one on the team—coach or player—has any qualms about returning with high-spirited exuberance. But they also teach night school and tutor and hold study halls and check grades every week, and there is a group of kids hanging around Al's van—and every other coach's car, as well—after practice for the lift home that he's been providing since he hired on here as the varsity baseball coach thirty-five years ago.

On Tuesday, it's a lift *to* practice as well as home because it's a no-school Veterans' Day that Al turns into a marathon film and practice session after he and his staff have made their early morning neighborhood rounds to pick up ride-less players. Al has already dropped off one load of kids to join their teammates in the portable Drivers' Ed classroom where a Nevada Union game tape is under way, and where the first-year running backs coach, Avion "Radio" Weaver, is already offering up commentary for the early arrivals. Today it is Del Campo that is getting their hat handed to them by NU's Wing T, and Radio, in a fervent, freestyle delivery that is part of what earned him his nickname, is shouting out things like, "We don't play like that! We do our jobs!" and, "When in doubt, tackle everybody!" Avion's brother, who coaches the basketball team at Grant, is married to Al's daughter, and so, when the rest of the staff rides him hard at practice about being Radio, Al has the chance to say, "He's getting angry. You guys gotta lay off. I can mess with him because he's family."

By the time Al and company get back to the Driver's Ed room, most of the rest of the team and coaches have arrived as well. But when Al scans the seats from his spot near the back door, he notices that his starting quarterback is absent and he says, "Where's Peewee?" No one knows, so Al says, "Well somebody's got to run," and as he says this, G grabs Bobby's shoulder, and he and a whole contingent say in near-unison, "Bobby's here," and Bobby sits a little straighter in his desk, as Peewee on his bicycle flashes by the smoked-glass window and up the ramp to the classroom door. He's here in time to retain his starting quarterback job.

"It's rare to see two high school teams that are good and that come out and play hard," Coach says. "The theme of this week is that there's no way to justify not coming up and playing hard. The thing we want to continue to work on this week is getting to 'mesh points'—to your gaps. The way to beat Wing T teams is discipline. Don't know what *his* job is. Know what your job is. If we do our job and stay at home when they run the 'double-reverse,' we'll be ready because our outside guys stay at home. Everything is inside. Have faith that the guy next to you is doing his job. When we win, we make everybody's day. When we lose, we ain't nothin'."

Despite Al's pep talk, the players struggle in practice this week. The team files out of the Drivers' Ed room and across the litter-strewn asphalt parking lot to get changed. While the players pull their blue and yellow practice clothes on, Al heads in to what used to be the shower room to start hauling out blocking bags for the day's practice.

When he's done, he leans back against the blue-painted cement balustrade of the ancient stadium and squints up into the early morning sunshine while his boys straggle down the steps and out onto the dead-grass field. Most carry their helmets and pads slung over their shoulders. Peewee and Bobby carry the bags of beat-up footballs and fall into a game of catch once they make it down to the yellow turf.

Most of the coaches, like the students, have the day off, but Carl Reed works with a special class of elementary-age kids who don't have the day off, so he has arranged a "field trip" that involves a three-hour visit to Grant's stadium so their teacher doesn't have to miss practice. "The administration'll love it. I'm gonna buy 'em some Egg McMuffins and say, 'Get your ass in the stands.' That's the only way I can be there," Carl says on Sunday when he hatches his plan. And as he arrives with his troupe of kids, whose challenges range from autism to bipolar disorders, he's in time to hear Al say, as he watches his linebackers "bite" on a Wing T fake, "Joaquin, you're a moron! How can you get a 4.0 in the classroom, and a 1.0 on the football field? If the fullback comes up this gap, and for some reason he doesn't have the ball, you melt his ass!"

"Damn," says Carl as he ushers his crew toward the bleachers, "my kids are gonna feel smart out here. This'll be like a self-esteem builder for them."

Then he turns his attention to the team's defensive practice and notices Sammy hanging back in the ranks instead of stepping into the huddle to run some scout team plays. "How you doin' there, Sammy?" asks Carl. "You look like you're still lingering from all those shots you took the other night." Sammy shakes his head and grimaces and Carl suggests tomorrow night after practice as a good time to pay off the bet.

Sammy's not the only one complaining today. Rumor has it that Nevada Union takes "snow days" for this entire week so their team can focus on The Game and nothing else, and these Grant kids, as they practice on this holiday morning, want to know why they can't have the week off as well. "Because," says Al, "you'd get in too much trouble—practice for three hours and screw up for four-teen. The only ones who wouldn't get in trouble are the Polynesians because they haven't discovered women." Then Al looks over at his giant but gentle nose tackle, and says, "James, you'd probably get laryngitis from singing in church … but that's not a bad thing."

What is a bad thing today, though, is that every facet of the Pacers' game seems to be at least a little bit off.

Carl is having little success working on the "motion blitz" with the outside linebackers. The idea is that they are supposed to anticipate Nevada Union's snap of the football, which usually isn't too difficult a thing to do because, on almost every play, the Miners break their huddle, sprint to the line of scrimmage, get set, put one of their wingbacks in motion, and, a split second later, snap the ball. But, as the outside backers practice against a skeleton scout team, "Urkel" keeps reacting late to the snap because he is busy feinting and backpedaling and performing all of the other tricks that usually work against teams that take a long time to get to the line. But Nevada Union doesn't waste time, and, even against his own guys pretending to be NU's offense, Urkel keeps getting caught flatfooted on play after play, until Carl gets tired of it and says, "You watch film? You see how fast they snap the ball?"

Al has the inside backers on his opposite side of the field going over the same "stunts" as the outside guys. He goes over the "reads" and the "motions" and the "blitzes" with his guys yet another time, and Joaquin says, "We already went over that." Al stops his explanation to reply, "I know that. But sometimes in a game people tend to accuse coaches that they weren't taught something."

Things don't improve when everyone reconvenes for "Team D," where Al has the scout offense run half-speed through some Nevada Union plays to give his guys a slow-motion look at what they'll be confronted with on Friday night. Even now, though, his defenders seem tentative in their reactions, but there are no takers when Al calls for questions. "When you're busy acting like you know what you're doing, and you don't know what you're doing," says Al, "that can kind of hurt us."

There is still no relief when the Pacers switch over to their offensive practice. G wears an extra lower back pad attached to his shoulder gear, and he has some yellow "Caution" construction-site tape stuck to that, and today it works as an advertisement for the way he wants to run the football behind his young offensive line, even against a thrown-together scout defense. Urkel is part of that defense, and he has lost all of the stutters and false starts he displayed earlier as he flies to the ball to make tackle after tackle and to cause Joaquin to observe, "Damn, he plays Nevada Union's defense better than he plays Grant's defense." Urkel and his fellow scouts are making the offense look sluggish and disjointed, so after yet another play where G stops and starts and spins and halts his way to the sideline for no gain, Al yells, "Just run as fast as you can! Don't think ... 'cause they're gonna fly to the ball every time. Don't think! Just run!"

And this is how things go for the Pacers for the remainder of the morning and well on into the afternoon until Lynn takes his offensive line in to watch more Nevada Union film, and all of the backs and ends choose a corner of the stadium to run their post-practice hills. Urkel and Freddy take a few more minutes to work on their reads, and, when they're done, Freddy asks Al for an NU tape to watch at home. Al thinks that's a good idea, and he says with a grin, "I'm a little leery about this because you might start thinking too much, and when you think too much you tend to lose that animal instinct."

Long after the rest of the team has headed back to the locker room, Bobby Bunfill is still out on the field. He's stripped out of his pads, but he's using one of the practice balls to go over a succession of fakes and sprints and sprint-outs and drop-backs that make Al shake his head as he watches his new quarterback go through his post-practice routine, and he says, "I hope we someday run the offense that Bobby works out in."

The offense that Grant does run works a little better on Wednesday, as does the defense and special teams, even though six of Al's principal players are still feeling the effects of their gargantuan early-afternoon meal up in Auburn, where they and Al met at the Marie Calendar's with Nevada Union's Coach Humphers and some of his senior starters for a game-week lunch that the two coaches began a few years back. After several rounds of steak and shrimp and pork ribs and burgers, each kid from both teams takes a moment to express what this game means to him, and what they all have to say boils down to, "This is an experience that not a lot of people get to have, and so we're lucky to be a part of it."

Then Al addresses the group about why the leaders of these two teams are sitting here today. "Rivalries are built out of respect, not out of innuendoes and stereotypes," he says. "We're going to work to beat you, just like you're working to beat us. But let's enjoy today, and we'll respect you as men for the rest of our lives. We want you to sit down across the table from each other and see that you're more than just a bunch of guys on tape or film or behind a helmet. You're young men."

By Thursday afternoon, Al is feeling better about his own young men, even though the weathermen are predicting a rain that could dampen not only tomorrow night's turf, but also Grant's advantage in the speed department that, says Al, "scares Nevada Union to death." They start off in the weight room for their last period P.E. class, and Al sits by the door and watches his team wander around the maze of rusted weights instead of picking one up, and he says, "That's a good sign. It means they're somewhere they don't want to be. Where they want to be is out on the football field."

Then, when the final bell rings to end the school day, the team reconvenes in the Drivers' Ed room to watch last year's Fog Bowl between Grant and Nevada Union, and again, everyone is antsy and no one can sit still, and Al says, "They're acting 'goofy' because they're thinking about the game."

The film ends, and that's it for today. The players drift out the door, and Bobby walks with Al over to the gym to open up the equipment room and check out his Pacers' game jersey and pants for the first time this year. While he searches through the stacks for a size to fit Bobby's slim frame, Al talks to his new quarterback about his role tomorrow night. "Peewee will start," he says. "And you'll play … but I don't know when. I hope that you both play well; that when we have Peewee in there, he does good, and when we have you in there, you do good. And," says Al as he hands Bobby his No. 12 road jersey, "you don't need to make up for nine games in one play."

And then it's Friday night and time for game number ten. By the time the final school bell rings, it has been raining for most of the day. A couple kids cut the feet out of their spare socks to wear on their forearms.

Carl walks in not too long before the buses are ready to start their pull up the hill. He had to stay late down at his job "because some racist parents tried to get my teacher aide fired. He grabbed a kid's arm to sit him down and the parents said he was too forceful, and they're going to call CPS and the sheriffs." And, Carl says, "This is the third time black parents have tried to get my aide in trouble because he's white."

All Al can say is, "Better get on the bus," and then as he watches Freddy head out the door, he says, "Don't forget your helmet. It's an important part of tonight."

It turns out that Freddy needs his helmet tonight because Nevada Union is ready for the Pacers. Rain beats on the Grant bus for the hour-and-a-half it takes to get to Grass Valley, and it beats on the team as they march from their dressing room on one side of the campus to the stadium on the far other side. There is a midway pause to climb down a muddy slope to the darkened expanse of the school's softball field, where they line up on the wet grass for their pre-game stretch with the dull glow of the stadium lights blossoming over the trees. "Let 'em hear it in the hills, ya'll," the captains call out, and then the cadence of the "Pacer Jacks" echoes across the valley.

They have already knelt on the cement floor of the dressing room for their long team prayer and their "Our Father," and listened with their fingers curled through their yellow facemasks as Al stood in their midst to say, "It's now time to set everything else aside. We are through wandering around. When we walk out that door, it's something we've spent a lot of time preparing for. It's not the beginning or end of your life, but it merits some time. They're not going to play harder than us. You can walk out on that field and you can look at it like a loser, and say, 'Damn, that's ugly,' or you can say, 'It's a beautiful night for a championship.' There are people who die every day in war fighting in the mud. That's sorrow. We can gain glory tonight fighting in the mud. We're not going on that field to prove ourselves. We're stepping out there to retain something that is ours. This is the night I wanted—dirty, mean, and ugly. And we can prove that we can play in any conditions and be supreme. Take care of the football, and hustle after everything. Once a mistake is done, we go on. The one thing we won't have to adjust is our effort. That's what tonight is about—effort."

And so it is. The team captains stride arm in arm in the gloom from both sidelines for the coin toss, arrayed in their Michigan-style black and gold for Nevada Union and all-white with gold helmets for Grant.

The Game spools out in pretty classic fashion. The Herrera Brothers slog onto the field for Nevada Union, and they are a couple of junior cannonballs at fullback and wingback that, as Al watched them beat up defenses on tape all week, he said, "See, here's the discouraging part, when they start running three or four yards a pop and they're wearing your ass out." And that's what they're doing to a Grant defense that wants to "chase" and wants to fly to the ball, and doesn't want to sit and wait and hold down their gaps and their mesh points where the Herrera Brothers find holes so recently vacated by overanxious Pacer defenders, and, before Grant can settle down and catch its breath, it is twenty minutes into the game, and they're down 13–0. But this isn't so bad, because Al had fretted all week about "being vulnerable to the big play," and the one time NU gives it a shot, with a halfback pass midway through the second quarter, Syd is downfield waiting to bat the deep throw away. And he also makes the acrobatic end zone catch that has guys on the sideline calling "Touchdown" even as he's leaping between the two defenders and the ball is still wobbling through the sky, and that gets the Pacers on the board with a minute left in the half. And then, when NU tries the double-reverse on Grant's kickoff, they drop the ball and Urkel sprints in to scoop it up and dash to the end zone, and when the Pacers gather in Nevada Union's fieldhouse foyer at halftime, they do so with a 14–13 lead. Everyone is covered with mud; the What-Whats and the coaches are up to their knees in brown paste and the starters look like they've been rolling in it, which they have. Everyone is slapping Urkel on the shoulder for his bold special teams play, but Al isn't so happy about it. "Tonight's not the night to pick up a fumble," he says to the gathered team. "Fall on it, and take care of the football." And then he says, "Let's go play football, gentlemen," and it's back out to the sideline slush where the P.A. guy is bleating over his loudspeaker like he's WWF, and Al says, "The guy I'd like to knock the hell out of is that damn announcer." Urkel is pacing and thinking, and Carl gets ahold of his jersey and says, "Remember, you're not Superman. You're Reggie Walker, playing weak-side linebacker for Grant High

School," and Urkel shakes his head in agreement and says, "I know. Stay at home."

Then it's the second half, where G dings his knee and is out for the game; Nevada Union scores to regain the lead after another one of their end-to-end marches; Bobby makes a hard-nosed run on a quarterback keeper to set up a one-yard TD plunge by Bully that gives Grant the lead back; and big James joyfully dances the Macarena on the sideline. But then Bully is stopped on another fourth down play to seal the game, and, with two-and-a-half minutes left, Grant turns the ball back over to the Miners, who have no timeouts and eighty-five yards between them and the end zone. They spend the next two minutes handing the ball to the Herrera Brothers, and watching them run with it down to the Grant thirty-seven-yard line.

With the clock continuing to tick away, they do something weird for them, which is take their time getting up to the line of scrimmage. But things slow down even more for everyone in the stadium when they finally do snap the ball, and their No. 10 drifts back and then flips a pass over toward the NU sideline, where his receiver and a whole contingent of Miner blockers are waiting, and where every one of the Pacer defenders converges in an all-out desperate sprint. Urkel is there, and Freddy and John and Syd and Corn and Willie, and Bully too, all of them running in their mudded-down clothes, and all wanting that ball, and as they splash through the mud and smash into the wall of Miners, NU's No. 10 drifts the other way, toward the Pacer sideline, almost in slow-motion—in actual slow-motion for the Grant faithful and for Al and Lynn and Reggie and Carl and a whole sideline full of guys who can see what's happening before it even happens—and then the ball is in the air again, spinning in the night sky, through the mist and the fog and the stadium lights, and then settling into No. 10's arms, where he cradles it on his solo run toward the end zone.

# Week Sixteen—The Second Time Around

## Bishop Manogue High School Miners: Reno, Nevada

**S**EVEN O'CLOCK MONDAY morning in Reno, Nevada, and sixty-seven boys stand at their stations in the Bishop Manogue weight room. They are waiting to be counted by Joe Sellers, their athletic period instructor and Manogue's head football coach, who walks between the weight benches with his wood clipboard and roll sheet, wanting to know who's here and who's not and why.

And today, there are a lot of guys who aren't here because the flu has got its grip on Miner football, and it's shaking hard and doesn't seem to want to let go. Thomas Peregrin, the senior quarterback, is out, just like he was out almost all of last week leading up to Saturday's game. Same thing with Manny McElroy, who Manogue relies on for his offensive and defensive play, but also, and even more importantly, he's the team's center for punts and field goals, and he's the one guy they've got who can "insert the spiral into the long snap," says Coach as he frets about his absence. And what about Anthony Farnsworth? Where's he? In Manogue's galaxy of football stars, it's "Farney," a 5'9" 160-pound noseguard, who Coach calls the "keg of dynamite," and who he feels the team can least afford to lose.

But today at 7:00 a.m., with the sun just starting to glint off the smoked-glass windows of the high-rise casinos along Virginia Street, Farney is nowhere to be found. And this, along with the kids who are here with their coughs and wheezes, has Coach worried and pacing and on the telephone in his office because, of all the weeks for the flu to hit hard, this is the worst week.

The Miners are scheduled to play on Saturday in the 3A state title game in defense of the championship they won last year, and also, more than likely, in their final game at Nevada's 3A level because, not only has Manogue not lost a game in the last two years at this level, but they haven't played in one that has been competitive. Their average margin of victory for this season is fifty-six points, and the other 3A teams in the state are getting tired of it, as are the Miners. So Coach has applied to the state commission for 4A status, the large-school level in Nevada that is populated mostly by Las Vegas and Reno public schools that are, at the very least, three times the size of Manogue's population of 450 students. But that does not matter because the Miners have got to find some competition and some teams who are willing to step onto the field with them. After Saturday's 49–8 semi-final victory over Spring Creek, the Spring Creek coach jogged across the field to thank Coach for not running up the score. And Coach's big challenge this week, beside fighting off the flu, might be convincing his guys that Virgin Valley—a team from down in the desert between Las Vegas and St. George, Utah—stands a chance on Saturday afternoon when the two squads square off on the field turf at Mackey Stadium. They'll be facing a Virgin Valley team whose own commute to the University of Nevada stadium will include a couple of buses and an airplane ride, which all seems like a long way to travel to play an "unbeatable" team. But there's no convincing Coach of this. He knows that good teams get beat by lesser opponents because they get complacent and cocky, instead of confident, whereas the lesser team is still hungry and preparing to win, and he says, "We got to work to combat that."

And then there's this sickness thing, which is really threatening to bring Manogue to its knees. But it's not the kids who are sick right now that Coach is worried about. It's the kids who'll be sick on Friday and Saturday that have him studying his whiteboard depth chart that isn't very deep. "If they're getting sick on Saturday or getting over getting sick on Saturday, that's okay," he says. "But if they're right in the middle of it, that's trouble."

Not that Coach hasn't faced this kind of trouble before, or faced the kind of competition the Miners will be going up against next year, when they make the leap to the large-school level. He spent most of his thirty-five years in education across town at Wooster High, a public school where the stadium is named for him, and where his Colts teams won seven state titles during his twenty-three-year tenure as head coach. After his four boys went through the program, Coach retired from football to become the school's discipline principal. He thought he was finished with high school sports.

But then the folks from Manogue called to offer him their athletic director and head football coach positions, two jobs that the fifty-year-old school normally filled with much younger men who got chased off by people who used the private school tuition they were paying as an excuse to treat the coach like a marionette. This wasn't a deterrent for Coach, who says, "Some 'a these people can be like wolves or vultures. They don't trust you because they're involved with Little League and some of these younger sports enterprises, and that's great because it's volunteerism. But then they think this makes them experts, and a lot of these young coaches get eaten alive listenin' to 'em and tryin' to do what they want 'em to do." Nor was he bothered too much by his outsider's view of Bishop Manogue as a "country club" kind of school. "I figured they'd have a lot of rich kids here," he says. "But they're still kids."

Most of all, he missed coaching football more than he ever thought he could miss it. So he and his wife had themselves a talk and decided, "Why not?" and then he got on the phone to make the four calls that would be the absolute deciding factor as to whether or not he'd take the job and get back into the game. Coach got a hold of Jack Brewer, Mike Jones, Mark Smith, and Casey Stevens—his staff from Wooster that called it quits when he did—and said, "What do you think?" and everyone agreed that, after a few years away from the game, it was time to get back into it. So, Coach signed on in June 2001, and he brought his staff with him, and what they found was a program in disarray. "The weight room was a mess and there were no storage cabinets and the field needed to be revitalized," says Coach. But even so, he still had it in his mind that Manogue was a playground for the rich. "I envisioned this place as a country club," he says, "with a parking lot full of Mercedes." Then, on the first early morning that he pulled up to the building, there was a flatbed truck parked in the lot and a guy out there in a flannel shirt and jeans and work boots with cement stains all over him, and he walked up to Coach to introduce himself, saying, "I'm Mike Poindexter, the Booster Club President." This brightened Coach right up, and all of a sudden he was saying, "This is my kind a place." And then he said, "Now let's get to work." They painted the weight room and picked up the trash and regrew the field and got a guy to build some cabinets, and they started the morning athletic period, and then they lost three of their first four games. But after that third loss, they went on a winning streak that took them to the state semi-finals where they narrowly lost to Moapa Valley, a team that had mopped up the field with the Miners early in the season. Two years later, they have yet to lose again. This year's seniors, Farney and Peregrin and company, had trouble winning a game their freshman season, but those same teams that dominated them three years ago have stepped onto the field for the past two years with hardly a prayer to stay on it with these Manogue steamrollers.

So what's the secret? Coach attributes it to the experience of his coaching staff and to the kids' ability to respond to a level of preparation and intensity and toughness previously absent in the program.

One thing that Coach can't stand is "chalkers," or offensive backs that run for the sidelines to avoid contact. Coach says, "When we first got here, we had to line the offense up facin' the trees to get 'em to run to the goal line." Now guys like Kenny Viser and Matt Virden avoid heading for the sideline at nearly all costs, preferring instead to bull-charge their way up the field, often leaving a whitewash of overmatched defenders in their wake. But on those rare occasions when one of his guys starts to move more laterally than forward, Coach finds himself hoping for a collision before his ball carrier can reach the safety of the sideline. "It's good when the opposition takes a hard shot at a chalker," says Coach. "Because that means I don't have to."

One kid that Coach doesn't have to worry about running for cover is Farney, and a half-hour after roll call, here he comes walking into the athletic office with his dark hair covered by a knit cap and his right hand wrapped in a splint and an Ace bandage. Not only is he laid a little low by the flu, but he also thinks he might have cracked a finger in Saturday's Spring Creek win. "Hey, Farney," says Coach. "You gonna be ready for us this week?"

Farney has his bad hand raised above his shoulder to keep his finger from filling up with blood and he says with a grin, "I'll be ready, Coach."

Even though neither the bad finger nor the bad stomach stands a chance of keeping him out of this Saturday's game, Coach still gets on the phone with his "guys" across the street at the UNR sports clinic to have a look at the hand, just in case, and, as he replaces the receiver in its cradle, he says, "Farney, you get over there about ten, and we'll get this straightened out."

"Okay, Coach," says Farney, as he departs the office to join his teammates.

After he leaves, Coach says, "Farney's so tough, he don't even know when he's injured."

Toughness goes a long way with Coach, and he thinks that it might be the main thing Manogue has to pay attention to in their preparation for Virgin Valley. "They're wrestlers," Coach tells his team during a post-practice film session. "They don't sit around and watch TV during the winter. They wrestle." And this is what Coach thinks will keep the Bulldogs in the game on Saturday, as well as provide a physical challenge for his players who have gone all season without having anyone stand up to them to say, "Come on, let's see what you got." Talent and size-wise, Manogue has got a lot, so much that Virgin Valley can't even begin to match up with the Miners, but, says Coach, "They're relentless. They're gonna be like playin' against a bunch a Farneys." And this is the angle he takes with his team all week. "These guys are Vegas guys," he says of the Bulldogs. "They're fast and they're talkers, and they're gonna want to run outside on you." But then he'll come right back with, "They're better than any other team we've played ... and you know why? 'Cause they play harder."

And all week, Coach takes the time with individual players to make certain that they're sure that Saturday will be no walkover. As they sit in the locker room and watch tape of a Virgin Valley wide receiver leveling a Moapa defensive end on a blindside crack-back block, Coach calls out to one of his own defensive ends from his front row swivel chair, "Tyler Higgins. Do you realize you can go out of that stadium in an ambulance?" When the Bulldogs' No. 20 moves along the line of scrimmage from his quarterback position before pitching to his trailing back in one of the option plays that make up a good chunk of Virgin Valley's offense, Coach says to Matt Virden, "I want you drivin' your forearm straight through his throat ever' chance you get. We'll see how tough he is." Then he adds, "Hell, he might kick your ass." When lanky John Hardwick, a swimmer who everyone calls "Doctor Death" because of his probable future in the medical profession, walks into Coach's office before Tuesday's practice, Coach asks of the Bulldogs' same No. 20, "Can you handle him, Doctor?"

The Doctor says, "I'll handle him, Coach."

When linebacker Jacob Stever drops a sure interception against Manogue's scout team version of the Virgin Valley offense, Coach says, "The headlines Sunday'll read, 'Stever Drops INT For TD.'"

Practice is hard this week, because Coach doesn't like to leave anything to chance—even as dominant as his team is, and maybe it's part of why they're as dominant as they are—and everyone watches a lot of film. On Monday morning, after they've finished their weight room workout, every kid on the team who has a chance of seeing the field on Saturday in a "meaningful" situation is issued a Virgin Valley scout tape. Coach yells out into the weight room, "We got linemen gettin' their tapes. You skill guys make sure you get yours, too."

"Why does he have to say it like that?" mutters Bobby Lepori. "'Linemen got their tapes.' I'm a skill guy. I've got skills."

The main skill Coach wants Lepori and his teammates to exercise with these videos is their ability to watch and chart and grade the guy they'll be going up against in Saturday's game. In other

269

words, they need to concentrate on what he's doing and how he's doing it, and to think about how they will go about getting the best of him. And they need to be able to relay this information and their own take on it back to Coach so he can "cross-check" his read of the game. "I want 'em to learn how to watch film," says Coach.

But they're not on their own in this endeavor. Coach Smith, who has been with Coach since 1989, comes in from his elementary school P.E. job in the early afternoons to sit with Peregrin and his corps of receivers in the coaches' meeting room, breaking down endless tapes on pass coverage, and talking about the formations and plays and routes that can beat them. "Early on, we run right at 'em, and we get their alignments, and then we go from there," says "Smitty" as he watches the way Virgin Valley creeps up to the line against Moapa. And then he says to Nathan Mendiola and Daniel Flocchini, his senior starters, "This is our last chance, our last time around the merry-go-round. Let's make it count. Run every route as if you're catching a TD pass." Then he leans back against the hard plastic of his office chair and really looks at these two kids who are a big part of this unstoppable Manogue machine, on offense as well as in the defensive backfield, and he says, "I don't really give a rat's ass how fast they are, or how tough, or whatever. We'll beat 'em by preparation; beat 'em by coaching. We're better than those guys are. I don't want you guys getting big heads ... but it's true."

This same feeling of barely contained confidence pervades the big group film sessions that go on every night in the locker room after practice. The kids strip out of their pads and find a seat, and the coaches settle in next to their position players, or, in Coach's case, front and center as the video starts to flicker on the whitewashed wall, so he can see exactly what's going on, and so he can say things like, "You're gettin' a lot of ink now: 'Greatest this' ... 'Greatest that.' But all that garbage don't mean nothin'. None 'a this ink stuff means anything unless you do your job. Then you can strut your stuff for a year."

The other coaches get their shots in as well. Coach Stevens, who started with Coach at Wooster back in 1978, watches one of Virgin Valley's defensive speedsters intercept a Moapa pass and motor with it toward the end zone, and he says, "It's plays like that that can cost you a championship, men."

Coach Jones is intently watching the Bulldogs' line-play, and he thinks he may have found something that could really hurt them. Jones was the head coach at Reno High until 1993 when he finally threw up his hands at his team's inability to beat Wooster. He kept his teaching job there, but quit his football position to work with Coach's tackles and ends, and the big thing he's noticing about the Virgin Valley defense is that their tackles "come hard" across the line at the snap of the ball. He thinks the way to counteract this ambitious defensive push is with "Brown Pro Right Dive 2," a quick-hitting off-tackle play that should be a "home run" because the Bulldog front line is so focused on getting off the ball that they won't have time to react to a play where the only backfield chica-nery involves the quarterback handing the ball off with flash-fire speed and the running back scampering across the line of scrim-mage with that same sense of urgency.

Later in the week, Jones strolls through the pre-practice stretch-ing lines until he stops in front of Kyle Martinmaas, who is reclined on the fading yellow grass in a less than classic "hurdler's stretch."

"Okay, Mr. Moss," says Jones. "Tell me one thing you learned in school today, one fact ... not a thought, because your thoughts are out there in the clouds."

There is no response from Moss, who is suffering from the strain of this stretch that was originally designed for liquid-limbed sprint champions, not stiff-jointed, thick-waisted fifteen-year-old backup offensive linemen.

But Jones is undeterred by Moss's agony, and he says, "All right, tell me how many degrees in a right angle."

Moss looks up from his uncomfortable pose and gasps out, "Ninety, Coach."

"That's right," says Jones merrily. "You did learn something." Then he strolls next door to cast his wide shadow over freshman Charlie Lepori, who shares Moss's discomfort and also the responsibility of being a future anchor of the Miners' offensive line. "How about you?" Jones queries. "What'd you learn today?"

"I learned about Shakespeare, Coach," says Charlie.

"Well that's good," says Jones. "Shakespeare would inspire your ass. He was one helluva dude."

These young kids like Moss and Charlie moved up to spend time with the varsity once their Frosh and JV seasons concluded, and, even as the coaches prepare their team for Saturday's match-up with Virgin Valley, they take time with these freshmen and sophomores who'll be helping to fill the shoes of this year's strong senior class next year against the much stiffer 4A competition, and this is something that has Coach nervous already.

During Monday's punt team practice, Coach sidles up to Chris Benvin on the sidelines and says, "When's the last time you hit someone?" And then, before the startled JVer has a chance to respond, Coach says to the underclassmen that are clumped around him, "Who here likes to hit?" When a few of these youngsters tentatively raise their hands, and still before Benvin can muster a response, Coach says, "Come on down here. Let's get some hitting in … whoever wants to play football." Then he leads a platoon of future Miner stalwarts in a slow trot down to the end zone, where he lines Benvin up on one side and lines the rest of the crew up facing him so the big sophomore can practice his drive-blocking technique, and, says Coach, "So we can see who has some toughness." As Benvin comes to life, and the two sides repeatedly smack into each other, Coach growls, "Drive! Drive! Drive! Drive!" in the clipped cadence that he says is a residual effect of his forty-years-ago Navy service.

On Wednesday morning, Coach walks upstairs from his office to the Manogue gymnasium to scan the floor that is strewn with football players going through what they call "The Torture Chamber" of their weekly Pilates training. The groans and complaints that emit from the islands of mats scattered across the hardwood don't bother Coach at all. In fact, he finds them encouraging and says, "That's how I know it's good for them. If they don't like it, then it's doing something for 'em." But what does bother him is that Trevor Richardson, his hefty offensive tackle, is absent. "He was wheezin' on me yesterday," Coach says. "If I lose any of my linemen, we're dead," says Coach. "The second guys aren't near what the first guys are. As a group, they're all right … but individually …" and here Coach does a head-shake/eye-squint/grin-grimace that translates into, "You know what I mean."

But Coach doesn't have long to contemplate life with a fractured front line because, as the rows of boys lift up into the neck-bridge portion of this morning's program, Trevor comes scuttling through the door and up to his relieved coach to explain that his car broke down. It's a 1988 Oldsmobile that his mom bought for him to get back and forth to school, and this isn't the first time he's had trouble with it. Trevor spends several minutes looking for a stray exercise mat. When he realizes they're all taken, he shrugs his ample shoulders and plops directly down onto the hardwood floor to join in with the neck-bridges and Coach calls out, "There's so much padding on that ass, the mat's no more than supplemental," and then heaves a relieved sigh as he heads back toward the stairwell.

It is down that stairwell and along a concrete corridor that leads to the stuffy locker room where the Miners devote so many after-practice evenings to watching film. And while Coach offers up his best critiques and observations, it is Coach Brewer who might watch more film than anyone.

Coach Brewer teaches history over at Wooster, where he started with Coach in 1983, and he drives "down the hill" every day from his home up in Truckee, on the California side of the border. On mornings when it's below freezing in Reno, it can very well be below zero at Brewer's house when he starts up the Toyota RAV to begin his commute. So what better way for him to spend a chilly Sierra Nevada evening at home than to fire up the VCR and watch hour upon hour of high school football? And those hours pay big dividends when the Miners take the field on Saturday afternoons, and when they slouch in their locker room seats on a Friday evening to study film with Brewer at the helm.

A Virgin Valley wideout makes a big catch for a big gain, and Brewer says, "When we see that, we'll just collide the receiver and make him pay." A fullback busts through the line of scrimmage to run roughshod into the Moapa secondary, and Brewer says, "We step up tough on the first back who's a wrestler, and there's no running lane there." Then it's a Virgin Valley punt. Brewer watches the "up-back" who stands as the last line of defense between the punter and the punt blockers and says, "Send his ass into the punter."

Then Coach Stevens breaks into the middle of this session when the Bulldogs' speedy No. 22 flashes across the screen with the football cradled in his arms as he tries to turn the corner along the sideline. "He's gonna run for the chalk every time," says Stevens. "If he runs up the middle, we oughtta stop the game and give him the game ball." And Coach thinks the same of some of the Bulldogs' other players. "A lot of these guys are good football players who'll give ya a shot when you're not lookin'. They will come into piles and hit you late. They're not afraid to cheap-shot ya. You see that No. 68?" he says of a big offensive lineman who'll be playing over Farney. "You gotta watch out for him. They're wrestlers. They're gonna do a takedown on ya."

As Coach talks, and as this final all-team film session draws to a close, Brewer ejects the Moapa tape from the machine and replaces it with a Virgin Valley game against Truckee, his hometown team. When he presses "Play," the Bulldogs are on defense, and the Truckee fullback slams into the line of scrimmage behind his mountain of blockers who mow over the defensive front. Brewer calls for the lights, and, as they flicker on, and as this roomful of coaches and kids shake their heads and blink their eyes in the electric glare, he says, "We want to end it on that one, with all those Virgin Valley guys on their backs, because that's where I want you to put them on Saturday." Brewer leans back against the wall, and Coach raises himself up from his chair to turn and address the team. The first thing he says is: "Remember, you're eatin' pizza for dinner tonight. Lotsa carbs." And this evening after he says, "Make sure you're eatin' that pizza," he calls out, "Mossy, you workin' tonight?"

Brandon Martinmaas—another of his imposing senior linemen, a part-time Godfather's deliveryman, and Kyle's older brother—answers, "Yes, Coach."

Coach says to his team, "All right, you call up Mossy. Maybe he can get you a deal."

Whether or not they need the deal, the Miners are going to need those carbs and all the energy that comes with them because the temperature has been plummeting all week, and it's supposed to go down even more on Saturday. "Nothin' cotton tomorrow," says Coach as he stands in front of the video cart and continues to address the team, "because it'll be cold. If you're too cold to play, then you aren't worth nothin' to nobody. You're burnin' more BTUs when it's cold. Your stupidity or lack of discipline will get your ass beat. Do what you're told. We ain't learned a lot from 248 victories, but we remember every loss, and we learned somethin' from all of 'em. When the game is over, we don't have no Gatorade or throwin' up No. 1 signs or makin' horses' asses of ourselves. We'll be tickled that we won, but we don't want to make too big a deal of it. We're supposed to win. I can't find anyone to make us underdogs. We're too good. I don't need you to be Superman. I need you to play smart. I need you to play disciplined. I need you to play like a team."

Coach takes a slow look around the quiet locker room and it's the last time they'll be in here together to watch film, just like today was the last time on their stadium field together because next year Bishop Manogue High School is picking up stakes and moving across town to their new $34 million facility where they'll have a new locker room and a new field turf stadium to host all of those 4A opponents. "Awright, men," Coach says. "Hay's in the barn. Anybody got any questions?" The kids start to fidget in their seats, and he says, "Okay then, one more thing—Don't carry Coach Jones off the field. We don't need anyone getting hurt after the game."

Besides the flu bug, and Farney's finger, and a Virgin Valley team full of tough-guy wrestlers, Coach is also worried that this week might turn into something like last week, when Spring Creek stacked the line of scrimmage to try and stifle the Miners' running game, and Smitty got to start calling pass plays that resulted in ten first half completions in eleven attempts, and four touchdown throws for Peregrin and his gang of receivers. "If I let Smitty run all the passes he wants to run," says Coach, "there'd be no time to run my 'powers' and 'wedges.'"

And, even though Smitty might throw the ball on every play if given the opportunity, he defers to Coach by saying, "The way this game is, it's 'pound ... pound ... pound ...' Then we'll throw for a flurry. Then, pound again. That's how it's gonna be."

When the team meets for their Saturday morning meal in a back banquet room at the "Silver and Gold" casino, Smitty has a clipboard of notes that is thin and manageable, which allows Coach to eat his French toast and eggs in relative peace. As Jones settles in to join them, kids stream by the coaches' table to say "Good morning" on their way to the buffet line. The Doctor stops by, and he says he's been worrying about how Virgin Valley might start the game.

Jones takes a bite of eggs and says, "Doctor, your analytical mind is just playing havoc with your poor soul."

Then Manny McElroy approaches the table. He's healthy again and ready to insert the spiral into the long snap. He's been watching film at home and is concerned that the Bulldogs might try something weird, like maybe a "Statue of Liberty"–type play. "You're on top of it, Manny," says Coach. "It's good for you to stay home. You haven't been here for a couple'a days and it's kept you from being around the resta this bunch and gettin' screwed up. Maybe some'a these guys would be all right if they tried that approach."

Then the boys are finishing up their meals and saying "Thanks" and drifting out the door to meet back up over at school where they'll start getting ready. Coach drinks his coffee and watches them move toward the door and he talks a little about what kind of crowd there might be at UNR's big stadium. The local ESPN station is broadcasting the game and the Catholic network will have a crew there as well. "This game's gonna be aired in Rome," Coach says, and he pushes away from the table and heads out toward the glass double-door.

If they are listening in Rome, they get to hear four full quarters of the closest game the Miners have had to play in two years, because, true to Coach's prediction, Virgin Valley refuses to give up. The Bulldogs come out for pre-game warm-ups in the sub-freezing weather, and they look like a miniature version of the New York Jets, as they shout and sprint and slap five, and do what appears to be everything they can to psyche themselves up to play Manogue. "Well," says Jones, "they're tryin' to get themselves ready."

Coach says, "We'll let them do the poppin' off. We'll do the hittin'." But the Bulldogs dispel any thoughts that all of this enthusiasm might wane once the game begins because they take everything the bigger and stronger Miners have to give, and they keep coming back for more. As Manogue prepares to exit the locker room for the opening kickoff, Coach says, "Don't do anything stupid that's gonna hurt our team. We're gonna see how tough these guys are."

Then the Miners find out how tough the Bulldogs are, which is plenty. When they come back into the halftime locker room, Manogue is up 21–12, all of their starters are still playing, and Coach says to his team, "We're in a football game," which seems for this squad to be more exciting than unnerving after their twenty-two–game streak of blowout victories. Then they head out into the cold for the third quarter and Manny McElroy gets welcomed back from his illness with the bone-rattling crack-back block that the coaches had warned about all week, and he staggers to the sideline with not too much idea of where he is. Virgin Valley's No. 20 takes shot after shot at his quarterback position, and then he does double-duty at defensive end, where the Miners run at him unrepentantly. "Every time we hit him on defense," says Coach, "it's like an offensive sack."

As late as the fourth quarter, the coaches are having to talk strategy on the sideline, with their team still up by only a couple of touchdowns.

"Maybe we ought to kick a field goal," Smitty says, as Manogue faces a fourth down call deep in Bulldog territory.

"We ain't kickin'," says Coach. "Kick a field goal, get it blocked, they pick it up and score … then we're in trouble." So they run the ball into the middle of the line instead, which keeps the clock going, and Manogue secures its second straight 3A title.

The Miners are happy, but also relieved, and there is no Gatorade and no throwing up No. 1 signs; just players and parents and friends milling around on the Mackey Stadium turf, snapping a few pictures and offering up a hug here and there.

Then it's back to school and one last time in the locker room. For the seniors, this is it, and Coach says, "I'm gonna miss the hell outta you guys," before he walks out the door and up the hallway to wait for them and their equipment. One by one, the kids file up the long hall to turn in their gear. There's Lepori, and Virden, and Peregrin, and Trevor Richardson, all with an armload of equipment. They shake Coaches hand and thank him, and they all give him a look that asks, "What do we do now?"

# Week Seventeen—Accept Excellence

## Mountain View High School Toros: Mesa, Arizona

**M**OUNTAIN VIEW HIGH School is the kind of place where everything is in place. The sidewalks are swept, the lawns are fresh-cut, and the shirts are tucked in. There are no freshmen here; they're all still over at Stapley and Poston, the junior high feeder schools. So the sophomores, the juniors, and the seniors—all three thousand of them—have the run of things. With its neat appearance and well-behaved students, the high school looks like a really nice state university, which is where most of these kids are headed after graduation and after their Mormon Church Missions. It is these Church Missions that they talk about more than anything else—certainly more than their Toro varsity football team that is riding a twenty-six–game winning streak, is ranked thirteenth in the latest *USA Today* national newspaper poll, and is currently preparing for a match-up with Peoria High that will send the winner to play for the 2003 state title.

All of this athletic success is expected. It is the Word of God and the Word of the Church that need to be worked at and trumpeted. So, when Max Hall, the All-State senior quarterback, reclines on a padded bench in the training room, while head trainer Matt Blackburn doctors his wobbly knee and says that he'll be departing Arizona State after his first scholarship year to fulfill his two-year Mission commitment before returning to college and to the football field, you believe him.

Coach Tom Joseph is on a mission of sorts himself, right here at Mountain View High School. He came aboard last year, intent on installing his own score-in-a-flurry offense at a place that was already winning plenty of games. He thought it'd be fun for the Toros to try something new. And that might be his greatest aim with these kids—to help them have some fun out on the football field. With a lot of programs, when a new coach comes in his primary job is to right the ship. But this ship was never listing. The new guy is supposed to clean house and lay down the rules, teach his team about the values of hard work and discipline, and set a stalwart example of consistency and accountability. But all of these things were already ingrained in these varsity Toros long ago.

So, what is there for Coach to do besides live up to this long-established tradition of excellence? As he stands on the thick grass of the practice field underneath the Arizona sun, he watches his guys in their perfectly aligned calisthenics formation, calling out numbers and stretches and cadences. Coach shakes his head and says, "I got a lot of good material that's going to waste. I got to get these guys to lighten up."

And he is trying to do just that. When reserve quarterback Tyler Mack executes a near-textbook "draw" play, Coach says, "You're gonna get arrested for impersonating an athlete." Then Max Hall steps up to the line of scrimmage to test out the new leg brace that he and Toro-backers everywhere are hoping will carry him through just two more weeks. The knee holds up, at least on this play, and Max leads his first-team offense through a repetition of "Z Screen," where he drifts far back in the pocket, his receivers fly at top speed down the field, a couple of his linemen "pull" to form a wedge, and the "Z"-back settles in behind them to catch the soft toss from Max and then heads upfield with the two linemen accompanying him as zealous chaperones.

The Z Screen comes off flawlessly, just like so many of their other plays do—in practice and in games—and Max contributes the added touch of lingering in the pocket for just that extra split-second to gaze downfield at his decoy receivers, as the scout team defensive linemen make their charge that is cut short when Max flips the ball to his Z-back. Coach notices this added bit of theater, and as Max walks gingerly back to the huddle, Coach says, "That was good. I liked how you looked him off. That was almost excellent."

But it would be really excellent, and really fun, if the Toros can pull off the "Z Reverse Pass" that they plan to use to start the game on Friday night. This play involves a quarterback hand-off to the halfback, who hands the ball to the Z-back on an around-the-end reverse, who pitches it back to the quarterback, who heaves it downfield to the "X" receiver, who has busied himself with a fake crack-back block before he headed toward the end zone. Coach has no doubt that the "Xs and Os" execution of the play will come off swimmingly because every day when he sits down to watch defensive film of the Peoria Panthers he sees a team that is overloaded with big, fast athletes but lacks the self-discipline that makes his own squad so difficult to beat. Coach isn't planning to begin the game with the Z Reverse Pass so much to catch the Panthers "off-guard" or to "gain an edge" as he is for the entertainment value and just to see what happens.

It's a given that the Toros will fool Peoria silly with their Z Reverse Pass; that the entirety of the Panther defense will react to the backfield assortment of hand-offs and fakes and pitches like a spider to a fly while the X receiver offers up his mimed crack-back block and then slips behind the thundering horde on a lone race toward the end zone that awaits only the express-delivered pass from Max Hall. This is the only moment that Coach is even beginning to sweat because when they tried this bit of razzle-dazzle a couple of weeks ago, a wide-open Brendan McGowan dropped the ball to the chagrin of a stadium full of Toro fans. That's why, all week, when they line up to practice their game-opener, Coach calls out to Brendan, "You'd better catch this. If you drop it, you'll never live it down." And that's why, all week, this play culminates with the X-man cradling the football as if someone had just tossed him a Fabergé egg.

The Toros are a small and unassuming bunch of kids, the biggest player being senior offensive tackle Devin Clark at about 280 pounds. But when the team lines up for any kind of group drill out at practice, or when they join together for something like this mid-day film session, Devin looms over the rest of the squad. So it's strange to watch the mite-sized Toros watch their semi-final foe on film as if they were seeing their own younger brothers in a Pop Warner scrimmage. Peoria is big and imposing, and yet all Coach and his band of achievers can talk about is how vulnerable the Panther defense is to the Toro offensive playbook. "Peoria doesn't read. They react," says Coach. "They have good athletes, but they're not very disciplined at all, are they? Look at 15." The Panthers' No. 15 has a habit of timing the snap of the ball and flying across the line of scrimmage in a wildly flailing beeline toward the opposing team's quarterback. This is an encouraging sight for Coach and his offensive players because it means that, with a lot of their misdirection plays, No. 15 will take himself out of the play, and the Toro offensive line won't have to block him. "15 isn't a team guy," continues Coach. "He wants to make the big hit, the big play.

He's not looking to play his position. He's interested in being an individual and standing out."

This idea of "being an individual and standing out" isn't a concept that the varsity Toros can easily grasp because everything they do is with an eye on the team. Take their game uniforms, for example. They wear the same style of jersey and pants and unadorned red helmets and high white socks and low black shoes that the first Mountain View varsity squad wore back in 1978. "When I came in last year," says Coach, "I suggested maybe an updated look and the answer was a polite 'No.' So, I guess this is just the way our uniforms are gonna be." No one wears tape or towels or gloves or wristbands or anything else that might distract from the plain uniform, unless it's a medical necessity. So when they march through the stadium gates in their wide, arm-locked, blue and red lines, they really do look like a band of brothers.

Despite their uniform appearance, this team is made up of individuals, the guys underneath the jerseys. There are guys like Max Germaine, who got the rare opportunity to wear some extra padding and tape and gloves early this season when he played on the defensive line with two broken hands. Once the hands healed up enough, he was moved back to his regular linebacker position, which wasn't always his position. Last year, Max played a lot of quarterback minutes in a lot of games during a season where the Toros set state records for most offensive points scored (602) and fewest defensive points allowed (34), but these minutes came in the second half of games—like the state title affair, where Mountain View beat Ironwood 50–8—that were over almost before they even got underway. So, after the season, he sat down with his coaches to figure out a plan where he could contribute more, and that plan involved him giving up his quarterback responsibilities and moving to defense.

"He just wants to help the team," says line coach Jerry Wheeler. "He'll do anything."

Max echoes that sentiment in a mid-week interview with *East Valley Tribune* reporter Les Willsey. The sportswriter asks, "Why the switch?"

Max straightens himself up in his seat, and he says, "I went to Coach and told him, 'I want to help the team, and I don't care how—I just want to win."

Max isn't alone in his single-minded sense of purpose. On Tuesday afternoon, Eric Sponseller, the Toro who comes closest in size to big Devin, his fellow offensive tackle, watches while his teammates go through their compulsory stretches and sprints. Eric chose not to stay home with the case of food poisoning that landed him on the sidelines. Instead, he's here at practice, watching and learning as he fights off the nausea and stomach cramps. But he is also trying, with his weakened voice, to call out encouragements and admonishments. "Atta boy," he says, and, "That's the way to step," and, "C'mon, boys. Let's pick it up."

As the days move toward their semi-final showdown, the Toros are focused on the upcoming game. Whereas Monday is dedicated to offensive practice and study of Peoria's defense in the lunchtime film session, Tuesday is given over mainly to Mountain View's defensive preparation. At 11:20, as the roomful of players digs into their first round of sandwiches and pizza, defensive coordinator Don Kramer pushes the video cart along the Annex hallway and through the meeting room door in the same unhurried fashion that he might wheel a shopping cart down the produce aisle at the local Basha's Supermarket. After he plugs in the machine, turns off the lights, and settles into his seat next to the projector, Coach Kramer says, "What is the importance of this game?" in his gravelly voice that has been a part of this program even longer than Wheeler's clipped cadence.

The team responds through mouthfuls of food, "It takes us to 'The Big House.'"

Kramer presses "Play" and images of the Peoria team begin to flicker across the big screen, and he says, "That's right, The Big House. But we got to beat the Panthers to get there."

Then, as they watch the fast-backs scamper around behind a Peoria offensive line that outweighs the Toro defensive front by an average of seventy pounds per man, Kramer explains this week's basic game plan for stopping the big, talented Panther team. He begins today's late-morning lesson by asking, "If you were Peoria, where would you try and run on us?"

The troops respond, "Outside."

"That's right," says Kramer. "No one can run inside us. We squeeze down too hard. People haven't got much outside on us, but they have got some, and so that's where these guys'll probably try and run. So we have to be ready for them."

The room grows silent for a moment as another Panther running play unfolds, where their No. 10, Keegan Herring, works to scoot around the end, and their split receiver tries to crack back inside on a pursuing linebacker. The block is ineffective on this play, and Herring is chased out of bounds, but that doesn't stop anyone in the room from noticing Peoria's assassin-like attempt, and it doesn't keep assistant coach Mark Swartz from calling out into the darkened room, "When he tries to crack like that, use your helmet to hit him in the jaw, and he won't do that again."

Then, on the succeeding play, Herring busts loose on an end run around the other side, and then doesn't slow down until he nears the goal line, so a few of his teammates can catch up and celebrate with him as he prances into the end zone. The camera holds on the play's aftermath long enough to show the yellow flags flying in response to the Panthers' choreographed jubilation, and Coach, from his chair near the back of the room, says, "That's a part of their game. But don't listen to it. Don't let them take you out of what we do. Focus on your job." Then Kramer rewinds the tape so they can figure out exactly what happened. As he continues to press "Rewind" and then "Play," it becomes clear that, beside the split receiver getting in a little more of a block than he had on the previous run, the pulling guard was able to clear the line and get around the corner to spring Herring on his gallop to the end zone. Coach squints around the room for McKay Carling, the Toros' weak-side defensive end, and he calls out, "Did you see the weak effort against that? When the guard pulls, knock his ass down, step over the top of him, and make a play. Don't let him block anyone else. Knock his ass down."

This invitation to wreak some havoc should be a welcome one for McKay. Even though he's already got one championship under his belt, he would like nothing more than to win it again in this, his senior year, in the same fashion that his three older brothers concluded their high school careers. But as much as he is into the tradition and work ethic of being a Toro, he is also considered to be something of a rebel on the squad, where his unshorn blonde hair and his white shoes that he has haphazardly streaked with shoeblack are enough to make him stand out. So, on Tuesday afternoon, as Eric huddles miserably underneath his hooded sweatshirt and the rest of the team takes its warm-up lap around the far goal post, it is not out of character for McKay to stumble out of the athletic building, still trying to tie his shoes and latch up his shoulder pads. He lopes onto the stadium grass, where Coach is watching McKay's practice-mates make their way toward the goal post. The team's job is to jog around it before heading back, and Coach has made the bold prediction that someone in that mass of battle-disciplined Toros will cut his lap short. But, while McKay finishes strapping into his gear, the tightly packed platoon of players circles the upright beam in true Mountain View solidarity, which causes Coach to say, "I hate it when they do the right thing."

There is still hope in the form of Spencer Perkinson, the senior strong safety, who made it onto the field only moments before McKay, and who, trailing in the distant wake of the pack, slows his trot to a walk before he slaps the goal post pad, and then about-faces to head for home. Coach gleefully shoves his whistle between his lips to give it a sharp trill, and then he calls out, "Another time around … courtesy of No. 11!"

By this time, McKay has secured his gear, and, as he begins his own jog up the field, he does so with the sense that this is his lucky day. "Thanks, Coach," he says, "for calling that before I started my lap."

But Coach replies, "No, you got two, too. You're late. And you're with Wheeler tonight when we're done."

Time with Wheeler after practice is less a punishment than it is a reminder that the team is what's important here, not one player's own fluid sense of time and space. And time with Wheeler means being around a man that might best embody what the heart of Toro tradition is all about. He is small and tough and disciplined and humble, and when he speaks in his clipped, direct sentences, it doesn't take too long for these Mountain View players to respond. When he tells McKay and his defensive line-mates, "Hey, you four guys make us better," they are looking for ways to get better. When he says to his gathered offensive linemen, "We gotta be foxy," you can bet that they are scrambling to figure out what "foxy" means and how they can be it. When he calls out, "Tuck in your shirt," to a wayward Toro, the other players standing around this recalcitrant are looking down to make sure their shirts are tucked in as well. He arrives at the Athletic Annex every school morning before sunrise, and what he does in those early morning hours alone in the office is watch film and diagram plays and concoct the blocking schemes that are at the very foundation of the Toros' offensive prowess.

But as much as Coach Wheeler contributes on the game field and in the strategy sessions, it is in the weight room where he is the absolute ruler. He and Coach and Swartz work together to run the Athletic Annex, but it is Wheeler who set up the state-of-the-art weight-training regimen ten years ago that made an already bulletproof team even tougher to beat. The Toros are in the weight room six days a week, conducting workouts that Wheeler programs and monitors with computer software. Next week, they will be "maxing out" on their big lifts in the days leading up to the state final at The Big House, something they do whether or not they are participants in the championship game. It is just part of being a Toro.

"A lot of people want maintenance lifting during the season, with the idea of keeping a certain strength," says Wheeler. "But you don't stay the same. You either get stronger or you get weaker. And we want our guys getting stronger."

A lot of people in the state look at Mountain View's consistent success, and they attribute it to other factor besides "work." Mike Sanchez was one of those people until he moved over from Westwood High at the end of last school year to head up the Toro junior varsity squad. He is standing behind the end zone of the Tuesday afternoon practice, preparing to dive in and start helping out, when Robbie Robinson, one of the junior team coaches, sidles up next to him. The regular season for both of their teams ended several weeks back, and yet here they are, along with their junior varsity and junior team colleagues, all with practice and game responsibilities for these varsity playoff weeks.

But who cares? Out here under these warm November skies, Sanchez is a part of this Toro team, when, just a few months ago, he could only ask questions and offer up speculations about "how they do it." "My job as JV coach is to keep them in the program, prepare them to play varsity, and then win games … in that order," says Sanchez. "The work ethic here is unbelievable, and you have to see the program from the inside to understand its success. From the outside, the view is that it's a rich school and they can afford to get the athletes and have whatever they want. But once you're here, you see that all of the success is based on hard work, and all that hard work pays off on Friday night."

Before Friday night there are a few questions to be answered, including one by Marc LeBaron, the senior running back who has gained at least a hundred yards in each of the team's twelve games this season. After spending last year playing for the junior team, Marc decided he wanted to do more to help the football program, so he signed up to assist Wheeler with his summer youth program, and, in every spare moment that he wasn't helping the Toros of tomorrow learn how to lift weights and run sprints and work hard, he devoted himself to lifting weights, running sprints, and working harder than he ever had in his young life. As a result, he added twenty-five pounds of muscle, dropped a few tenths of a second off his running times, and is now as important as any individual can be to the success of the Toro team. He's important enough that Coach walks up to him toward the end of Tuesday afternoon's practice and asks Marc, "What part of your body hurts the most? And don't say, 'Nothing.'"

Even with his new twenty-five pounds, Marc still looks more like the kid at the end of the bench than the ball carrier at the bottom of a running play pile. Marc grins up at his coach and says, "Nothing, Coach."

At the very least there is his ring finger knuckle that pops out of place and a thigh bruise that makes for an extra-stiff roll out of bed each morning, so Coach peers down at his senior workhorse with his own half-grin until Marc says, "My hand, I guess," to which

Coach's smile widens and he says, "Conversation over. That's all I wanted to know."

The defense is working on shutting down the "Scat" and the "Option," the two plays that make up a good portion of the Panther offense. The Scat involves a deep hand-off to the tailback who, for Peoria, is usually Keegan Herring. His job, once he receives the ball, is to bounce along the line of scrimmage until he finds a hole in the defense to slither through, a ploy that has worked so far this season to the tune of almost 1,600 yards. The Toros plan to stymie these improvisations by squeezing down on every gap along the line of scrimmage so that Herring will end up bouncing until he bounces out of bounds.

Against the option, where almost every other team tells its defensive ends to hit the quarterback and to make him not want to tread that path again, the Toros have a different idea in mind. What they do is called "feathering," where the defensive end forces the quarterback to pitch, and then leaves him with no more than a slap on the shoulder pad, as he "feathers" out to help the cornerback and trailing linebackers corral the pitch-back. "If you tackle the quarterback when he doesn't have the ball," says Coach Kramer, "you're taking yourself out of the play."

As good as McKay and Kyle Kilpatrick, his fellow defensive end, are at this technique, it might be linebacker Bryce Hardy who is the king of the feather, as well as one of the few seniors on the team who sees football in his future beyond next weekend at Sun Devil Stadium. But he is going to have to wait to find out where he might be playing next year, because, at 5'9" and a little over 200 pounds, he plays mostly on guts and instinct, and the big colleges are looking for 6'4" 240-pound guys who play on menacing physical size and frightening speed. "We have to be patient," Coach says to Bryce's father when he calls to check on recruiting progress.

"When some of these schools don't get the big kids that they want, then we'll start to hear from them."

But right now, Bryce isn't waiting to hear from anyone. Instead, he's the one doing the talking. He's standing with Kramer in the Annex hallway to report his findings after spending the evening watching a Peoria game tape. "A couple things I noticed, Coach," says Bryce, "is Herring gets down in a four-point stance when he's gonna get the ball, no matter where he is, in the 'I' or 'split backs,' or whatever. And when he's dropped back in the 'I,' he cheats up a yard or two when he's gonna run the ball inside, and he backs up some when he's gonna sweep or scat or option outside."

"Hey, that's some good studying," says Kramer. "We'll be able to use those things."

And on Friday night, they do use those things and a whole lot more, and what happens to Peoria on this Friday night is not pretty. The Panthers do experience a few instances of sunshine, like the opening kickoff, where Herring takes a hard shot that causes him to fumble the ball into the arms of a startled teammate, who plucks it out of the air and races down to the Toros' forty-yard line; or Herring's punt block late in the game that comes on the heels of his twenty-yard touchdown sprint against the backups' backups, and that raises the Panthers' point total for the game to eight. Between these Panther highlights, it is all Mountain View in an affair that Coach Swartz sums up when he says on the bus ride home, "They were getting their ass driven all over the place. Before, they didn't understand. Now, they understand."

The Toros wake the Panthers up from their dream-sequence opening kickoff good fortune when Bryce Hardy says to the defense that he captains, "First play to last ..." and then they smother Herring for a two-yard loss on his first run. Peoria tries to pass on their next play, and Hardy's linebacker mate, Bryce Bunker, intercepts the ball, which gives Bryce Hardy the chance to level the intended receiver, and every other Toro the chance to turn on their heels and sprint upfield to find someone of their own to level, all while Bryce Bunker negotiates his way down to the Panthers' forty-yard line. Then it's time for Max Hall and the Toro offense to trot onto the field.

This is how the first half goes: the Toro defense flusters the Panther offense, causing fumbles and interceptions, which result, a few plays later, in a Toro touchdown. Things don't work out perfectly though, because Marc LeBaron takes a helmet shot to the hip that ends his string of hundred-yard performances. But he doesn't care. "We're going to The Big House," he says. "And that's all that matters." Behind the chain-link fence, a Peoria fan shakes his head under the brim of his gold Panther ball cap and says to a companion, "They just a well-coached team ... NFL-style."

Maybe not quite NFL-style. There are no end zone dances or Gatorade jugs dumped on Coach's head; just a bunch of kids working hard to be really good at the game of football, and a few middle-aged men who are committed to helping them do just that. But that doesn't mean the Toros aren't entitled to a little fun.

On the school bus ride home, Coach is leaning back in his bench seat. He is feeling pretty good and thinking, not just about Hamilton, the team they will face in the finals, but also about the final moments of tonight's game, before the two teams met at midfield to shake hands and offer up a few hugs and congratulations, and for the Toros to pat Peoria's Herring on the helmet and say, "Good game." Coach's guys were on the sideline with their helmets off and broad smiles across their faces and they were cheering themselves on and calling out, "We're going to The Big House," and Coach is smiling now in the dark of the bus, and he says, "That was good. Our kids got a little excited there for awhile."

# Week Eighteen—Forty-Eight Minutes for Redemption

## Mayfield High School Trojans: Las Cruces, New Mexico

**B**Y **TWO O'CLOCK** on Sunday afternoon, the old coach, Jim Bradley, has parked his black pickup truck in the schoolhouse parking lot and made his way through the locker room door and into the athletic offices. He's already been to church and to eat, and now he's got a Federal Express package in his hand, and he's ready to open it up and have a seat in his office chair to start watching film.

As he stands in the doorway, he glances down at the desk nearest the locker room door where Michael Bradley, his son and defensive coordinator, sits with his green ball cap tilted back on his head. Michael studies the television set, where the La Cueva Bears are running roughshod over one of their New Mexico State 5A opponents. It seems as though each play comes to a crashing conclusion after a hefty La Cueva gain, or, almost as often, a La Cueva touchdown.

He's trying to get a read on the La Cueva offense and their tendencies, but, says Michael, "When you're beating somebody by forty-five points, it's hard to get a read on that." In almost every one of these several game tapes that the Mayfield staff has collected on La Cueva, the spread is at least forty-five points. One of the games that didn't make it to quite that margin was their week four contest, where they beat Coach's Mayfield Trojan team 35–7 up in Albuquerque.

Now, on this Sunday afternoon, besides trying to put together a plan of attack for Saturday's state title game against these La Cueva Bears, Coach and Michael and the rest of the Mayfield staff are wracking their brains to put a positive spin on the early-season thumping they took at the hands of the Bears.

But as the afternoon drags on, this goal proves daunting. "We gotta find something on these guys that'll show us what they're doing," says Michael. "They cannot be perfect." He's watching La Cueva's Friday night semi-final victory over Rio Grande, and the more he watches this and other tapes, the more he convinces himself that there is no rhyme or reason to the Bears' offensive scheme. He looks up from his work to see his younger brother, Gary, walk into the office with a bag of tacos clutched under his arm. Gary works with Coach to run the offense, and, like Michael, he has already spent several morning hours studying La Cueva game tape.

Coach is sitting in his back office listening to his telephone messages, but when he hears his youngest son come in, he pushes himself out of his chair and trudges into the main office with the latest shipment of La Cueva tapes. He rips open the FedEx package with a flourish, pulls out two videocassettes, and then drops the plastic bubble wrap onto the frayed office carpet, where he then performs a slow motion jig that fills the room with popcorn pops and prompts Michael to look up from his yellow pad and say to his father, "That's the liveliest I've seen you in months," which elicits a laugh from the rest of the staff.

But Coach's impromptu dance performance and Michael's commentary also serve as a sobering reminder of the weekday morning earlier in the season when Coach's intestines exploded and he had to undergo emergency surgery to save his life.

# WEEK EIGHTEEN—FORTY-EIGHT MINUTES FOR REDEMPTION

That day was the first day in forty-five years as a football coach that Coach missed practice, and then he missed a lot more practices in the following few weeks, as well as the Trojans' next two games. Gary took over the offensive play-calling in his absence, which prompted Coach to bestow the official title of offensive coordinator on Gary. "It was something I shoulda done a long time ago," says Coach. He did do it in time, though, for his Trojans to beat a previously undefeated Las Cruces High team 30–7, and to spoil a possible championship game match-up between Cruces and La Cueva that sportswriters across the state were already dubbing "The Dream Game." Instead, the two teams wound up on the same side of the playoff bracket, where they faced off two weeks ago in a first round game that La Cueva won 63–0.

Michael presses "Play" once again on the Rio Grande tape, and then starts to chuckle after La Cueva rips off three consecutive big gains against the Raven defense. But then Michael checks himself as a fourth play results in another thick chunk of La Cueva yardage, and he says, "I can't really laugh, because the first time we played them, it looked like we weren't reading anything. It looked like our guys hadn't even been coached to read what they were doing."

"That's true," says offensive line coach Dan Howard. "So we're lucky we've already played them. Everybody who's only played them once has had a big shock."

That big shock comes from a La Cueva team that has an abundance of size and speed and varsity experience not usually seen in the state, combined with a swaggering arrogance that has given the Bears a free-pass license to roll up high double-digit scores against more than a couple of overmatched teams. "Last time we played 'em, they ran over our ass," says Michael. "We didn't see the damn thing coming until it was in our face."

"Well this time around it's gonna be a hard-hitting game," says Gary.

"The first game was hard-hitting," replies Michael. "But we weren't doing any of the hitting."

Gary is still moping over his offensive squad's lackluster showing in Friday night's semi-final victory over Carlsbad, where the Trojan offense managed only twelve points, where the defense had to muster three goal line stands to preserve the win over the Cavemen, and where Coach was prompted to say of the gallant defensive performance, "You gotta have a lousy offense to have such a good defense."

Michael presses "Play" again on the remote control, and the Bears spring into offensive action on the big screen, ripping off another impressive hunk of yardage on a "Buck Sweep" running play. Instead of following the path of the ball, Coach watches the backside action, and he asks Michael to rewind the tape so everyone can see what he sees, which is a hulking offensive tackle going through the motions of his assignment on the play, and then standing back to watch the outcome on the far side of the field. "We don't have any players that play like that," says Coach. "No matter how good those guys are supposed to be, it's still Albuquerque football."

It's been eleven years since an Albuquerque team has won a big-school state title, and the last team that did it was the La Cueva Bears, who beat Coach and a Roswell High School team that he headed up for fifteen years before he retired from teaching and came back home to Las Cruces to take over the Mayfield program. And Las Cruces is home to Coach and his family. He was born here, he grew up here, and he played football for Las Cruces High School, and then at New Mexico State, playing his Saturday afternoon games in an early version of the Aggie Stadium, where his Mayfield boys face off against Las Cruces every year in their traditional rivalry game that can't be held in the school district's own thirteen thousand seat "Field of Dreams" stadium because, for this week at least, it simply isn't big enough.

But the Field of Dreams is where Saturday's state title game will be held, and this is good news for the Trojans because the school district's new sports complex is both within view of Mayfield's football practice fields and, after last year's loss to Las Cruces in the state final, and their nearly as stinging defeat in the same game the year before to Clovis, Coach and his team are looking for any edge they can get in their third straight trip to the championship game. The loss to Clovis in 2001 came by a touchdown, and then last year they went into the final game minus both their starting quarterback and cornerback against a pass-happy Las Cruces team that they had narrowly beaten three weeks before. When the final gun sounded, the Trojans were down by three points.

And so this season has been all about getting back to that championship game and, this time, winning it. They have the banners draped around their meeting room and coaches' room and training room and locker room that read, "Make Up For Two Years!" They made their way past that Las Cruces team in a game where no one gave the Trojans a chance except for the Trojans. They beat Carlsbad in the semi-final game with those measly twelve points and the three gut-wrenching defensive stands, and Carlsbad is the team that everyone around the state, including Coach himself, was picking as the pre-season favorite to win it all.

So now here they are, an undersized, overachieving Mayfield team, preparing once again to play for the title, but this time against a La Cueva juggernaut that has already handed them their lone, lopsided loss of the season. Why then are the coaches down at school on a Sunday, with their cups of coffee and their Taco Bell lunches and their stacks of game tape? Why the full week of before school, at lunch, and after school all-team film sessions in the meeting room? And why the three-and-a-half-hour practices, with the junior varsity on hand to run scouts, and the freshmen with their coaches on the next field over, a full month after their own playing season has concluded? And why do they gather around Howard and defensive coach Henry Carillo in the post-practice weight room?

Howard pulls them in close, and he says, "You gotta prepare. You gotta practice. And on game day, you gotta want it more. Emotion ain't gonna win no damn ball games. Intensity is ... and focusing on that next play. There ain't no room for doubt."

And then Carillo says, "One play at a time. It's just a long ways to go. Don't get caught up in all that other crap. We don't just want this. We deserve it. We live as a team. We live as one big family. Football's life, man ... before, during, and after school."

After all of this, they're still here, this Trojan team in their sweat-soaked shirts and shorts and socks, and with their hair matted down from their helmets. The senior leaders face their team, and Bobbye Matthews says, "Beginning of the season, we said we're ready. Here we are."

James Suter chimes in, saying, "We never turn our backs on our family,"

Jackie Ruiz finishes up with, "If you got to break your leg ... break it! After we leave this place, the only thing that'll bind us together is that ring. Every year, the last two years, we lose one game. Well we already lost our one game!" And this brings the whole crew to its sweat-socked feet, and to the middle of the room, to unleash one unrehearsed and exuberant growl of "Yeaaaahhh!" and this is at last enough to get them out the door and down the hall and through the locker room and out to their cars and trucks that are smeared with green and gold "Good Luck" paint.

And here they are, this team that Coach calls, "A bunch a puny little guys," looking dead up the barrel of Interstate 25 toward Albuquerque at the mighty La Cueva Bears, and saying, without even the hint of a flinch, "Come on down … because we're ready for you."

And maybe, in the end, that's what it's all about. It's not about being big or being fast or being tough or clever or intimidating. It's about being ready. It's about Michael sitting in front of a television set for twelve hours on a Sunday with his yellow legal pad and his pencil and his stack of tapes, and then turning to his fellow defensive coaches to say, "Okay, this is how we're gonna stop them."

It's about an offense that features senior Jackie Ruiz, a kid who played almost exclusively on the scout team last year. Gene Priestly credits that time on the scout team with Ruiz's thousand-yard success on the field this year. Priestley is the Mayfield freshman coach, as well as Coach's best friend since he moved to Las Cruces when he was in the seventh grade and Coach was in the eighth. But right now Priestley is standing back to watch Jackie work with the first-team offense and he says, "Old Jackie, he ran mainly scouts last year and the year before against two tough defenses, and he ran hard every time, searching for a hole, and sometimes he'd get through and sometimes he wouldn't, and every once in a while he'd break one, and those were pretty to watch. It'd bring tears to your eyes watchin' him. But it taught him to run hard and smart, and to be patient and tough." And, as Priestley gazes in his mind back to those autumn afternoons where Jackie would charge into the line to get beaten into the ground and then get up to make them do it again, Coach is watching the Jackie of the present slip up on another pass block and he's watching his senior quarterback, Jeremy Lawson, step right into the collapsing pocket when he should be stepping away from it, and his linemen let up on their own blocks to turn around and see what happened, and the whole thing looks like a mouthful of chewing gum instead of a football play, and Coach says, "Damn! Get your damn mental job going. This is a fifteen round damn boxing championship. And we gotta go fifteen rounds. It ain't no amateur fight. It's the full fifteen rounds. No gloves ... bare knuckles!"

Coach and Priestley are a couple of guys who look like they know what it's like to go through a fifteen round fight. The days when Coach used to tape up his helmet ear holes so he wouldn't have to listen to his own coach are long over. And what about all the baseball they used to play on Sunday afternoons in Las Cruces, and down the river in La Mesa, and over in El Paso and Juarez, and as far away as Alpine, Texas ... the dusty car rides and the dirt fields and the pretty girls and the cold beer, all of it so long ago that it almost could have been someone else.

But it wasn't. It was Coach, who sits in his office chair, talking on the telephone in his windbreaker and comfortable shoes, and saying to Ray Apodaca, another friend of days gone by, "That Priestley, I just can't get through to his damn head. He can't take instructions. He's old like you are, Raymond."

But Priestley doesn't seem too old when he stands in the middle of the athletic office at lunchtime and says, "Vamos a Chope's," and then he zips up his green jacket and walks to his truck to make the drive that he and Coach have made so many times over the years to La Mesa and Chope's Bar, where he can sit at a back table and think about those long ago days of him and Coach and their old car and just enough money for gas and beer, and the feeling that this would last forever.

Coach gets a mid-week call from an Albuquerque reporter who wants to know what people can expect from the atmosphere of Saturday's game. "I don't know what to tell you to 'expect,'" says

Coach. "Naturally, their fans like them and'll be cheering for them, and our fans like us and'll be cheering for us. We'll be in the green and white. They'll be in the blue and silver ... very nice-looking, very regal uniforms." Then Coach leans forward in his chair and takes off his glasses and says, "At least you're calling three or four days before the game so I can talk to you legitimately and with common sense. People get a bad impression of me, a terrible impression, when reporters are asking me after a game, 'Did it hurt you to lose your quarterback going into this game?' What was I supposed to do or say? What would Bobby Knight have done? He'd have punched his lights out, probably."

On Tuesday night, Coach stands up before the Booster Club meeting in the Trojan film room and says, "I don't have too many friends in here. You can always tell a friend—it's someone that, if your fly's open, he'll tell you. Last week, I stood up here with my fly open, and nobody told me." He looks around at all these people who support his team, and he talks about the ten or so seniors who don't see a lot of playing time, and he says, "It hurts. They work as hard as anybody else. But what are you supposed to do? And it's tough on them and tough on their parents, and it's tougher on the parents than it is on them."

Later in the week, Coach picks up his office telephone to call the Carlsbad coach, who was his assistant at Roswell for fourteen years, and whose son, Jason, played in Friday's semi-final game and then waited for twenty-five minutes to say hello to Coach. As he dials, Coach says, "The best thing about old Potter is his wife and kids," and then, when Potter picks up, Coach says the same thing to him, and then he tells Potter about his son. "Yeah," Coach says, and he smiles into the telephone. "He's a great kid. It's a good thing you got a good family, Potter. I don't know what you'd be if you didn't have them."

And it's a good thing for Coach that he's got his family because he very well might be lost without them. There are Michael and Gary out in their office chairs taking notes and diagramming plays and watching film; and there is his other son, Jim, coaching football over in Spring, Texas; and all their wives and kids; and his daughter, Debbie, a P.E. teacher in town, and her daughters, and her husband, Jeff.

And then there's Phyllis, Coach's wife, who leans, exhausted, against the kitchen counter at Michael's country house. It's Saturday night, and the big game is over and decided, and family and friends are everywhere and Phyllis is surrounded by all of them, and she is tired, and this world of hers, this world that she and Coach have made together, is getting close to the end, and she knows it.

Right now, though, Phyllis can gaze out the kitchen window at her husband, who stands just outside the glow of the backyard firelight, and he's got Michael and Gary, each beside him, and all of them wearing their Trojan ball caps and jackets, and they are shoulder to shoulder and drinking beer and listening to the laughter of their friends around the mesquite-wood fire, and this is a good picture for Phyllis to have tonight, and to hold onto for all the days after this one.

But what about everyone else? What do they think about when they think about Coach? Do they think about this night, at the end of this long season, when he talks about the surgery he's got coming up to put his insides back in working order, and when he stands back for a moment from the party to watch his grown sons and their families and all these people who cheered their lungs out today for the Mayfield Trojans?

Maybe they want to remember him in the Saturday pre-game locker room with his team all around him, looking at his kids and saying, "You're gonna go out there and play your ass off, and after it, you're gonna tell somebody you love them. There's no greater thing than to love and be loved. Now let's go play some football."

Or perhaps they think about Coach on the spray-painted-green stadium field, caged in by TV cameras, with tape recorders shoved in his face, and all wanting to know, "What happened? Why this third straight title game loss?"

Coach stands there, engulfed by it all, almost lost in his green and gold windbreaker, and all he can think is, "Maybe forty-eight minutes was too much." Because Mayfield owned the first half, with Gary and Coach's offense coming to life to score three touchdowns, and Jackie running the ball like no one had run on the Bears all season, and Michael's runty defense standing up to La Cueva.

In the halftime locker room, Michael said, "Don't even dream about winning the state championship. Don't even think about it. Think about the next play."

Then Coach said, "Let's finish it," and the Trojans stormed back onto the field, and their packed stands were rocking and the kettle-drums that lined the stadium track were bumping and those faithful Mayfield students were screaming in their seats, and this is when that scary La Cueva giant shook itself awake. With time running out, another one of those Mayfield goal line stands was not enough to keep the La Cueva kicker from trotting onto the field to knock through a chip-shot field goal that won the game.

Or maybe they should think of him in that after-game locker room, after this dead-quiet team, in their game pants and cleats and undershirts, takes a knee around Coach, and he's on a knee too, and he says, "You guys played your ass off … you played your ass off. About a hundred and twenty plays in the game. It come down to one or two. You start playin' football, you take a risk of gettin' your heart broke."

But there's also this picture, a couple of hours before the game, with the tailgaters still out in the parking lot, making noise and roasting carne asada on their charcoal grills, and with the Field of Dreams mostly empty, and the players in the locker room strapping into their pads, and in the training room with Doc, getting tape for their ankles and wrists. Coach sits alone on a folding chair just outside the locker room door. The sun shines warm on his face, and there's a football game getting ready to get played, and he's hanging on—fighting really, with everything he's got—for this moment right here.

# Week Nineteen—The Long Run

## Fort Davis High School Indians: Fort Davis, Texas

**G**ERRY GARTRELL HAS a cold, which puts him in bed on this clear-skied Sunday morning instead of down at the fieldhouse, where several of his varsity players are gathered to get ice and heat for their Saturday night aches and pains from Don Cook, who volunteers part-time as the trainer for the Fort Davis Indians football team. John Liddell sits waist-deep in an ice bath, soaking his pair of hurt knees, and Mitch Aufdengarten is seated on a wood-plank bench, massaging his tender foot with a Dixie cup icicle. Trini Granado is here also, stripped to the waist and with an ice bag Ace-bandaged to his shoulder. While these sore players, along with teammates Cody Stewart and Forrest McLain, lounge around the locker room, David Rueda, the Fort Davis principal and athletic director, is on his way to meet with representatives from Strawn High School so they can agree upon Ratliff Stadium in Odessa as the site where the Indians and the Greyhounds will play on Saturday night for the six-man state football championship.

That's right, six-man football, and the six-man game in Texas features the same basic aspirations as the eleven-man variety, but the way those aims are pursued is a little different. There is the shrunken field—eighty yards long by forty yards wide—and even though a touchdown still gets you six points, the point after attempt is worth one point if you run or throw the ball into the end zone, and two points if you complete a kick through the uprights. A field goal is worth four points, and the reason for this is that, in six-man, with the holder and kicker set up behind the line, and only four players on the line of scrimmage to block the six on-rushing defenders, the ball-snap, the hold, and the kick, all have to be even more perfectly executed than they are in the eleven-man game. But this dip in scoring odds in the kicking game is more than balanced out when most offenses get their hands on the football, where all six players are eligible to run, throw, and catch the ball during every play from scrimmage in a mad dash to the end zone, which Coach Gartrell describes by saying, "It's like basketball, but you can hit people." Also like basketball, there is a lot of scoring, and scores in the sixties and seventies are not uncommon. So it's not really a stretch, as the Indians make their preparations this week to face Strawn, for assistant coach David Donnell, to belt out in his shrill Texas brogue, "We'll score eighty, and hold 'em to seventy-nine!"

And why not? It's been that kind of a year for Fort Davis, where they bring a 13–1 record into their final match-up with Strawn, and where each of their four playoff wins have featured a lackadaisical first half performance by the Indians, and then a second half where they roared back to take the lead. That just might be the most beautiful thing about six-man football because, no matter how far down you get, you're never quite out of it.

Two years ago the Indians looked like they were out of it. This was back when Fort Davis still played eleven-man, and when those same seniors who are reclining in the locker room on this Sunday morning, prepping to play for a state title, could reflect back on their freshman and sophomore years where they were integral components of a fifteen-member varsity team that never came close to winning a game in their West Texas district that included small-school powerhouses like Rankin and Iraan. Coach says, "There was no way we could win, or even be competitive. When you got 140-pound freshmen lined up at guard and tackle across from 200-pound upperclassmen, that doesn't bode too well for your team."

The problem was that Fort Davis had dipped below the 100-student cutoff for small-school eleven-man competition and was trying to compete against schools with as much as twice their enrollment, and this yawning disparity was enough to put the varsity Indians at 0–20 for that two-year stretch, and for the town of Fort Davis to begin the debate about whether or not it was time to make the move back to the six-man game that they had played up until the early 1970s, when the school census nudged them up into eleven-man territory and plunged them into thirty years of mostly losing.

On the surface, the decision should have been a simple one. The six-man game in Texas is designated for schools with a population of less than a hundred, and Fort Davis qualified with their eighty-six–student enrollment. They could "drop down" and ease right in with the other 130-plus schools that compete in the state in this modified brand of football. But that word "modified" brought visions of ice ballet and rhythmic gymnastics to some of the ranch-hardened denizens of this mile-high town, who'd be damned if their boys were going to trade in their helmets and shoulder pads for leotards and legwarmers.

But the perception of six-man as some kind of inferior cousin to the eleven-man game was only part of the battle. There was also fierce resistance to the switch by the parents of big kids, who were afraid that there would be no room for their children in this game designed more for speed and agility than for size and brute strength. After an unhappy battle, it was agreed that Fort Davis would go to six-man, and Coach and his team were able to make believers out of pretty much everyone in Jeff Davis County, especially out of a vocally opposed couple whose lineman-sized son got into a seventh-grade game last year and had a pass thrown to him in the end zone … which he dropped. But Coach called for a pass on the next play as well, and this time the young man caught it for a touchdown, and he exclaimed, "This is the best day of my life." Since that "best day," his parents have been on board with the swelling contingent of Fort Davis Indian true believers who can barely contain their giddiness over their ball team's ascension to the upper reaches of the Texas six-man universe.

These days, six-man is the weapon of choice for the Indians and their legion of fans. "If you brought up the suggestion of going back to eleven-man," says Coach, "almost everyone would be against it." And these days, the town newspaperman, Bob Dillard, can march into the Monday morning locker room to see how the troops are shaping up for Saturday night, and he can report to Coach the rumor that Strawn has already ordered their state champion rings. "Do you think it's true?" he asks.

"I don't know," replies Coach. "But tell the guys. That'll get 'em fired up."

Coach has his green and gold windbreaker zipped up, even in the warmth of the fieldhouse, as he battles his illness, and in these early morning minutes before the start of the school day he is surrounded by "the guys," and by Donnell and Cook and the team's other assistant, Lonnie Flippen, to watch a little Strawn video. Strawn has already been predicted as anywhere from a five-point to a seventeen-point favorite over the Indians, and, in the latest statewide rankings, Fort Davis is ranked third, behind Strawn and behind Richland Springs, the team the Greyhounds beat to make their way into the finals. "I like bein' the underdog," says Coach.

Donnell grimaces and shakes his head in a show of mock concern. "It's a shame you all can't play football like they can in East Texas," he says.

Coach Cook looks up from his orthopedic work with Liddell's creaky knees and says, "See, we still don't get the respect. There's only two teams left, and we're ranked third." The bell rings, and Cook shuts off the VCR and says, "Time for you boys to get to class."

The boys head off to their math and English and history periods and Bob prepares to drive back to the newspaper office, where he has the pleasant dilemma of trying to plan enough space in his next edition for the influx of "Good Luck" advertisements that have increased each week as the Indians have made their way deeper and deeper into the playoffs. It seems like the whole town has gone football crazy.

Down at Mary Lou's Diner, for example, Ed Dutchover leans back in his breakfast chair and grins. He played on the last really good Fort Davis team that won a regional championship back in 1963, in the days before there was a state title game for six-man, and he looks at this season like salad days for the little town that he's called home for almost all of his life. "This is the most excitement around here in forty years," Ed says. "A lot of times people are lukewarm about football. But this success gives people the chance to see the dedication of these kids and it helps the kids to see, 'Hey, we are winners.'" Ed's family has been a part of Fort Davis history since 1854, when Ed's great-grandfather witnessed a murder across the ocean in Belgium. "He was fifteen years old," says Ed, "and the killers shanghaied him and brought him over here. We been here since the 1800s," he says of his family and his town. "And it's not every day that a little place like Fort Davis makes it to the state championship game. But our guys makin' it, maybe it helps to show people that we don't plan to blow away in the dust."

On Thursday afternoon, after the daily pre-school Strawn Show where they watch Clifton Baker rumble over Zephyr and Gordon and Richland Springs, and after morning classes and the one-hour school-wide lunch break, the varsity Indians, along with their three coaches and three junior high team managers, board the well-traveled Bluebird bus to make the three-hour drive up to Odessa to get in a practice on the artificial turf of Ratliff Stadium.

There are about ten people there to greet the Fort Davis contingent, as Coach Flippen wheels the school bus through the chain-link gate and up alongside the concrete blocks of the stadium walls. One of these people is Trini's uncle, Elisar Alvarado, who works as a maintenance man for the Ector County School District. One of them is the Ector County Athletic Director, Mark Anderson, who says, "We're proud to have you all." And then there are the sports guys and their cameramen from the three local TV stations, and a crew from the Odessa newspaper, and even a reporter dispatched down here from *The New York Times*—all wanting to know, "What's it like?"

While Coach and Mitch and John Liddell talk with the media contingent, Donnell and Flippen take the rest of the team through their pre-practice stretch on the field, which is already modified for Saturday night's game, featuring the low-slung six-man goalposts.

At the end of a long season, here they are in Odessa, another West Texas town rich in football tradition, a town that has never hosted a state title game or a six-man affair, and that actually seems tickled to get a peek at this small-town version of tackle football. Odessa has positioned itself squarely in the Fort Davis corner, the only West Texas team still alive in the playoffs on any level. All this positive mojo has Coach feeling pretty good, and as he squints through the December afternoon sunlight at the cavernous high school football stadium, he says, "This location worked out perfect, like somebody orchestrated it."

But then Coach shakes himself out of his good-vibrations reverie to have a look at his team's early-practice performance, and it is apparent to him, to his fellow coaches, and to the small coterie of on-lookers, that things have started off a bit out of key. The Indians have moved from their stretching line to their passing lines where everybody gets the chance to catch the ball, most of the players take turns throwing it, and nobody is having much success with either pursuit. Coach watches a consistent succession of wobbly throws and bumbling drops, and he says, "Is this the 'no-catch' line over here? If anybody came out here and thought this's the champion of six-man football, they'd laugh. We gotta have some concentration."

So the Indians drop out of their passing lines and try to concentrate on some defense and how they plan to stop Strawn's big No. 5. This is Donnell's realm, and to watch him almost skip out to gather the boys around him is to watch a man who loves everything about the game of football. "Oooh, man! You gonna be movin' on this turf Saturday night," he says as he performs his ex-athlete's shimmy across the slick artificial surface. Then, as Flippen gathers together a collection of JVers for the scout offense, Donnell starts to review the strategy that will slow down No. 5, and, Fort Davis hopes, the entire Greyhound offense along with him. The Indians plan to close off the inside gaps with their big noseguard, Tim Salcido, and with Mitch coming up hard to fill a lane, and they want to herd the Strawn runners toward the sidelines.

"Let me tell you somethin' about a power runner," says Donnell as he steers Tim and Mitch and Jaime Garcia into position. "You got to get him runnin' east and west. You let him run north and south, we're in trouble. He want to dive, we'll get six hats on the ball. He want to stand up and run, we'll knock the dawg out of him. The next time someone hit him, he'll be lookin' for that ground." And then Donnell turns to address Liddell and Trini and Clay Tom Gibson, who are responsible for those outside lanes. "The only way they can beat us on a sweep or anything like that, is we start givin' ground. We win the line of scrimmage; we win the ballgame. We don't put pressure on that quarterback? He'll hurt us all day long." Then Donnell gestures toward the offense at the scout who is designated Strawn's No. 5, and he says, "Let me tell you somethin'. You see that big old boy runnin' an 'Out'? You better be thinkin' 'bout steppin' in front of him and takin' it to the House. That boy heads out on his own toward the sideline? You think he's headin' over there to talk to a cheerleader? I don't think so. You got to get over there."

And "getting over there" is what the Indians excel at. Their team speed has been probably the biggest difference for them all season, and they are confident that it will be the difference on Saturday night. All week, as they watch Strawn film, the main thing that the Fort Davis crew seems to notice is how long it takes the Greyhounds to move across the TV screen. When big No. 5 perpetrates another one of his patented plunges into and through and beyond the line of scrimmage to lumber for another fifteen yards that equal a first down in six-man, Coach remarks, "There ain't a whole lot of speed out there on the field."

So when the Indians switch to offensive practice on the Ratliff Stadium turf and Coach says, "Okay, it's time for a review and a preview," the emphasis is similar to what Donnell wants to accomplish on defense: to use the Fort Davis team speed to get to the outside. "Right off the bat," says Coach, "we're gonna send Trini and Liddell straight up the field and throw it to 'em and see if they can cover 'em." This opening-salvo tactic will test Coach's theory that the Fort Davis receivers are better than the Strawn backs; it will put the Indians on the attack right away, and they'll have a chance to score fast. "That first play is gonna tell us a lot," says Coach. "If it goes off like I think it will, we'll have Strawn where we want them. But if it don't, it's gonna be us that's got to adjust."

The big thing the Fort Davis players have to adjust to today is Ratliff's plastic grass. It has a completely different feel to it than the real stuff they play on back home, and this might be Coach's biggest concern as he gazes out across the stadium's playing surface. As fancy as it is, Coach can't help but think about his home field, and he says, "I like playin' on that brown grass. You know you're in December when you're playin' brown-grass football."

As the Indians skid and stumble through their passing lines and defensive schemes, Donnell says, "I don't know why we're slippin' and slidin'. We gotta figure it out. Either we got too much cleat, or not enough."

The players agree with him. When Trini tries a stutter-step move on Coach's game-opening deep route, his plant foot slides out from underneath him, and he collapses in a heap. "It's too slippery," he says, and he shakes his head and pushes himself up to jog back to the huddle. Then David Lara, the team's 200-pound junior quarterback, experiences similar results when he tries to plant and throw off a leg that is already encased in a knee brace. After Coach helps him up off the turf, David readjusts the Velcro straps of his brace and then studies the bottoms of both shoes to discern the culprit of his mishap.

Mr. Anderson, the Ector County AD, watches these football follies from his station on the sideline and calls out, "This is gonna be the perfect place right here. When we get the right shoes on ya, you won't slip." Another guy watching from the sidelines is Coach's son, Greg, who has driven over from Midland, where he works for an athletics supply company. On Saturday afternoon, he'll have a stack of boxed turf shoes leaning against the concrete-block benches for the Fort Davis runners.

They don't know that yet though, and on this Thursday afternoon, as the sun dips behind the smoked-glass of the Ratliff Stadium press box, casting the playing field into chilly December shadows, and as the mystery of the slippery turf gains in suspense, Coach decides they've had enough for today. He calls the squad around him in the fading light of the end zone and says, "Whose field is this?"

They chant back, "Our field!"

And Coach says, "Okay men, loud and proud."

They respond with, "Champions!"

And then it's time to load up the bus and head into the heart of Odessa for supper at WhataBurger, where Coach sits in his orange vinyl booth with his orange tray of food on the table before him, and his coaches and players all at their tables, joking and talking quietly, and eating their franchise restaurant sandwiches that you can't get in Fort Davis, and he nods his head sagely and says, "Yeah, we like to do it up big time."

After Saturday night's game Coach will be hanging it up for good, both his coaching and his teaching duties at the high school. He spends two days of this championship week in a cubbyhole room at the back of the school library, finishing up his stint as the in-school suspension supervisor and saying, "This is crampin' my style." It's not the duty that bothers Coach; rather, it's the administration's refusal to allow his one student to serve the time down at the fieldhouse where Coach could take care of the details surrounding Saturday's big game. But they want to be consistent, and that consistency includes the small library room and the hard stool and the no talking, all of which could be compromised down at the locker room.

So Coach sits and waits and looks at the wall clock and glances at his watch and cell phone until the Thursday morning of the Odessa trip, when a kid named Michael earns his second day with Coach this week, and Coach gets the green light to escort the young man down to the fieldhouse. Michael begins this tour of duty seated at the folding conference table in one of the stuffed swivel chairs, and with the Strawn-Richland Springs game on the television set as he opens his math textbook to start solving problems. But when Coach sizes up Michael's plush accommodations, he frowns, and when Rhonda Babb walks into the room, Coach asks her to search out a brother stool to the one in use over at the official ISS site, and then he tells Michael, "We don't want Dr. Rueda to come in here and see you sittin' in the lap of luxury."

A few minutes later, Rhonda breezes in with the stool in tow, and she helps Michael get set up on his new perch. The library stool has his shins level with the conference tabletop, and when he hunches over to resume his math work, he takes on a Bartleby-the-Scrivener air of industry that causes Coach to click off the television set and purse his lips in satisfaction and say, "Dr. Rueda'll be real proud."

Real proud is how Coach feels when he settles into a chair next to Michael and has a chance to think about this week, and all the years that have led up to it. He sets his stack of play cards down on the table and stretches, and then he sits back and says, "This is a special time for me." After decades of working and coaching in just about every corner of the state, the Gartrells have decided that their house up on Delores Mountain is home for good. And after Saturday's game, he'll be spending a lot more time around that house and down at The Desert Rose—his wife Judy's coffee and clothing and knick-knacks business—and in his old Ford truck, beating around yard sales and flea markets to keep the store stocked. "My wife has followed me all over Texas," says Coach. "And now it's time for us."

Before that time can start though, there is this week, which tops off a magical run for Fort Davis that Coach couldn't have conceived of in his wildest imaginings. The town will shut down on Saturday for the en-masse migration to Odessa, where almost everyone will join the team at the Elegante Hotel after the game to "partake of a steak" and take a dip in the indoor pool and maybe rent a room for the night at the place Coach likes to call, in his most refined tone of voice, "The premier hotel in Odessa … but that ain't sayin' much."

There's also all that media attention, the TV cameras and the big-town reporters, and the Odessa photographer who sets up a sports-page picture of Coach and his seniors on the summit of Coach's home mountain. There's also a British film crew that is roaming the state, in search of scenes that say, "Texas!" and they find the Fort Davis Indians on Tuesday afternoon. Coach spends the day saying things like, "Cheerio," and, "Repair to the loo," and, "Nip down to the pub for a pint with my mates," in his best British accent. After a stretched-out practice on the wind-blown field, they contact Coach on his cell phone, and he gives them direction before snapping the phone shut and saying, "The blamin' limeys are comin'."

When the crew arrives, their cameras trace the path of a few six-man plays, and then the Brits' man-in-charge says to Coach, "We are doing portraits of people with Texas faces, and you sir, have a Texas face."

By Saturday afternoon there is hardly anyone left in the town of Fort Davis. They have already filled up the gymnasium for the Friday pep rally, where the players stand in a long receiving line for everyone to file by with hugs and handshakes and solemn wishes of, "Good luck," and, "We're proud," and, "Go up there and whip 'em," and where Coach accepts a goodbye plaque of appreciation from Dr. Rueda and then stands alone in a spotlight's glare. He holds the plaque out before him like a hymnbook, and it flashes gold in the dazzle of the single light, and he sucks in a breath and says, "My wife should be here to stand next to me. She's the only reason I ever did anything good."

People have crowded around Coach at his Saturday morning biscuits and gravy breakfast at The Drugstore, where he eats without Judy and their daughter, Tess, because they're in Odessa, Christmas shopping before the big game. Coach is alone, but not really alone, because they won't stop coming up and saying, "You made this year," and, "Who'd of thought it?" and, "Why not stay on, Coach?"

And he says, "Thank you," and, "We got some good boys," and, "That's a tempting thing to think about." But when they drift away, smiling, Coach takes a sip of iced tea, and he says, "They do want me to stay on. They say, 'You know football.' And they say, 'We need you.' And it makes you feel good to think that they think that. But you know how they say, 'You kind of know when it's time'? Well, I'm startin' to know it's time."

And those same people have lined the Fort Davis main drag under the glorious midday Saturday sun to whoop and holler and cheer the bus as it steams out of town. They wave their signs and honk their horns and float their green and gold balloons up into the blue sky. "I feel at peace," Coach says. "I feel good about giving myself and my team over to our destiny. There are no worries or fears about this game or what might happen, or about anything else. What's supposed to happen will happen."

What happens is that the largest crowd ever to watch a Texas six-man game shows up at Ratliff Stadium, and the Fort Davis Indians play as hard as they've ever played, and Strawn is as big and tough as predicted, but also much faster and more prepared to win than Coach and his team could have known. The first play from scrimmage that Coach has planned to see if the Greyhounds can keep up results in a Strawn defensive back snatching the ball out of the air and returning it to set up his team's first of many scores. The Indians start off in a hole and they stay there, until late in the fourth quarter and with the Indians down by three touchdowns, when Coach calls his guys together and says, "We got 'em right where we want 'em, men," and they really want to believe him, especially after Trini catches a scoring pass from David Lara. But Strawn covers the next on-side attempt, and that's all there is for this highest-scoring-ever title game, where Trini alone accounts for five touchdowns in the Indians' sixty-two–point effort, and the best team wins.

For Coach, this isn't a bad way to go out. The Strawn kids are way happier than his guys are sad. This is new territory for Fort Davis, and it feels pretty good just being here and, for the first time, having the eyes of Texas upon them. Coach gathers his team underneath the shadow of the goal posts, and he says, "I will always think of you as champions because you are champions." There are a few tears and shakes of the head, but by the time Coach and his Fort Davis kids emerge from the locker room, showered and changed and ready to get on the bus, it's mostly tired smiles all around.

And then there's the Elegante, with the big steak buffet and the swimming pool and rooms for the night and people everywhere, all those people that they've known all their lives, they're all here, eating and talking and saying, "You boys mean so much to us," and how can anyone argue with that?

Coach can't. He's seated in a booth, with a steak dinner in front of him, and his family all around, and he is relaxed and content. "I'm a lucky man," he says, and he smiles at Judy, and she smiles back, and all that's left to do is get a good night's sleep in this nice hotel and then get up in the morning and head for home.

# Week Twenty—Finish Strong

## Katy High School Tigers: Katy, Texas

**I**T'S 6:30 A.M. down at the Katy football office, and Coach Mike Johnston stands at the lectern surrounded by his staff. This is the final week of the football season, a championship week that will conclude at the Alamodome in San Antonio, where the Katy Tigers will face the Southlake Carroll Dragons on Saturday, with the Texas 5A Division II state title on the line. But that doesn't really matter because, whether this was football season or not, Coach Johnston and his staff would be right here in the predawn hours of the morning, already well into the first two pots of coffee from the office percolator, and ready to talk some football. "On the last day of the school year," says receivers coach Scott Svendsen, "we'll be in here, meeting at 6:30."

The last day of the school year is a ways off right now, but the calendar year, and with it the official Texas football season, is drawing to a close as these twelve assistant coaches turn away from their computers and play sheets and morning newspapers to settle in and listen to Coach. He has already been back to his own office to drop off an armload of paperwork and hang up his change of clothes. By the time Coach opens up one of the three-ring binders where he keeps track of every facet of the program, Justin Landers, Katy's head athletic trainer, and Chad Haug, the school's strength and conditioning supervisor, have made their way down the hall from their own offices and have taken their seats at the conference table, and Kent Bruno, the Tigers' burly linebacker coach, has asked, "Do ants carry disease?" as he returns from his own foray into the coffee kitchen. He settles in behind his desk with his steaming cup and says to the room, "'Cause that sugar in there's fulla ants."

Roll call is already underway, as defensive backs coach Todd Moebes stands at the back whiteboard with a red dry-erase pen and calls around the room to each of his fellow staffers, "How are your children?" And each coach in turn reports back any kid who was absent the day before and why, and with a crew of almost two hundred varsity and JV and sophomore team players still practicing in this middle part of December, the list that Moebes compiles with his red pen contains no more than five names. One name that gets reported by offensive coordinator Chris Massey, but that doesn't make it onto the whiteboard, is Donny's, a sophomore offensive line "project" who has reached the conclusion that football isn't for him. "Donny decided he couldn't handle those afternoon practices," says Coach Massey. "And he heard there's a bus headed to San Antonio, and he's not on it."

Actually, there are a lot of buses headed to San Antonio. There are the three chartered team buses that will make their way west along Interstate 10 on Friday morning in a convoy that will also include a school district police car, a full-sized Budget rental truck, and Coach's black Chevy Tahoe. There is the "Whitehead" bus that will follow on Saturday, arriving just before game time with a load of sophomore and junior scout teamers who have had a big part in preparing the varsity on its march through the five playoff games leading up to this weekend's finale. There are the buses for the two hundred–member marching band, and for the girls in the Bengal Brigade drill team, and for fans who are getting used to making this late-December trip for a Katy Tiger football game. This is the sixth time since 1994 that the Tigers have devoted this week leading up to Christmas Break to preparing for the state title game, which they won in 1997 and 2000.

Coach knew early on that what he wanted to do in life was coach football, and when he played for a state title in his senior season at Galena Park over on the east side of Houston, the experience planted a goal in his mind that he carried with him to Stephen F. Austin University, where he played college ball, and to Beaumont and Nacodoches and Abilene, where he worked as an assistant coach, and then here to Katy, where he hired on as the offensive coordinator in 1980, before taking over as head coach in 1982. "All along," he says, "my goal was for my players to have the opportunity to play for a state title like I had the opportunity to play for it when I was in high school."

That's why Saturday will mark the one hundred fifty-fourth straight day that the Katy coaching staff has reported to work. But, says running backs coach Jeff Dixon, "That's nothing special because everyone else does it too. You have to do it." That's why they'll also be here on Sunday at one o'clock to grade tape and figure out their end-of-the-year awards, just like they did last year, the morning after they lost in the semi-finals, and in 1998, the year a kid forged a grade on his grade-check sheet and then played three "Celebration Time" plays in one of the Tigers' playoff victories. His teacher discovered the discrepancy and reported it to the administration, with no malice against the young man or the football team, but with the intent of doing things right. And Katy's administration wanted to do things right as well when they reported the incident to the state's University Interscholastic League. And the UIL wanted to do things right when they ruled on the case and called Coach on the Friday morning before Saturday's noon game to hand down their decision. Then Coach had to walk out of his office and along the fieldhouse sidewalk and step onto the team charter buses that were already loaded up for the journey up Interstate 45, and he had to tell his players that they weren't going to Dallas because they were disqualified from the state title game. "That whole deal," says Coach. "Tellin' them boys they weren't goin' up there to play, that was the second hardest time I ever had in football."

And it's why Gregg Miller and Todd Thompson hustle into the football office from their teaching assignments a few minutes before fifth period athletic P.E. to write out the script for the "Defensive Team" period, only to find out that Gary Joseph, the Tigers' defensive coordinator, has already completed it. So Thompson has a bonus five minutes to work at his desk, and Miller can take his time changing into his coaching clothes. He swings open the door to the coaches' locker room and disappears inside, only to reappear almost instantly and ask, "Are we red and white, or red and gray today?"

Coach Joseph glances up from his stack of computer printouts and says, "Red and white."

This is a serious question at Katy. Back in 1997, when Massey first started here, he figured one day that he'd have his linemen come straight down to the meeting room in their school clothes for athletic period without taking the time to "dress out" so they could get ten or so extra minutes of film work accomplished. As Massey thinks back to this day, he is sitting in that same meeting room with this year's group of his "Hawgies." Everyone is dressed in their red and white shorts and shirts and their athletic shoes, and Massey is outfitted in his red and white nylon Katy sweat suit. The lights are dimmed, so it's difficult to make out the "Hawg Parking Only: All Others Will Be Crushed" sign on the white wall; and the whole crew is reclined in plastic chairs, watching tape of yesterday's practice. Massey presses "Rewind" on the remote control, and while the players and plays run in reverse on the white wall, he says, "This was about the time Coach came down to see what was goin' on." As he clicks "Play" and everyone on the wall starts moving forward again, Massey whistles his abbreviated version of Clint Eastwood's *The Good, the Bad, and the Ugly* theme, and then he shakes his head and says with a sideward glance, "That's *not* how we do things here at Katy High School."

Part of how they do things includes a swim in the school's natatorium on the Monday afternoon after a Saturday game to "flush 'em out" after the pounding of a forty-eight minute football contest; but on this early Tuesday morning, Coach Haug has to report to Coach that that didn't happen yesterday because there's something wrong with the pump system, so instead of laps in the pool, it was laps around the practice field. As the players and coaches jogged out to begin their run, they had to step over and around the equipment that the maintenance crew is using to drain all the excess water that is not only preventing the team from using the pool, but also keeping them from the washing machines where they clean all of their practice and game gear. This is even more of a serious problem because no one likes to go around without clean underwear and socks, especially with the rash of artificial turf–induced staph infections that they have been trying to fight off over the last several weeks.

But up until a few weeks ago, the washing machine dilemma wouldn't have been a problem because the team had Earnest Stevenson, the Katy School District maintenance worker assigned to the fieldhouse, who would have found somewhere else on campus to get the boys' clothes clean for tomorrow. Earnest is the guy you need around the fieldhouse in a program like this, where everyone does at least exactly what they're supposed to do, or they get out.

The backed-up water pumps are backing up into the drains, and the drains are starting to flood the floors, and as he sloshes his way through the thin skein of water that covers the linoleum in the fieldhouse hallway, quarterbacks coach Jeff Rhoads says, "This'd be taken care of if Earnest was here." Senior cornerback Ryan Mouton agrees, and as he changes into his school clothes and adjusts the bandage he wears to protect a damaged forearm, he says, "It'd be a lot nicer if Earnest was here." "That's right," agrees senior defensive lineman Tate Stewart. "We should have Earnest at the state championship game. We should all pitch in and buy him a ring." "That's a good idea," agrees Coach Svendsen.

So why isn't Earnest here? Why do the coaches have to figure out how they're going to get the laundry done because there's no way the new guy is going to go out of his way to do it? Why is the locker room not quite up to par, and the towels folded not quite the way everyone is used to, and the hallway a slippery maze of puddles? Why isn't there anyone standing at the glass doors to the fieldhouse to greet the players as they come in from practice, to shake hands and slap shoulder pads? Because in the days leading up to the Thanksgiving holiday, Earnest and Coach Dixon were saying their goodbyes one night in the fieldhouse hallway, and Dixon said, "We gonna see you over break?"

Earnest said, "You know if you need me I'll be here."

Dixon replied, "Well you know we always need you around here." So Earnest was there, showing up on his own over the weekend to wash clothes and sweep floors and pick up around the locker room for no extra pay, at the same time the coaches were putting in their hours at the office. And whereas the coaches' "off-the-clock" work is accepted and even required, Earnest's extra service to the team violated the rules of his district contract, so he was transferred to another shift at another district high school and put on ninety days probation. Now Earnest is sick about not being able to do his part for the Katy Tigers, and he's also sick about the possibility of losing his job. Coach misses Earnest as much as anyone, and he is working to try and bring him back into the fold because he was a true part of things here, and in the way he worked and conducted himself around these boys, he was another model of the values that the Katy Tigers hold dear. "Discipline is the basis of everything we do with our football team," Coach says. "The idea of submission and conformity is what we try to instill in everyone involved in the program, the idea of selflessly giving to a greater good, and, if you can do this, you see how it works when everyone submits and conforms to the cause."

The "cause" this week is to try and find a way to slow down the Southlake Carroll offense that features All-State junior quarterback, Chase Daniel, his backfield running mate, Aaron Luna, a disciplined offensive line, and a whole array of competent wide receivers that get equal opportunity to catch Daniel's precision passes. "The wideouts are all good, but none of them stands out from the rest," says Moebes, as he sits alone in the dark of the film room. He is frustrated because the last three weeks the Tigers have faced teams that had one dominant receiver, and so it was easy. "We'll put our best guy on your best guy," says Moebes.

Katy's "best guy" back there is Mouton, who Coach is confident could cover anybody in the state. "I think in time," says Coach, "he'd be able to defend the Alamo." But on Saturday, the Southlake Carroll coaches up in the Alamodome's press box won't be peering through their binoculars to find out where Ryan Mouton is on the field so they can avoid him. They run their "Spread" offense by the numbers, so if there are three defensive backs covering two receivers on the left side, and two covering two on the right, Daniel might flick a short "bubble" pass to his slot man on the right.

If the defense decides to drop an extra man off the line so they have three against two on both sides of the field, then this is when the Dragons get really excited because it means they can take advantage of the shorthanded defensive interior with a hand-off to Luna, or a fake hand-off and a run by QB Daniel that allows him to show off his speed. It is not difficult to surmise that the Dragons have an emphatic response for any rampart an opposing defense might try to construct in their path.

But, as far as Coach Rhoads is concerned, as he sits in another one of those darkened-room meetings with his eight quarterbacks, "path" isn't the right word to use when you talk about the Southlake Carroll offense. "It's like a Superhighway," he says. "You ever been on I-10 about twelve o'clock? That's what it's like." And as Moebes sits in the dark at the other end of the building, watching more film, one of his players pushes open the door to sit with him, and then asks after a few minutes and a couple of Southlake Carroll touchdowns, "They punt much?"

Moebes shakes his head in the glow of the reading-lamp light. "So they're not used to goin' three and out?" the player continues. "They're not used to bein' stopped," says Moebes. "Well," says the player, "let's make them work this game." "I'm all for it," replies Moebes.

The Dragon scoring machine is so much like Rhoads' "Superhighway" description, and it is so discriminatory against its punter that it is a serious point of discussion for Katy's offensive coaches and players as they plot out their part in the strategy to try and stop it. As Rhoads and his quarterbacks watch a replay of their semi-final win over Schertz-Clemens, in which Katy trailed 12–7 at the half, only to prevail 33–12, junior James Aston tiptoes out-of-bounds on one sweep play in the midst of his 230-yard rushing performance. "Clock's runnin', men," reminds Rhoads.

"We get in this situation, we gotta be able to run these plays straight ahead ... keep the clock runnin'. 'Cause let me tell you ... Whooh! Their offense, about six plays, they can make somethin' happen. We wanna stay in bounds. We wanna keep the clock runnin'."

The Schertz-Clemens film moves forward, this time to a play where Ben Johnson pivots back in their I-formation to hand the ball deep to James, who powers across the line of scrimmage behind senior fullback Bryan Thompson and Joseph Longacre, the Tigers' 310-pound senior strong tackle. Aston stays in bounds and picks up a nice gain on the play "Okay," says Rhoads. "That's what we need to do. We need to keep 'em on the sideline. We need to move the ball. Take a long time doin' it. And score. That's how we'll win the ballgame. Their offense is better than their defense. We have to take advantage of that. Our defensive coaches say, 'Just score.' But it's more than that. We have to march the ball down the field. Southlake's gotta understand momentum. We gotta score, but we gotta take six minutes a pop with it. Sometimes it won't take them thirty seconds to score. Those guys have got to be on the sideline for us to win."

Katy's offense might be more qualified than any other team in the state to execute this type of game plan necessary to keep the Dragons' Blitzkrieg off the playing field. It's a plan where ten four-yard gains are infinitely more desirable than one forty-yard gain, and straight-ahead plow horse is the transportation of choice over around-the-end thoroughbred. In an epoch where many teams are almost maniacally intent on gobbling up big hunks of yardage on each play, and then holding their collective breath while the opposing offense utilizes much the same strategy against their defense, Katy's approach is slow and steady, using their old-fashioned I-formation, their mammoth offensive line, and their unflinching work ethic to grind out win after steady win. Says Coach, "I'll tell you what. People ought to be careful about entertaining folks and think more about winning football games. Teams need to be thinking about sticking to things they're good at." And this is exactly what Katy has done for the twenty-two years that Coach has been at the helm and that Coach Joseph has been his defensive coordinator and first assistant. This is a team that isn't blessed with a cornucopia of flash-fire speed or big-time college talent, but which integrates the desire of its kids to excel as a team, its coaches' skill and willpower to show them how to do just that, and its school's and community's unflagging support.

The Tigers take kids like Ben Johnson, who Rhoads describes as "totally unflashy," and turn them into starting quarterbacks because, Rhoads says, "Since his freshman year, he's done everything the coaches have asked him to do and more. He's got a 4.0 in the classroom, but he doesn't run fast and his arm's not strong. But he knows who to get the ball to, and how to do it."

They take kids like Bryan Thompson, who everyone agrees is the best player on the team, and turn them into fullbacks who usually carry the football about two times a game. "But Bryan does all the things that people don't notice," says Rhoads. Like he did in the Schertz-Clemens game, where the coaches credited him with eleven "cut blocks," a below-the-waist chop at the legs of an onrushing defender that is only legal at the high school level in this state because, unlike everywhere else, Texas follows the same rules as the NCAA. "We call 'em 'stingers,'" says Rhoads. "And it's a devastating block and defensive coaches hate it, and there ain't no one can execute it like Bryan can." So that's Bryan's job, the best player out there—to remain invisible to everyone in the stadium except the defensive end who has to think more about protecting his legs than about covering his gap. And he does it, week after week.

And then there's Tate Stewart, who moved from tight end to defensive tackle after the Tigers' season-opening loss to Lufkin.

Coach likes to play at least one tough out-of-district opponent early in each season "just to see where we're at," and this year it was Lufkin, who had more team speed and slicker execution than Coach had ever witnessed in an early-season opponent. They blew Katy's defenders off the ball in a lopsided victory that had prognosticators across the state crossing off the Tigers from their December calendars and penciling in this Lufkin team that these Katy kids can't stop talking about, even four months after they played them. But what Coach did see, as far as "where his team was at," was that his defensive line was being dominated. "They did their jobs and filled their gaps and were coachable and responsive," says Coach. "But physically, they couldn't match up."

So Coach explained to Tate that he was needed on defense, instead of at tight end, where he had been honing his play since the first four days of summer practice before his freshman year, when the coaches work out the incoming ninth-graders on both offense and defense. Afterwards, they hold a draft to try to get the kids they want on their side of the ball. Tate was one of Coach's picks, both for offense and for the tight end position that he is personally responsible for, and now he was saying goodbye for the most part. So these days, Tate wears the defensive white jersey out on the practice field, and, Coach says, "Technically, he's still not there. But as a physical presence and an anchor, having him in the middle of the defensive line has made all the difference."

Or what about Joseph Longacre and his gang of Hawgs up front? They just keep moving forward, keep lifting weights and running sprints and perfecting their "gap hinge," and their "kick-slide," and their "good base." They keep listening to Massey when he says, "Frank Comito. Don't slide to block air. Slide with your eyes. What're you doin' there? You look like a blind bull tryin' to horn somebody," and when he says, "The Dragons have won thirty-one in a row, but that don't mean nothin'. You get 'em out on the field, and then you find out who's better. This is the type of game where you can't miss an opportunity to score. That's just the way it is. They're tellin' their guys the same thing. The fact is, though, that when we line up, our guys should physically push their guys off the ball. We should push them back. We need to execute. We can't have any communications breakdowns 'cause that's what gets us off schedule. So this week is all about stayin' on schedule and gettin' that four yards a play."

There is a certain freshman football player who will be undertaking a similar systematic approach on behalf of the Katy Tigers, but he won't be doing it in the form of off-tackle runs and "Two-Route" pass patterns on the Alamodome field-turf on Saturday afternoon. Instead, he'll be performing "Bear Crawls" and "Up-Downs" on the desiccated Katy practice field. This young freshman with his varsity dreams will be tasting copious amounts of dirt from that field because he chose this week of schoolwide final exams to "act the fool" in his English class, where he incited a miniature gang of his classmates into the type of rude behavior that they don't like here at Katy, and they especially don't like it when the teacher is deep into a pregnancy. She forwarded an e-mail to Coach Rhoads, her departmental colleague, that outlined the miscreant's indiscretions, which concluded with him standing in front of her, luxuriantly gulping down a can of Coca-Cola that he wasn't supposed to have in the room in the first place. "We're gonna find out how bad this young man wants to play football," says Rhoads as he digs through the English room trash basket for the crumpled aluminum canister.

When he finds it, his colleague says from her desk, and through all of her brink-of-vacation fatigue, "I want him to pay." "Don't you worry," replies Rhoads. "I'll set this Coke can next to his nose while he's doin' his log rolls." This is good enough for this young woman who wants nothing more than to get home and take off her shoes, and after Rhoads exits the room, he says, "We got a philosophy here that we want to win 'em over, not lose 'em. But at the same time, we're not runnin' a rehab program. So this is one of those times where we'll be walkin' that line."

By the time Coach Rhoads walks through the football office door and deposits the offending can in his desk drawer, he is giddy with enthusiasm over the picture in his mind of what tomorrow will bring, when the soda can's owner shows up at his sixth period athletic P.E. class with the rest of the freshman squad in the Katy red and gray shorts and shirts, and the white socks and running shoes, and when Rhoads will sidle up to him and say, "You and me got some business to take care of." And when he relates the chain of events, as well as his proposed antidote, to Coach Svendsen, Svendsen tips his bottle of Propel fitness water toward Rhoads in a brotherly salute and says, "I know where I'll be tomorrow."

But when tomorrow comes, the young recalcitrant is nowhere to be found, and when Rhoads calls his house, there is no answer, and so he has escaped the justice that he certainly knows is coming his way, at least for this calendar year. But, says Rhoads, as he opens his metal desk drawer to take another peek at the evidence, "I called his house so he knows that I know, and now he's got somethin' more to think about over break." Rhoads leans back in his chair, thinking about what he'll make this kid do when school starts up again, and he glances over to Svendsen with the knowing nod. Svendsen grins in a way that suggests two weeks isn't too long to wait for the re-education of this young man, and he says, "Oh yeah, that'll be happening."

There are some things happening with the Southlake Carroll defense that begin to form a pattern for the Katy offensive crew as this championship week wears on. There are the Dragon cornerbacks that QB Ben Johnson watches on the videotape of their playoff win over Irving. He's looking for how they line up against different offensive formations, and even though he's not finding much he is noticing a consistent blind spot in the way they cover. "It looks like they're a little negligent on the 'Out' routes," he says. "They play a little soft, and they turn their hips and their face inside, even when there's a threat of the receiver going outside." He fast-forwards through a couple of running plays, and then slows down the motion on a play where the Irving quarterback drops behind his pocket protection and his receivers scurry down the field to test the Southlake defensive backfield waters. True to Ben's hypothesis, the cornerback on the bottom of the screen reads "pass" and swivels his hips and his head toward the middle of the field as he braces to address Irving's hard-charging receiver. He rewinds the play where the bottom-of-the-screen cornerback has left the slightest of outside advantages to the Irving offense and says, "I suspect the corner on top is doing the same thing," which, as Ben presses "play" on the remote control, it becomes immediately clear that he is also a soft seven yards off the line of scrimmage, and that he's got the same inside swivel going that leaves the sliver of advantage for a Katy offense willing to attack the perimeter.

Says Rhoads, "I know it's tempting to throw the ball down the field on them. It's almost as if they invite you. But you cannot get into a slingin' match with them. We been throwin' Two-Routes all year, and I believe throwin' the Two-Route is what's goin' to do it for us."

And as Massey and his Hawgs watch their own stack of Southlake videotapes in their constant search for how best to hammer the Dragon defense, they seem to have found their own small but important "tell." On play after play, it appears as if the two Dragon defensive ends stand over the football while the opposing offensive squad breaks its huddle and approaches the line of scrimmage, in a vigil that lasts until the offensive tight end veers toward either the right or left side of the ball, at which point the Dragons' No. 85 hustles to settle in front of him, while their No. 84 skirts to the opposite side of the line, where he is outside the offensive tackle, and thus uncovered, at least until the snap of the ball. Coach Massey isn't certain exactly why the two defensive ends flip-flop in this fashion, but he is pretty sure that it has something to do with No. 84's relatively small size—215 pounds—as compared to everyone else in the trenches. It also might have something to do with his quickness, which is enhanced when he begins a play uncovered. Massey *is* sure of what his offense needs to do to make No. 84 play "heads up" against a tight end, and that is to set their tight end up on one end of the line as the offense approaches the line of scrimmage and settles into their stances, where he'll doubtless be covered by No. 85, and then to put him in motion and flip him to the other end of the line as Ben calls out his pre-snap signals, where he'll be heads-up with the lithe No. 84. On many plays when they don't use this flip strategy, Massey wants to employ a "double tight," where he'll pull an outside receiver off the field and send in an extra tight end to bookend the front line so that both defensive ends will be covered and faced with immediate contact at the snap of the ball. Beside these tight end measures, Massey wants to create a number of situations during the game where No. 84 will be lined up across from a tight end, as well as on the same side of the line as big Joe Longacre, so he is caught in a crossfire between the tight end that he has worked all season to avoid and a 310-pound offensive tackle whose favorite thing in life is running people over. "Basically," says Coach Massey of the Dragons' gifted but undersized No. 84, "we want to wear his ass out."

The Katy Tigers are a little worn out themselves in this twentieth official week of the Texas football season, and despite all of their precautions to ward off injury and illness and fatigue, the wear of all those weeks is taking its toll on kids like Michael Parker, who curls up in the back of Coach's Tahoe and sinks into a dead sleep on the way home from a Monday afternoon photo shoot with other Houston area players at Rice Stadium. Coach reports this from his lectern spot at the Tuesday morning meeting and he shakes his head in amazement at how tired Michael is, and how tired everyone else must be as well, and he says, "These boys, if they could just make it through one more game."

And what a game it is. On Monday night, Coach tells a Booster Club gathering, "If ya'll are wantin' to see a train wreck, there's gonna be one in the Alamodome on Saturday at high noon." On Wednesday night, Coach stands before his Leadership Council in their weekly meeting after Drew Zeiler speaks for his teammates to say they'd like to go out to a movie on the night before the game, instead of watching a video in the hotel banquet room, and Coach says, "That'll be fine." Then he leans forward over the meeting room lectern to look around at his senior leaders and to say, "The most precious thing God gave us is our spirit. And it's your responsibility to nurture that spirit and protect it. The greatest thing about this team is the character you all display out there. There are more talented teams out there, but no better teams. Otherwise, they'd still be playin'. Your character is what's gonna carry you through."

When Coach shows up in the Thursday morning dark to announce at the 6:30 meeting that Gordon Wood, one of the people that Coach looks up to most in this world, died in the night, he asks, "Will you join me in prayer?" So the fifteen men shut their eyes and bow their heads, and Coach says, "He was a great man, a great role model for this profession that we've all chosen." And then it's back to work, and by the end of Thursday's morning meeting, Bruno has found a theater, and by lunch on Thursday he has talked to the manager about a show time and a method of payment and a Katy-only screening that the manager suggested.

On Friday night, after the morning chartered bus caravan along I-10 and a pre-planned rest area stop for sandwiches and ice-bucket-chilled Gatorade, and then the early afternoon Alamodome practice, after an hour at the undisclosed hotel, the hydraulic doors of the three chartered buses hiss open and 135 boys and men in red polo shirts pour out onto the sidewalk and into the mall and up the escalators and through the theater's velvet ropes and into their seats. Before the movie starts, they're all thinking about what Bryan Thompson said after their Alamodome practice, which was, "We're finally here. Keep it under control. It's gonna be fun tonight, goin' out to the movies with the boys. We're gettin' ready for the biggest day of our lives. Let's be ready for it."

And then that day comes, and the picture they've grown up with in their minds is real: the marching bands with their high-stepping drum majors, and the rows of brass instruments flashing in the indoor stadium lights, and the drill girls in their glitter and high boots, and the pom-poms and megaphones and the tens of thousands of people, and everything festooned in Dragon green and black and in Tiger red and white. The crowd is roaring for the teams long before the game is even thinking about getting started, when the boys come out in their undershirts to "walk the field," to stretch out in little belly-down circles with their position-mates, to look and listen and feel what it's like, that feeling of possibility, of work and Team, and as Coach said to them early in the week, "Men, I'll tell you what, you got a opportunity to live your dream. Not a lot of people get a opportunity for that."

But before they live their dream, they have some time in San Antonio, for practice, and heaping platters of buffet dinner, and *The Last Samurai*, and then an evening walk beneath the hanging lights of the old Christmas town, and sleep and breakfast and a Katy preacher's lesson from Colossians 3:23 ("Whatever you do, work at it with all your heart, as working for the Lord, not for men"). And then it's time to get taped and get the FosFree that helps with cramps, and the short bus ride to the stadium, and there are all those people, already here to greet them, cheering and calling out, and waving their red and white banners, and the Whiteheads are here, too, dressed-out and seated on the concrete floor outside the locker room.

Coach Rhoads starts his countdown for quarterbacks to take the field for their warm-ups, "Quarterbacks, six minutes," he says, and then, "Quarterbacks, four minutes," and then, " … two minutes," and then they're on the field with their centers, and with the rest of the team following at their appointed times and with their coaches.

Bill Bundy, the Katy AD, is standing on the sideline, and he was here earlier to witness Southlake's All-State kicker boom a field goal from Katy's side of the fifty-yard line, and he says, "It sounded about like a baseball bat hittin' a watermelon." And the kicker is only one of four Dragons named to the All-State team that came out in this morning's newspapers, and which had no Katy Tigers on the first team, and only one—Ryan Mouton—on the second, but Coach is happy with the timing of the selections, just like he's happy to hear about the big pep rally they held up in Southlake on Thursday night. And he is feeling good right now on this Saturday morning because he was able to avoid the pep rally spectacle that Katy enjoyed back in 1994 when, says Coach, "We came out Saturday, and we couldn't have been any flatter," and that's why

338

he told the parents all week, "We'll celebrate after the game," and, "We don't need your intensity on Thursday evening. We need it Saturday at noon."

And now here it is, Saturday at noon, and the Southlake Carroll Dragons sprint onto the stadium floor through their inflatable tunnel and green and black balloons. And there is Coach's team, amassed in its own end zone, locked hand in hand in long red and white columns, and behind a butcher paper sign that erupts in red and white as the Katy Tigers run out.

After Coach says to his mustered team, "Let's play a football game," Southlake returns the Katy kickoff to its own nineteen-yard line, and the All-Stater Chase Daniel launches a deep sideline pass over the top of sophomore Will Thompson that results in a sixty-six–yard touchdown barely a minute into the game and a collective gulp from the Katy faithful. Then, Katy has to begin its own first offensive possession on its eight-yard line, but here is where the offense starts its long day of doing its part of the defensive game plan. They keep the ball in James Aston's hands, between the hashes and behind Bryan Thompson and Joe Longacre and his determined Hawg-mates, and they drive it, like a tractor furrowing a clod-dirt field, and, although they don't score, they hold on for almost nine minutes and conclude with a punt that leaves the Dragon offense on its own four-yard line, where Coach Joseph begins to slip the cover off his defensive scheme, and where the Dragon contingent, led by their head man, Todd Dodge, begins to sweat. The Dragons are used to doing what they please with their offense, so much so that the early touchdown pass was, to them, no big deal, until Coach Joseph and his Katy defensive charges start to throw the numbers game that a Spread offense counts on right back into the Dragons' face. Coach Dodge, on the other side of the field, changes play-call after foiled play-call from his sideline post that Coach Joseph has rooted out before the snap and signaled to Ryan Mouton and Will Thompson and their backfield mates to "Move! Move!" and they are hauling across the field, changing up their coverage. And all of this works for the Tigers, because the rusty Southlake punt team trots out onto the field twice in the first half, and both times the long snap is low and bobbled by their punter, and Katy narrowly misses notching a blocked kick, and between those short-lived Dragon possessions, Katy puts together another workmanlike drive that ends with Coach stepping up to say, "Throw the Two-Route," and with Ben delivering an arcing strike to Chris Pedlar, and then Morgan Beckendorff punching through his sixty-first straight PAT of the season, and, after Katy ends the first half with another long possession and no more points, the two teams trot into their respective locker rooms tied 7–7.

Things could hardly be much better for Katy, as Coach tells his staff in their early-halftime meeting room, "Tempo-wise, we're doin' what we want to do."

Bruno says of the Southlake offense, "They only got in fourteen plays. That's the first time that's happened to them in two years," and then he's reminded of the early Dragon touchdown, and he says, "They found our soft spot—big surprise. Our sophomore sat down, and they ran by him." "Aw, Lawdy," replies Coach, "We just got to pet him, stroke him, hug him, pump him up. Will's playin' hard. All the kids are playin' hard." Then Coach turns his thoughts to the Southlake punt problems, and he says, "Two straight low snaps. We might challenge 'em in the second half on that."

And then the coaches break off to meet with their players. There is Coach Bruno, who says to his linebackers, "They're over there freakin' out right now. I'm a tell you how this one's gonna go. It'll probably come down to who has the ball last. It sounds stupid. But it's that simple. They got a great kicker, but he's never kicked one with the game on the line."

Coach Massey says to his Hawgs, "We need more plays this half than ever before. Keep wearin' their ass out. Keep knockin' on that door, and eventually that sucker'll open."

And then there's Coach, who gathers everyone around him in the long narrow locker room to say, "This is the way a championship game oughtta be played, between two really fine teams."

Joseph Longacre chimes in and says to his fellow Hawgs, "We got 'em. Let's pound 'em. Hey, I'm not even tired."

That's a good thing, because after the Tigers burst through their "Sleigh the Dragons" banner, and after more magic from Coach Joseph's defense that results in the Tigers getting their blocked punt for an out-of-the-end-zone safety, a 9–7 lead, and possession of the ball, Southlake goes back on the offensive late in the third quarter, and the Tiger defense starts to give ground, enough so that Aaron Luna dives over the goal line for Southlake a couple minutes into the fourth quarter. They convert a two-point play to go up 15–9, and they hold the Katy offense in check, and then they've got their All-State kicker, the boy with the baseball bat leg, lined up for a forty-five-yard field goal try with 3:23 left in the game, and the chance to seal things up for the Dragons, and the crowd is roaring, and it's a good snap and a good hold, and he drives into the ball . . . and he hooks it. There is enough hope left for Katy that they plow their man, James Aston, into the line on a couple straight plays to get the Tigers up to their forty-nine-yard line, and then they send in Ryan Mouton at wide receiver, and he flies down the left hash mark on a deep post pattern, and there is no one on the Dragon defense who can keep up with him, or with Ben Johnson's sturdy throw that settles into his arms and, coupled with Morgan Beckendorff's sixty-second PAT in a row, puts Katy back on top with 2:30 left in the ballgame. But this is like a lifetime for the Dragon offense, and it seems much longer than that for the Katy Tigers, until Ryan Mouton knocks down a pass to his sideline, and then Will Thompson scoops the next pass off his kneecaps and bobbles it, and then cradles the ball in his arms, and Drew Zeiler is on the sideline, hobbled and on crutches and hollering, "He picked it off! He picked it off! He picked it off!"

So James Aston and the Hawgs step back onto the field, and it takes four straight-ahead running plays, four big pushes by the offensive line, and by Bryan Thompson and James Aston with the ball master-locked in his arms, to get their ten yards, and to run down the clock, and to earn the Katy Tigers the 2003 Texas 5A Division II State Title by a score of 16–15.

# Acknowledgments

**A** GRATEFUL NOD OF appreciation to Mark Weinstein and Erin Kelley at Skyhorse Publishing for giving this book about high school football a shot and for making it the book that it is. A tip of the cap to the towns, schools, and teams along the route of *Hometown Heroes*. And, to the coaches, who picked up the telephone, listened to someone they'd never met ask to spend a week with them and their players, and said, "Come on," an inestimable "Thank you."